Guns and Violence

Other Books in the Current Controversies Series:

Guns and Violence

Henny H. Kim, *Book Editor*

David Bender, *Publisher*
Bruno Leone, *Executive Editor*

Bonnie Szumski, *Editorial Director*
David M. Haugen, *Managing Editor*

CURRENT CONTROVERSIES

Cover photo: © Shepard Sherbell/Saba

Library of Congress Cataloging-in-Publication Data

Guns and violence / Henny H. Kim, book editor.
        p. cm. — (Current controversies)
        Includes bibliographical references and index.
        ISBN 0-7377-0065-3 (lib. : alk. paper). — ISBN 0-7377-0064-5
(pbk. : alk. paper)
        1. Gun control—United States. 2. Firearms ownership—United States.
3. Firearms—Law and legislation—United States. 4. Violence—United
States. 5. Violent crimes—United States. I. Kim, Henny H., 1968–   .
II. Series.
HV7436.G8774   1999
363.3'3'0973—dc21   98-56515
                                                                        CIP

©1999 by Greenhaven Press, Inc., PO Box 289009, San Diego, CA 92198-9009
Printed in the U.S.A.

Contents

The Problem of Gun Violence Is Exaggerated

Chapter 2: Does Gun Control Reduce Crime?

Yes: Gun Control Reduces Crime

No: Gun Control Does Not Reduce Crime

Chapter 3: Is Gun Control Constitutional?

Yes: Gun Control Is Constitutional

only the right of a legitimate state-run militia to utilize guns for protection. Gun control measures do not violate constitutional rights because they merely limit gun ownership under certain conditions and ultimately fulfill the Second Amendment's intent to ensure the physical safety of the nation's people.

The National Rifle Association (NRA) insists that the Second Amendment protects the individual's right to bear arms and, subsequently, the freedom of the American people. The NRA, however, rarely offers compelling evidence for its interpretation. On the other hand, by supporting the banning of handguns and other gun control measures, the Supreme Court has provided substantial proof for the fact that the Second Amendment is not a guarantee of gun ownership.

No: Gun Control Is Not Constitutional

The original intent of the Second Amendment to protect individual rights has been too often ignored by federal courts. History shows that an armed citizenry has been an accepted or even necessary part of American society. This belief has been upheld in various courts in which an individual's right to bear arms was protected. However, the tyranny of regulation continues. Gun control laws betray constitutional freedoms by maintaining ill-gotten government powers at the expense of individual rights.

The media's uninformed and hypocritical degradation of the Second Amendment threatens to strip the nation of not only the freedom to bear arms but of all freedoms which individuals enjoy and take for granted. Younger generations should be provided with educated information instead of with misguided attacks on an inalienable right that must be upheld if freedom is to continue into the next century.

Gun control advocates justify limitations on gun ownership in the name of protecting the common good. However, gun control regulations, such as the Gun Free Schools Act of 1994, have merely stripped citizens of their ability to protect themselves and enforced punishment inappropriate for the "crime" of lawfully owning a gun. Gun control laws are not effective for public safety; at best, they display the extent to which state governments have compromised their power to the federal government, which has gained absolute control over personal freedom.

Although gun control fanatics believe otherwise, the Second Amendment is a basic right that cannot be revoked. Gun owners have already yielded to gun control laws that at the fundamental level are unconstitutional. In the interest of attaining the freedom American citizens were meant to have, the government's encroachment on gun ownership must be revealed as the tyranny it really is and fought to the end.

Chapter 4: Is Gun Ownership an Effective Means of Self-Defense?

Chapter 5: What Measures Would Reduce Gun Violence?

Foreword

By definition, controversies are "discussions of questions in which opposing opinions clash" (Webster's Twentieth Century Dictionary Unabridged). Few would deny that controversies are a pervasive part of the human condition and exist on virtually every level of human enterprise. Controversies transpire between individuals and among groups, within nations and between nations. Controversies supply the grist necessary for progress by providing challenges and challengers to the status quo. They also create atmospheres where strife and warfare can flourish. A world without controversies would be a peaceful world; but it also would be, by and large, static and prosaic.

The Series' Purpose

The purpose of the Current Controversies series is to explore many of the social, political, and economic controversies dominating the national and international scenes today. Titles selected for inclusion in the series are highly focused and specific. For example, from the larger category of criminal justice, Current Controversies deals with specific topics such as police brutality, gun control, white collar crime, and others. The debates in Current Controversies also are presented in a useful, timeless fashion. Articles and book excerpts included in each title are selected if they contribute valuable, long-range ideas to the overall debate. And wherever possible, current information is enhanced with historical documents and other relevant materials. Thus, while individual titles are current in focus, every effort is made to ensure that they will not become quickly outdated. Books in the Current Controversies series will remain important resources for librarians, teachers, and students for many years.

In addition to keeping the titles focused and specific, great care is taken in the editorial format of each book in the series. Book introductions and chapter prefaces are offered to provide background material for readers. Chapters are organized around several key questions that are answered with diverse opinions representing all points on the political spectrum. Materials in each chapter include opinions in which authors clearly disagree as well as alternative opinions in which authors may agree on a broader issue but disagree on the possible solutions. In this way, the content of each volume in Current Controversies mirrors the mosaic of opinions encountered in society. Readers will quickly realize that there are many viable answers to these complex issues. By questioning each author's conclusions, students and casual readers can begin to develop the critical thinking skills so important to evaluating opinionated material.

Current Controversies is also ideal for controlled research. Each anthology in the series is composed of primary sources taken from a wide gamut of informational categories including periodicals, newspapers, books, United States and foreign government documents, and the publications of private and public organizations. Readers will find factual support for reports, debates, and research papers covering all areas of important issues. In addition, an annotated table of contents, an index, a book and periodical bibliography, and a list of organizations to contact are included in each book to expedite further research.

Perhaps more than ever before in history, people are confronted with diverse and contradictory information. During the Persian Gulf War, for example, the public was not only treated to minute-to-minute coverage of the war, it was also inundated with critiques of the coverage and countless analyses of the factors motivating U.S. involvement. Being able to sort through the plethora of opinions accompanying today's major issues, and to draw one's own conclusions, can be a complicated and frustrating struggle. It is the editors' hope that Current Controversies will help readers with this struggle.

Greenhaven Press anthologies primarily consist of previously published material taken from a variety of sources, including periodicals, books, scholarly journals, newspapers, government documents, and position papers from private and public organizations. These original sources are often edited for length and to ensure their accessibility for a young adult audience. The anthology editors also change the original titles of these works in order to clearly present the main thesis of each viewpoint and to explicitly indicate the opinion presented in the viewpoint. These alterations are made in consideration of both the reading and comprehension levels of a young adult audience. Every effort is made to ensure that Greenhaven Press accurately reflects the original intent of the authors included in this anthology.

> *"Tragic events involving guns rarely seem to speak for themselves or to point directly to the effectiveness or ineffectiveness of firearms; rather, what the incident 'proves' depends largely on the speakers and whether gun control or gun advocacy is their primary agenda."*

Introduction

As far as most parents were concerned, an informal prayer meeting, held every morning in front of Heath High School, was a safe, nurturing environment for their children. But on December 8, 1997, that perception was profoundly altered when a bizarre shootout brought tragedy and unwanted attention to the 27,000-person town of Paducah, Kentucky. Fourteen-year-old Michael Carneal, armed with a pistol, two shotguns, two rifles, and 700 rounds of ammunition, gunned down eight of his classmates before anyone could stop him. In the aftermath, while families mourned the loss of their children, others attempted to understand why this senseless tragedy occurred. Few could offer satisfactory explanations for a motive or factors leading to the event but most could not deny the extent to which gun violence had made its way into contemporary society.

There are more than 223 million firearms in the United States. With an increase in the number of incidents involving guns and children, the heated debate over gun control continues, not necessarily producing definitive answers but more often generating new arguments about the legitimacy of guns in modern society. Tragic events involving guns rarely seem to speak for themselves or to point directly to the effectiveness or ineffectiveness of firearms; rather, what the incident "proves" depends largely on the speakers and whether gun control or gun advocacy is their primary agenda. In the Paducah shooting, for example, gun control groups have argued that the availability of guns made it too easy for a high-school student to attain so many guns and, subsequently, too easy to murder his classmates. Gun advocates, however, view the event differently, asserting that gun availability had little to do with a tragedy that probably resulted from parental neglect and a lack of personal responsibility.

Behind the heated arguments surrounding gun control are motivations rising from very personal experiences with guns. For example, Carolyn McCarthy became an activist for stricter gun control laws after tragedy forever altered her life. In 1994, a gunman shot at twenty-five people inside a crowded Long Island Rail Road commuter train, killing six people including McCarthy's husband and leaving her son partially paralyzed. Grief over the loss of her husband and the pain of struggling with her son in his recovery propelled her on a mission to prevent similarly devastating tragedies by curtailing the availability of assault weapons.

Others who have experienced tragedies emerge with very different attitudes toward guns. After suffering a violent attack by a rapist, Nancy Bittle founded Arming Women Against Rape and Endangerment, which advocates women's gun ownership as a form of self-protection. "I was raised to view guns as symbols of evil," says Bittle, "but now I look at them as tools—like fire extinguishers."

Gun lobby groups, such as the National Rifle Association, have claimed the stories of people like Bittle to build their case to protect gun ownership. Women especially have been recognized as a group whose safety could be ensured most effectively by responsible gun use.

Personal experiences have acted as motivations behind gun advocacy but the "evidence" needed to further the passage of pro-gun policies comes from statistics-based studies by criminologists and social scientists. A 1996 study by John R. Lott and David B. Mustard, presented in the *Journal of Legal Studies'* article, "Crime, Deterrence, and Right-to-Carry Concealed Handguns," provided the "proof" for which gun advocates had been waiting. According to Lott and Mustard's study, states that allowed citizens to carry concealed handguns showed a marked decline in violent crimes. Furthermore, concealed handguns did not result in more gun accidents but deterred potentially violent incidents and prevented future crimes.

While gun lobbyists embraced Lott and Mustard's study, others criticized it, pointing out that unreliable statistical methods ultimately invalidated the study's pro-gun evaluations and, therefore, should not be employed in making policy decisions. Franklin Zimrig and Gordon Hawkins, authors of a critical analysis, "Concealed Handguns: The Counterfeit Deterrent" in *Responsive Community* assert, "The benefits and costs of permits to carry are marginal to the tremendous costs we already pay for the high ownership and use of handguns in the United States."

Many agree that gun violence is still a major problem that can be alleviated with gun control measures. "A little thing like a background check can prevent a murder. And a little thing like a waiting period can save a life," states Sarah Brady, chair of Handgun Control, Inc., the United States' largest citizens' gun control lobbying organization. Brady, whose husband, former press secretary James Brady, was left partially paralyzed during the 1981 assassination attempt on President Ronald Reagan, was responsible for the passage of the Brady Handgun Violence Prevention Act of 1993. The Brady Act requires vendors to impose a five-day waiting period and perform a background check on a customer before selling that person a gun. The Brady Act has faced opposition from gun lobbyists but still is considered a major success as a gun control measure. "We never said the Brady law would stop all forms of gun violence," asserts Brady. "But the Brady law *has* contributed to a major decline in gun-related crimes."

The relationship between guns and crime is just one of the issues addressed in *Guns and Violence: Current Controversies*. Contributors such as Bob Herbert, Sarah Brady, David B. Kopel, Charlton Heston, and John R. Lott also examine the seriousness of gun violence as a cultural phenomenon. They debate the constitutionality of gun control, the effectiveness of gun ownership, and measures to reduce gun violence.

Chapter 1

How Serious Is the Problem of Gun Violence?

Chapter Preface

Deaths and injuries from gun violence have been the focus of increasing attention in America. Examples pervade the media. A laid-off employee returns to his company to gun down former managers and co-workers. A troubled graduate student chases after his engineering professors and shoots them point blank. A thirteen-year-old boy, planning revenge against a female classmate for breaking up with him, goes on a shooting spree at school and kills four girls. Violent incidents involving guns make their impact on the general public and influence thoughts on personal safety and moral responsibility.

To some, such tragic events signal a disturbing era in which communication is lost and guns become a means to settle disputes. For other opponents of firearms, the fact that so many people, including children, have access to guns indicates that the potential for gun violence is prevalent even for those who are not intent on committing a crime. "More than ten children are killed by handguns every day," says Jann Wenner, founder of Cease Fire, a national public education campaign. Statistics indicate that 41 percent of American households contain one or more guns. According to the federal Centers for Disease Control and Prevention, by the year 2003, gunfire will be the leading cause of injury death in the United States. For many people, these findings support the contention that gun violence is a serious problem.

Some critics, however, are reluctant to accept what they feel is needless fear about guns. To people like John Lott, who studies the impact of guns on crime, the problem of gun violence is exaggerated by anti-gun groups. Guns, according to Lott, more often are used by responsible owners to prevent crime. Subsequently, such effective means of self-defense and prevention contributes to a reduction in the level of violence that occurs in the country. Studies do indicate that gun violence may be subsiding. The Federal Bureau of Investigation's 1996 crime survey showed a decrease in the number of violent crimes committed with guns, and a decline in violence overall.

In the following chapter, viewpoints from various arenas address the seriousness of gun violence in the United States.

Gun Violence Is Becoming an Epidemic

by Bob Herbert

About the author: *Bob Herbert is a syndicated columnist for the* New York Times *and a former NBC News reporter.*

The first thought of Police Officer Michael Robbins in the swirling, eerily quiet aftermath of the ambush was that he was going to die. He and his partner, Talmitch Jackson, were in their patrol car, the headlights off, in a dark alley on Chicago's South Side, and both had just been riddled with bullets. They were moaning and they were soaked in blood.

As Officer Robbins sank toward unconsciousness and what he believed was death, he thought of his mother, who had died several years before. He had a vague sense that he could see her, that perhaps in his extreme distress she was there, encouraging him, somehow conveying to him that he should struggle harder and that he would not die.

The attack occurred on the night of Sept. 10, 1994. An ex-convict with a semiautomatic weapon opened fire on the officers as they pulled into the alley to investigate a report of a gang disturbance. Officer Robbins, who was behind the wheel, was hit 11 times and Officer Jackson four times. Although grievously scarred physically and emotionally, both have since recovered.

As Officer Robbins put it, referring to the extensive surgery he has undergone, "They opened me up like a fish, but I'm O.K. now."

Presenting the Case

For several days Officer Robbins had been working on a brief speech to be delivered in prime time at the Democratic National Convention. On Aug. 26, 1996, he told delegates and the nation about the work he had done since the shooting as a leader in the fight against gun violence, which he called a "modern plague."

Officer Robbins heads a Chicago-based program that is part of the national HELP Network, an organization founded in 1994 by Dr. Katherine Kaufer

Christoffel, a pediatrician, to deal with the devastating public health consequences of gun violence in the United States. Simply stated, HELP's goal is to reduce the carnage, especially among children.

The statistics are appalling: More than 5,000 juveniles and 33,000 adults die each year from gunshot wounds. More than a million latchkey kids come home to a house or apartment in which there is a gun. The firearm homicide rate for males tripled between 1984 and 1993.

Calling Attention to the Problem

"This is an epidemic," Officer Robbins wrote in a draft of his speech, "that is about 10 times as big, in terms of lives lost, as the great polio epidemic of the first half of this century. This new scourge paralyzes at least as many as polio did at its worst. It needs to be stopped."

Gun violence on television and in the movies is quick and clean and often glamorous. No approximation of the agonizing pain of the victim is ever conveyed. And seldom are there true accounts of the all but unbearable sadness that settles over the lives of the parents, wives, husbands, siblings, friends and lovers of those who are lost.

"I'm one of the fortunate ones," Officer Robbins said in an interview. "I've been spared. I feel there has been some divine inspiration and you couldn't convince me otherwise. But it's been difficult. I've had to go through enormous changes. And not just physical, but emotional. Despair. Distress over my being assaulted like that. The anger. And just wondering about the recovery. You know, how much of my old self would I be able to get back?

"The statistics are appalling: More than 5,000 juveniles and 33,000 adults die each year from gunshot wounds."

"I was fortunate to have relatives, friends and co-workers who were able, sort of like Humpty Dumpty, to put me back together again."

Living Proof

Officer Robbins has bullets and fragments of bullets—what he calls "debris"—in various parts of his body. One bullet is lodged less than an inch from his spine.

The weather, he says, plays havoc with him. "This is Chicago, man. The weather here is rough, and if you have all that metal inside you, you're going to be affected. You get very stiff, very sore, and there's a lot of, sort of, achiness."

When he walked to the podium, Michael Robbins carried with him the honest and simple notion of public service. He talked about the problem of gun violence because he would like to spare others the fate that befell him.

"Convalescing," he said, "I felt as I did when I was in the Navy. I wanted to do something to help my country. That's all I'm trying to do."

Gun Violence Is Increasing Among Children

by Sandy Grady

About the author: *Sandy Grady is a writer for the* Philadelphia Daily News. *Her column is syndicated in newspapers throughout the United States.*

Their names were Natalie, Brittany, Stephanie and Paige Ann. In photos they wear fresh, impish smiles of 12- and 11-year-olds peddling Girl Scout cookies or heading for a pajama party.

You look at their pictures—and the placid smile of heroic teacher Shannon Wright, who shielded another child—and every face comes at you with a jolting puzzle.

The faces of the dead ask, "Why?"

Answers don't come easy. The faces strike you with baffled anger. Why would a couple of pint-size Rambos in camouflage outfits grab an arsenal of rifles and fire 27 high-powered slugs—as though the crowd of school children was just a video game?

Shooting mayhem by a crazed adult can be unraveled by shrinks. But kids blowing apart kids is ultimate, numbing horror. We're stumped how innocence got twisted into evil. Until we know the nightmare visions in the heads of Mitchell Johnson, 13, and Andrew Golden, 11, we grope in the dark.

Searching For Reasons

Maybe it will come down to guns. Usually does. Hard to imagine the March 1998 Jonesboro, Ark., kid murders happening any place but America, where weaponry is ubiquitous as Big Macs. Maybe we'll wait for Bill Clinton's experts to figure out the pattern of these kid shoot-'em-ups. Don't hold your breath.

Maybe Arkansas Gov. Mike Huckabee, a Baptist minister, got close to the truth in blaming the child gunners on an epidemic of TV and movie violence.

"I don't know what else we'd expect in a culture where children are exposed to tens of thousands of murders on television and movies. We've desensitized

Reprinted from Sandy Grady, "The Questions After Jonesboro," *Philadelphia Daily News*, March 27, 1998, by permission.

human life," said a bitter Huckabee. "It's a cultural disease."

He's right. A National Television Violence Study says gunfire and gore on TV, despite the ratings, isn't declining. Worse, says Northeastern University criminologist James Fox, are computer and arcade videos in which kids play-act at wasting people.

In TV crime shows, gangsta rap and videos, victims get knocked off cleanly: No pain, gaping wounds, screams. Is that what the Arkansas tyke shooters saw on the school ground—symbolic targets?

Who Else Is Responsible?

Pull the trigger, man, it's a game. Or maybe we should blame schools. They don't gear up enough security, cops and metal detectors. Don't spot and counsel troublemakers before the firing starts. Sure, in hindsight, there were signals the Arkansas kid gunmen were destined to explode.

The 13-year-old told a girl, "Tomorrow you find out whether you live or die." He vowed to shoot a sixth-grade girl (who survived) because she broke up with him. "Nobody breaks up with me," he boasted. (Hey, it's the TV code: Cross me, you die.)

No shock the kid assassins weren't taken seriously. The national average is one counselor for 800 middle-school kids. Not easy to detect suicidal or homicidal dynamite.

What about parents? Early accounts say parents of the 13-year-old

"Shooting mayhem by a crazed adult can be unraveled by shrinks. But kids blowing apart kids is ultimate, numbing horror."

shooter were hard-working, middle-class folks, both postmasters. And yes, the dad raised his boy as a hunter and competition marksman from age 6. Here, I'd agree: When juveniles turn killers, the law should come down hard on parents. Seventeen states have such laws, not Arkansas.

Too Many Guns

In the end, it may come back to guns—too many of them, too easy for a wacko kid to grab and go bonkers, a culture where shooting others becomes TV fantasy.

The 11-year-old's grandfather said in a CNN interview the boy stole three rifles from him. Doesn't matter. Guns are a way of life in Arkansas (75 percent own them).

But shooting hardware is as plentiful on the streets of Philly, D.C. or Chicago.

Will we ever do anything about this ballistic epidemic in over-armed U.S.A.? Oh, the Jonesboro effect will dwindle.

There'll be no disarmament or even toning down the firepower while the National Rifle Association cowers politicians.

Except for "deep sorrow," the NRA stonewalled as though the Arkansas kid murderers used slingshots. "Lawful gun ownership had nothing to do with this tragedy," insisted gun-lobby spokesman Bill Powers.

(Next NRA bumper stickers: "Guns don't kill kids, kids kill kids.")

Sure, there'll be hand-wringing by congressional blowhards about the Jonesboro deaths.

They won't defy the NRA while campaign bucks flow. The gun lobby would even like to dismantle the Brady Bill and assault-weapon law.

Perhaps a Lost Nation

Look at Australia, a tough, gun-happy country. In 1996 a nut case killed 35 people in Port Arthur. Within two weeks, the country banned sale and possession of assault-type guns and pump-action shotguns. Not in America.

"If the Jonesboro tragedy doesn't move Washington beyond tears and into action, what will?" fumed Sen. Frank Lautenberg, D-N.J.

Nothing, senator.

You can blame TV crime shows, bloody videos, school counselors and parents. But the Jonesboro horror will fade—until the next child gunner goes berserk.

Those smiling faces of Natalie, Brittany, Stephanie and Paige Ann ask for answers. They'll get silence.

Gun Violence Is Overwhelming the Nation's Health Care System

by Susan Headden

About the author: *Susan Headden is a staff writer for* U.S. News & World Report. *Her feature stories focus on prominent economic issues.*

One glance in the rearview mirror of his 1978 Cadillac Eldorado and 21-year-old Dewayne Bellamy knew that his evening was over. Approaching the car near a decaying corner of the nation's capital was the teenage son of a woman with whom Bellamy was having an affair. The boy had a gun. Before Bellamy could draw from his own arsenal of semiautomatic weapons, he heard the familiar pop of a 9-millimeter pistol. There was no pain, no blood. Only after he awoke from a coma three days later did Bellamy receive two pieces of news. The first was that he had been shot 13 times. The second was that he would never walk again.

From the moment paramedics lifted him into the ambulance, Bellamy became the charge of the nation's taxpayers. And for the next eight months, the meter would never stop ticking. Covering everything from $3 scalpels to $2,283 CT scans, Bellamy's hospital bills would ultimately total $562,561. Doctors' fees would add tens of thousands more to the tab. For Bellamy, a onetime car thief who used to earn $5,000 a day selling crack cocaine, that's big money. But he doesn't worry about it. After all, he's not paying the bills.

In emergency rooms and rehabilitation centers across the country, Bellamy's is a depressingly familiar tale. By the year 2003, according to the federal Centers for Disease Control and Prevention, gunfire will have surpassed auto accidents as the leading cause of injury death in the United States. In seven states, it already has. But unlike victims of car crashes, who are almost always privately insured, 4 out of 5 gunshot victims are on public assistance or uninsured. That means taxpayers bear the brunt of medical costs that have spiked nearly ninefold since 1986, to a stunning $4.5 billion a year.

Nationwide, the number of violent crimes has held steady since 1992, yet gun sales continue to soar. While most gun owners buy their weapons legally, keeping them for self-protection and recreation, a flourishing illegal-drug trade has caused a dramatic rise in the number of powerful semiautomatic weapons used to commit crimes. The result is a flood of new gunshot victims to the nation's emergency rooms.

Multiple Wounds

Although injuries from military-style assault weapons are rare, multiple wounds inflicted by semiautomatics such as 9-millimeter pistols are becoming so common as to make some trauma specialists practically nostalgic for the days of the cheap Saturday night special. "It seems like we never see just one shot anymore," says orthopedic surgeon Andrew Burgess of the University of Maryland's shock-trauma center in Baltimore. The increased firepower means doctors are saving fewer patients—and seeing greater damage to those who do survive.

Today's gunshot victims are a distinctive breed. Headlines highlight shootings of innocent bystanders, but the fact is that probably half of gun homicide victims—in some cities as many as 70 percent—are offenders themselves. They are due no less care, doctors say, but they confront modern medicine with an unsettling paradox: Physicians invest countless hours at huge expense to bind wounds and even heal their gunshot patients, only to return them to the streets, where many promptly resume a life of crime. "About 20 percent of our gunshot victims are what we call our 'frequent fliers,' says Burgess. "It's not as if they leave here and find Jesus."

Criminals or bystanders, those shot by semiautomatic weapons can test the limits of even the best emergency care. Lamarr Wilson of Newark, N.J., was one such victim. Shot seven times with a semiautomatic, the 23-year-old was riddled with so many holes that doctors in the trauma unit of the University of Medicine and Dentistry of New Jersey couldn't treat them fast enough. "We'd plug up one hole, only to find two more," says Tonni Glick, an emergency room nurse. The perforations caused the contents of Wilson's bowels to spill into his lacerated vital organs. Wilson's abdominal skin eroded so badly it had to be replaced with a sheet of plastic wrap. Altogether, he endured 14 different surgical procedures. "This one, we never thought he'd make it," says Glick. "But these young guys are tough. We saved his life." A Medicaid patient, Wilson spent 61 days in the hospital. The bottom line: $268,181.

> *"While most gun owners buy their weapons legally, . . . a flourishing illegal-drug trade has caused a dramatic rise in the number of powerful semiautomatic weapons used to commit crimes."*

In the seemingly endless debate over gun control, one fact is unassailable: Gunshot patients are far more expensive to take care of than are victims of other kinds of crime. A typical stab wound, for example, cost $6,446 to treat in 1992; the average gunshot case cost $14,541. Although gunshot wounds account for fewer than 1 percent of injuries in hospitals nationwide, they generate 9 percent of injury treatment costs. That's because more than half of all gunshot victims require expensive emergency surgery. Typical are laparotomies (average cost at one urban hospital: $41,000), thoracotomies (average cost: $26,000) and procedures on the neck and extremities. And that's often just the beginning: About a fifth of all gunshot victims require additional surgery later on.

"Disruption"

One reason for the higher treatment costs is physics. A bullet causes trauma to human tissue by transmitting energy beyond the capacity of the tissue to absorb and dissipate it. That causes what doctors call "disruption." The extent of the damage depends on the size and speed of the bullet and the type of tissue affected. A bullet can stretch human tissue, creating an opening that in the most severe cases may expand to many times the size of the bullet. Whether the cavity is temporarily or permanently damaged depends on the body area affected. Elastic tissue like that of a bowel wall is more resistant to permanent damage; inelastic tissue like that of the liver and brain is less so. "If a rubber ball and a raw egg of equal weight are dropped on a cement floor from the same height, these two missiles of equal kinetic energy will sustain different degrees of damage," explains Dr. Jeremy Hollerman of the Hennepin County Medical Center in Minneapolis. "The rubber ball behaves like skeletal muscle or lung, the raw egg like the brain or liver."

> *"Gunshot patients are far more expensive to take care of than are victims of other kinds of crime."*

At higher velocities, bullets pack more destructive force, causing more extensive damage to soft tissue. Bullets fired at high velocity also tend to create a kind of suctioning action when they strike human tissue, carrying external bacteria deep into internal wounds.(Contrary to popular belief, bullets are not sterilized in the heat of firing.) Slugs are often left in the body when their removal poses a greater danger to a victim, but they can cause lead poisoning and degenerative arthritis if lodged in a joint. Bullets fired at high velocity are also more likely to shatter when they strike bone or metal, producing multiple and even more destructive projectiles. Says Dr. Kenneth Swan of the University of Medicine and Dentistry of New Jersey: "In the face, these secondary (bullets) often cause more damage to the brain and eyes than the primary bullet."

When they survive, victims of multiple gunshots almost always go on to live more complicated—and more expensive—lives. Nestor Cantor, 22, of Brooklyn, N.Y., took seven shots in the small of his back from a 9-millimeter semiautomatic fired by a hit man in Richmond Hill, Queens. The bullets exploded, driving lead fragments deep into his spinal cord. Extensive operations repaired lacerations to his bladder and liver and drained fluid from his lungs. The doctors call Cantor a "T10 complete"—paralyzed from the waist down. Two weeks in the intensive care unit, 3½ months at Bellevue Hospital and 1½ years in a public rehabilitation facility have generated a

> *"When they survive, victims of multiple gunshots almost always go on to live more complicated—and more expensive—lives."*

Medicaid bill in excess of $300,000. "I never see what it costs," says Cantor. "I haven't paid anything out of my pocket."

At George Washington University Medical Center in Washington, D.C., former Medical Director Keith Ghezzi, an emergency room physician, totes up the financial toll of a weekend of violence in the nation's capital. A typical gunshot patient spent 16 days in the intensive care unit at $1,487 per day. The patient required drugs costing $13,580, X-rays at $2,738, and bandages, tubes and miscellaneous supplies totaling $16,280. Nursing care, physical therapy and other services added thousands more to the bill. By the time the man was discharged from the hospital, he had racked up a bill of $100,838, not including doctor's fees. Medicaid will pay about 70 percent of the bill; the patient will pay nothing.

The story is repeated every few days. In 1995, a homeless man who had served time for armed robbery and assault was taken to George Washington after he was shot while wielding a knife outside the White House. In just two days, the man received more than $70,000 in medical care. He died. The hospital ate the cost of his treatment.

Cost Shifting

Such cases show how handgun violence affects Americans who have never even seen a gun or heard one fired in anger. Like most institutions, George Washington covers the costs of treating uninsured and underinsured patients by increasing the bills of those who do pay. Such cost shifting, a report to Congress estimated, forced private patients to pay an average of 29 percent above the actual costs of their care in 1993. According to one study, the University of California-Davis Medical Center, despite incurring three-year losses of nearly $2.2 million on gunshot victims, actually made a profit on its trauma center, so heavily did it shift the burden to patients who could pay.

As health maintenance organizations demand more and more savings, however, hospitals are finding it more difficult to pawn off on anyone the costs of the uninsured. The consequences for trauma units are dire. Once sure-fire moneymakers, more than 60 urban trauma centers have closed in the past 10 years, leaving less than one quarter of the nation's population residing anywhere near top-flight trauma care. In a study by the General Accounting Office for members of Congress, all the shuttered trauma centers blamed their troubles on the growing burden of uncompensated services—millions of dollars of which resulted from treating indigent victims of handgun violence.

For every patient who dies from a gunshot wound—and there were 39,720 in 1994—three others are injured seriously enough to be hospitalized. Of those, one on average suffers from a disabling, lifelong injury. The worst injuries are to the spinal cord, and the higher on the cord the blow, the greater the area paralyzed. If a patient is injured anywhere between the first and third cervical vertebrae, for instance, he may lose all feeling from the neck down. Most spinal-cord-injured gunshot victims are paraplegics, paralyzed only from the waist down.

Million Dollar Man

Eddie Matos was unluckier than most. In the past six months, the 21-year-old former drug dealer has not moved from his room at New York's Goldwater Memorial Hospital, where he keeps the shades pulled tight and watches soap operas and videos all day. He could motor around the grounds in the $5,000 electric wheelchair he operates by puffing on a straw. But why bother? he says. He sees the same old patients, and they all look like him. Before his accident, Matos was a prospering businessman. He had four "spots": three for crack, one for cocaine. One spot could make $11,000 on a weekend; Matos kept $2,000. The money bought cars—a Cadillac, a Pathfinder, a Mustang and a Volvo. It bought jewelry and his own apartment. It also paid for a 9-millimeter semiautomatic pistol. "My favorite," Matos says. "It does damage."

He should know. One night in September 1990, another man with a 9 millimeter jumped Matos outside a grocery store and shot him once in the neck. The gunman has since "gotten his," Matos says. But his own life is shattered. Lying in the quadraplegic ward of the aging city-run hospital, his only movements are the painful spasms that convulse his muscles every so often. He cannot feed himself

"Handgun violence affects Americans who have never even seen a gun or heard one fired in anger."

or breathe without a ventilator. He must clench a wand in his teeth to turn the pages of a book. Matos has stayed at Goldwater longer than any other gunshot victim. His treatment has cost the public well over $1 million.

Aiming to Maim?

For patients paralyzed by gunfire, bills like Matos's are not uncommon. Quadraplegics, paralyzed from the neck down, require round-the-clock care. They need aides to change catheters, tracheotomy tubes and bladder bags; to feed, bathe and clothe them; to help wean them, if possible, from their ventilators. Unable to cough, their lungs must be suctioned several times a day to prevent pneumonia, which threatens lives already shortened by ventilator dependency. Bladder infections, which strike with troubling frequency, must be attacked aggressively or they will spread. Beyond medical care, there is arduous physical therapy to prevent muscle atrophy and occupational therapy to help patients function in a nonhandicapped world.

"So common are spinal cord injuries among gunshot victims today that some health care providers suspect gunmen are deliberately aiming for the neck."

All in all, a bullet in the spinal cord is an expensive proposition. In 1992 dollars (the most recent figures available), the National Spinal Cord Injury Statistical Center estimated first-year medical costs for a high quadraplegic (injured in the uppermost cervical vertebra) at $417,067, plus $74,707 for each year thereafter. The first-year costs for a paraplegic were $152,396, plus $15,507 for each year thereafter. For a 25-year-old quadraplegic, that would amount to lifetime medical costs of $1.3 million; for a paraplegic, $427,700.

So common are spinal cord injuries among gunshot victims today that some health care providers suspect gunmen are deliberately aiming for the neck. "It's as if the gunmen are saying, 'We don't want to kill you; we just want to paralyze you,' says Glick of the University of Medicine and Dentistry of New Jersey. "We want to keep you alive so you will always remember what happened to you." In Los Angeles, at least half of all spinal cord injuries are caused by gunshots. Since most insurance plans have lifetime benefit caps, even those patients with private health insurance eventually end up on Medicaid. Roughly 75 percent of all gunshot victims are under 30, as are half of all spinal cord victims. That means better survival rates, of course—and many costly years ahead.

At the Kessler Institute for Rehabilitation in West Orange, N.J., whose stellar reputation for treating head- and spinal-cord-injured victims has attracted celebrities like dancer Ben Vereen and actor Christopher Reeve, gunshot survivor Talmadge Conover improved steadily under a rehabilitation program that costs $1,000 a day. But once the 18-year-old paraplegic returned to his drab third-floor apartment in a fading section of Newark, N.J., with three bullets still in his abdomen, he found it harder to keep doing the pull-ups that flipped his skinny body from side to side. The result: bedsores so infected they started eating away at his bone. Now, Conover is recovering from a successful skin-graft operation, studying for a high school equivalency degree and working the phones from a $30,000 Clinitron bed, a sort of heated hammock of delicate silicone balls. He says he has stopped dealing cocaine. Estimated cost of his treatment: more than $134,000.

Carrying a Nine

That Conover was shot with a 9-millimeter semiautomatic weapon would come as no surprise to anyone who has spent time in an urban trauma center.

Introduced in the early 1980s to revive a sagging gun industry, "nines" are the weapon of choice on city streets. They are cheap and concealable, and, with extended magazines, they allow the shooter to fire up to 36 rounds without reloading. "You carry [a nine] to get a rep," explains Matos, "to get respect."

The Treasury Department's Bureau of Alcohol, Tobacco and Firearms lists two brands of 9 millimeters—the $410 Ruger P89 and the $609 Glock 17—among the top 10 guns found at crime scenes. There are more than 3 million 9 millimeters on America's streets, and while many of those are arming law enforcement officers, the number of 9 millimeters used by criminals has nearly doubled since 1987. In Philadelphia in 1987, 9 millimeters sent 57 victims to local trauma hospitals; by 1993, the number of victims hospitalized by 9 millimeters had soared to 351.

Gun Violence Is Proliferating

Vernon Parker, a 31-year-old Brooklyn man, still carries nine bullets in his right thigh from the 17 rounds of an Intratec TEC-9 semiautomatic fired into him outside a housing project in the Bedford-Stuyvesant section on Oct.19, 1993. (The manufacture of TEC-9s, along with certain magazines, was banned under the 1994 assault weapons law, but thousands made before the ban remain in circulation.) Slugs from the TEC-9 struck Parker's groin, buttocks and shoulder, necessitating three operations and two years in the hospital. The cost: well over $500,000. Today, there is little hope that Parker will walk again. "It used to be that just flashing a gun was enough," says Parker, a convicted drug dealer who speaks from experience. "But these young guys today, they'll shoot a whole crowd in broad daylight just to get one dead."

> *"These young guys today, they'll shoot a whole crowd in broad daylight just to get one dead."*

To doctors after a while, the entries on emergency-room-admissions forms start to look the same: *GSW, BL, M, 1976, MA*—gunshot wound, black, male, 20 years old, medical assistance. Only the faces change. "There is a lot of frustration and angst about these injuries," says Stephen Hargarten, an emergency room physician at the Medical College of Wisconsin in Milwaukee. It is no longer enough, he says, for emergency room doctors to simply treat gunshot victims and release them. "Doctors must leave the bedside," he says, "and go to the legislatures."

Solutions?

And so they are. Physicians are lobbying for restrictions on U.S. handguns as strict as those for imports. They want childproof guns, a heavier tax on ammunition and other reforms.

In their more discouraging moments, however, doctors admit the prognosis is

Chapter 1

poor. Nestor Cantor, after all, says he knows seven people who have been shot, six of them killed. Eddie Matos counts at least five. Talmadge Conover says he knows more than a dozen victims of handgun violence, three of them dead. He has had days when he wanted to join them. But in a country where there is one handgun for every other household, even those relegated to wheelchairs show no inclination to disarm. The phenomenon, says Cantor, "is just too big. It's out of control."

Gun Violence Is Killing Many Young People

by Jennifer Weiner

About the author: *Jennifer Weiner, staff writer for the* Philadelphia Inquirer, *has written about the entertainment industry as well as women's issues.*

You could hardly find four girls with less in common than Jackie, Taniesha, Nikkie and Lenorra.

Taniesha Roane was 15. She lived with her grandmother in a rough Philadelphia neighborhood where friends were falling, one by one, to the streets. Jackie Przybylski, 17, lived a world away in a small Wisconsin town, a bubbly girl with a Mickey Mouse shirt for every day of the week who amused her close-knit family with her string of short romances. Fourteen-year-old Nikkie Bastan-Siar was a quiet girl whose life was neither as harsh as Taniesha's nor as carefree as Jackie's. Her parents split when she was a baby, and she grew up with her big sister and her single father, a truck driver whose long hours often kept him away from home. And 20-year-old Lenorra Koung survived a mass murder in her native Cambodia only to confront violence, American-style—more random, but just as fatal.

Their talents and hopes were unique. The only thing these girls shared was the terrible way they died: by gunfire. You might argue that their deaths were tragic mistakes, that each was just in the wrong place at the wrong time. If only Jackie had gone home when that boy started showing off his shotgun. If only Taniesha had listened to her grandma and chosen different friends—ones who didn't carry guns. If only Nikkie had not been feeling so sad the night a boy she didn't know had brought a gun to her best friend's house. If only Lenorra hadn't been visiting her boyfriend at his video store the night a guy armed with two guns came looking for revenge over a petty quarrel.

Nikkie, Taniesha, Jackie, and Lenorra died because they lived in a world where there are guns in the hands of too many kids—guns that float through high school lockers and backpacks and parties as easily as cigarettes or car keys. Fifteen Americans younger than age 20 die from gunfire *every day*.

"These girls died because of the unsupervised, unregulated gun industry in this country. They would be alive if the United States had laws to prevent the easy availability of guns," says Tina Johnstone, one of the organizers of an event to remind lawmakers of this epidemic of violent death.

> *"Nikkie, Taniesha, Jackie and Lenorra died because they lived in a world where there are guns in the hands of too many kids."*

On September 30, 1996, in Washington, D.C., nearly 40,000 pairs of shoes were lined up around the reflecting pool of the Capitol. That's the number of people in this country who are killed every year by gun violence. Organizers called this the Silent March, since the victims themselves can no longer speak in protest.

For every empty pair of shoes, there was a story—the girl who never got to wear her dyed pumps to the prom, the boy who will never shoot hoops in his high-tops again.

Nikkie, Lenorra, Jackie and Taniesha will be remembered with tears, but also with determination. These are their stories.

Jackie: Missed at Home

"It's so quiet now," says Marian Przybylski (say it shuh-BIL-ski).

It doesn't *seem* quiet in her home in Stevens Point, Wisconsin. There are the sounds of television and passing traffic, kids on their bikes outside.

Then you realize what Przybylski no longer hears: the stereo playing Clint Black, the telephone ringing constantly, the door slamming as her 17-year-old youngest daughter makes her way in and out.

"You wait for her to come through that door," says Jackie's oldest sister, JoAnne, "and it just never happens. It still doesn't seem real."

Jackie's room is almost exactly the way she left it on a Friday night in September. Her James Dean poster hangs on one wall, her elementary-school track ribbons and collection of porcelain masks on the others. Her bed is neatly made—typical of a girl who'd visit her sloppier friends and, without prompting, start vacuuming their rooms. "That's just the way Jackie was," says her mom.

You can drive through town on this June Saturday, when Jackie would have celebrated her high school graduation, and trace her history. There are the streets she drove—too fast, her friends admit, laughing and remembering Jackie piloting the gigantic black Oldsmobile that her family called The Boat, calling out to cute boys in other cars, getting stuck in snowbanks or driving into ditches.

There's the dentist's office where she'd worked since she was 14, the Hot 'n Now where she'd scarf down double cheeseburgers, the YMCA where she studied Tae Kwon Do, the gym where she'd work out. "She was the liveliest person

I know," says Sarah Smoker, 18, who was one of Jackie's best friends since first grade. "She was never bored. She always had an idea of something to do. She'd call me all the time—'Let's go for a walk! Let's go get gas!' "

An Active Life

Jackie sported a total of nine earrings, and was the first one on her block to pierce her navel—by herself, with a pin. In high school Jackie dated a half-dozen boys in quick succession, breaking things off before they got too serious because she didn't want to settle down, but managing to remain friends with all her exes. "Every few weeks, you'd hear the slam of the back door and a car zooming off . . . but they'd always be back," says her mom.

Jackie also had a serious side. When she was 13, she announced to her own dentist, in the midst of an appointment, that she wanted to be a dentist, too. He hired her the next year to help in the office, and Jackie never got bored, or grossed out by the blood.

She also shared a special bond with her father, David. Of the three girls in the family, Jackie was the only one who was interested in hunting. She didn't mind waking up at four in the morning to go out with her dad in the cold and silent woods. She went to hunter's safety school, and by sixth grade she had her own rifles. "She respected guns," says her mother. "All of my girls knew they weren't something to play with."

An Unfortunate Meeting

But not everybody shared that respect. On a Friday night after the first high school football game of Jackie's senior year, she and some friends gathered at the home of a classmate she didn't know very well. His name was Ryan Murphy. Police say Ryan's father ran a gun dealership out of his house. It was sometime during the party that Jackie saw Ryan trying to show off by picking up a pump shotgun and holding it to the head of her friend Alicia Bembenek. Jackie saw the threat immediately: "Hey, the safety's not on," witnesses say she cried. Ryan turned and put the gun to Jackie's head, police say, and pulled the trigger.

The other kids started screaming and ran. Ryan dialed 911 and told the operator that he had been screwing around with a gun, and that a girl named Jackie was dead. Then he shot himself in the face, first with the same gun, then with a rifle. Neither shot killed him, and he eventually surrendered to police. At press time he had been charged with first-degree homicide for Jackie's death, and reckless use of a dangerous weapon for putting the gun to Alicia's head.

> *"[Jackie] went to hunter's safety school, and by sixth grade she had her own rifles."*

A police officer knocked on the Przybylski's door at 3:45 A.M. "I thought she was sitting in the car, that he'd tell us Jackie had done something and was sitting back there, too scared to come out and tell us," her mother says.

Now Jackie's family, and her wide circle of friends, are acutely aware of the silent spaces in their lives where Jackie, with her bright smile, used to be.

"I remember," says her mother, "how that phone would be ringing all the time, and I'd say to Jackie, 'I'm not your secretary!' Boy, I wish I could say that now."

Nikkie: A Party Appearance

Her family knew that Nikkie had been upset about her breakup with her boyfriend, and that she was sometimes unsettled by the situation at home. But the person who was closest to her in the world—her older sister, Angee—thought she was coping pretty well.

Angee and her dad definitely didn't see any sign that Nikkie was depressed on that Saturday in June. Nikkie and her sister (14 and 15) had arranged to go to their friend Debbie's house for a party and then spend the night. Nikkie was going to shower and dress there, and she couldn't decide what she wanted to wear, so she walked out of her house with a big pile of potential party outfits. She didn't look like she was planning anything desperate. Who knows what would have happened if a gun had not shown up at the party?

> *"Who knows what would have happened if a gun had not shown up at the party?"*

Up until that night, Nikkie and Angee were always together. Born in September, a year and three days apart, the sisters shared a room, shared clothes, shared secrets. They dated best friends, did 60 sit-ups a day to keep in shape and talked about becoming models. They were both planning to be bridesmaids in their father's wedding. "We were together 24-7," Angee says.

Not an Easy Life

Her parents had split up when Nikkie was 2½. Her dad, Hugh Bastan-Siar, was a truck driver who'd emigrated from Iran. Although he and his ex-wife, Marie, shared custody, Hugh raised the girls, and it wasn't easy for anyone. He worked long hours, and Nikkie and Angee were often with sitters and live-in caretakers or, later, on their own.

By the time Nikkie started ninth grade at Arundel Senior High, outside of Baltimore, she'd moved more than a dozen times, hopping from suburb to suburb. "It was hard, making friends, then losing them and having to start again," says Angee. It was especially hard for Nikkie, who was quiet and shy, and who let her sister take the lead.

Nikkie was an excellent student, a talented gymnast and also more of a straight arrow than her sister. 'When I was in middle school, I'd go out, but she never would," Angee says, remembering how her sister would chide her for drinking. "She'd say, 'Angee, why do you do that?'" But by the time she was 13, Nikkie's attitude was changing. Maybe she was worried that her big sister, one of the only sure things in a life full of new apartments and new schools, was leaving her behind.

Soon Nikkie was joining Angee in using their father's frequent absences to stay out late at parties where parents weren't around. But Nikkie was still herself, "the quiet one who'd sit in the corner," her sister says. "Everywhere we'd go, I'd get all the attention."

Finding Love

Nikkie fell in love the summer she was 13, with a guy who was 17. They went out for eight months. "He's tall, real good-looking," Angee says. "She was head over heels with him."

But being in love wasn't easy. Her boyfriend wanted sex. Nikkie wasn't ready—and she confided in her father that the guy she loved was pushing it. "She told me that when she had sex, she wanted it to be with someone who loved her," her dad says. "She would tell me that her feelings for him were strong, and that she wasn't sure he felt the same things back."

Nikkie's boyfriend broke up with her in December of her freshman year and started dating Debbie, one of the sisters' best friends. Janet Bastan-Siar, then Hugh's fiancée and now his second wife, says that Nikkie took the breakup hard.

"She pined for him," she says. "I would tell her, 'Nikkie, it's going to pass,' but she always felt things so passionately."

A Convenient Gun

Nikkie's ex was expected at Debbie's house that Saturday in June. Also coming to the get-together were some guys Angee and Debbie had known in middle school, guys that Nikkie didn't know. One of them—Chris Stillman—brought a .38-caliber revolver to the party.

> *"Taniesha had been shot to death as she sat in the living room of Angel's apartment with a bunch of older neighborhood guys, 18- and 19-year-olds."*

Police say that Chris took the bullets out to show the gun around, and then loaded it again. Nikkie had gone into a bedroom and was adding a few last words to a note she'd written some time before, police say. At some point Chris and another boy joined her. In the note, she was telling Angee she was the best sister anyone could hope for. She was saying goodbye to her mom and dad. She was telling whoever would read it about her broken heart. Maybe she was imagining that the guy who dropped her would be the one to find her on the bed.

Police believe Nikkie picked up the gun Chris had placed beside him on the bed. Angee was in the kitchen when it went off. "I heard this *pop*, and I ran to the bedroom. There was blood and brains all over the wall, and I knew. . . . I knew she was dead."

Someone called an ambulance. Chris took off, tossing the gun as he ran. It's never been recovered. Police say the case is an open-and-shut suicide.

The family doesn't believe it. Angee insists that Nikkie had no way of knowing there'd be a gun at the party that night. Her father keeps coming back to that stack of clean clothes she took with her, and the $7 he'd given her. "If she wanted to die, why would she have bothered?" he asks.

And as for Angee, the big sister Nikkie loved and left behind, her whole life is different. "I can't turn around and have her be there. I'm by myself." She moved out of her father's house for a while, she says, because he's still so grief-stricken over Nikkie's death that it's hard for her to be around him. "He's so used to me and Nikkie, not just me," Angee says. "And I don't like to see him cry."

> *"When the family was told Lenorra had been shot, they didn't panic. Not until a doctor came to break the news."*

Taniesha: A Passing Victim

When Angel Wright saw the police cars and ambulances outside her apartment, her first thought was of her friend and sometime roommate: "Where's Taniesha?"

Taniesha loved action and excitement, and Angel expected to see her right in the center of things.

Then the paramedics carried a body out the door. One hand dangled from underneath the sheet. Angel recognized Taniesha's fingernails—long, pink, airbrushed, the second nail on the right hand broken. They'd just had their nails done together.

The paramedics jostled the stretcher. The body appeared to move. Angel thought for a moment that her friend was "cool." She wasn't. Taniesha had been shot to death as she sat in the living room of Angel's apartment with a bunch of older neighborhood guys, 18- and 19-year-olds. They'd been passing a .22-caliber pistol back and forth. Somehow the gun went off. The bullet hit Taniesha in the chest, killing her instantly—this pretty, petite girl who liked pink K-Swiss sneakers and *Waiting to Exhale*, who dreamed of being a hairdresser and loved to go dancing and was two weeks away from turning 16.

Fragile Childhood

Taniesha was essentially raised by her grandmother. Her own mother was 16 when Taniesha was born, and she had no steady job, no permanent home and a drug habit. So Sarah Crocker took Taniesha into her two-story yellow row house with photographs of children and Jesus Scotch-taped to the walls. Miss

Sarah, as the grandchildren and great-nieces and nephews who were continually in and out of the house called her, was the one constant in Taniesha's life.

Growing up, her grandmother says, Taniesha was a lovable girl, funny and easygoing. She went to Catholic school through sixth grade, sang in the church choir, stepped with a local drill team and loved to wrestle with her cousins.

The year Taniesha turned 14, something happened that she'd been almost afraid to hope for: Her mother had given birth to a baby boy and had gotten clean. She took custody of her youngest son and started getting to know Taniesha, her oldest daughter. The family says that year, Taniesha was the happiest she had ever been. She and her young mom were more like sisters than mother and daughter. Taniesha would braid her mom's hair. They'd go shopping together and even went on a mother/daughter outing to get their names tattooed on their legs.

Getting Worse

It lasted a year and a half. The family can't say why Taniesha's mom went back to drugs—only that addictions are hard to beat. "She hid it from me, but Taniesha knew she was using again, and it hurt her," says her aunt Charlene. "She'd beg me to go find her mom, to go get her off the streets . . . but I couldn't. I just couldn't."

When her mother abandoned her for the second time in her life, Taniesha seemed to give up. Her friends were dropping out of school, and for girls in her neighborhood, happy lives were something you saw on TV, not something you could plan for yourself. Taniesha started a quick slide into the party life, trying to dull the pain. "She was searching for love," says her aunt. "And she wasn't getting it from the people she needed to get it from. She wasn't getting it from her mom."

Things went bad fast. Taniesha started arguing with her grandmother about curfews, about the friends she chose. By April, before she could finish her freshman year, Taniesha had quit going to school most days and was staying with Angel, who was two years older and almost like an adopted sister. "She said that she couldn't put the burden on me anymore, that she shouldn't be my responsibility," her grandmother says.

Angel says the two of them had fun. There were late nights and house parties, music and dancing, and a boy named Ty, whom Taniesha loved. "He was her heart," says Angel.

But as Mother's Day approached, Taniesha seemed to get sadder, more careless.

Unending Regret

The really puzzling thing about the way Taniesha died is that she'd always been extremely afraid of guns. Her family says even a realistic-looking water pistol would terrify her. It's a sign of how low she was feeling—and how accustomed she'd become to seeing young men with weapons—that Taniesha didn't panic and run when 18-year-old Marion Gibbs, a neighborhood guy known as Rock, brought a gun into Angel's living room that Saturday night. He's been charged with murdering Taniesha.

And now her family has nothing but regrets. Her baby brother has started pulling his hair out, crying for a sister he'll never see again, and her grandmother talks sadly about how she never gave up hoping that someday she could get Taniesha out of the city, on to a better place.

"She has no idea," says Sarah Crocker, "how much she is missed."

Lenorra: Escape From Violence

By the time she came to this country, Leab "Lenorra" Koung had known more violence than most of us will experience in a lifetime. When she was a baby, Lenorra escaped from Cambodia—where millions of civilians were killed in a civil war—with her mother and seven siblings. They spent a year running to Thailand under the cover of night, amid gunfire and buried mines. "Have you seen the movie *The Killing Fields*?" her sister Leendavy asks. "We were worse. Mountain to mountain, through the rain, running and running. . . . We suffered a lot." The family didn't think baby Lenorra would survive. "She was very, very sick. . . . We had no food, her belly was swollen."

Lenorra spent her childhood in refugee camps. She went to school there, and also came under the tutelage of her father, Peang, who had been a famous performer in Cambodian folk opera. Like the rest of her siblings, Lenorra started learning in the camps to play traditional instruments, sew elaborate costumes and practice the folk dances.

She was 7 years old, a timid girl who didn't speak any English, when her family moved to South Philadelphia. But right away she began performing with her family at weddings and parties. She learned English quickly and started walking the path that her siblings had paved—hard work, study, rehearsals after school, performances on weekends and, eventually, college.

Lenorra loved to teach. She taught Cambodian dance to the kids in the neighborhood, and English to other Cambodian refugees. "Even when she was a little kid and we'd play, she'd always want to be the mother, the teacher—the leader," Leendavy says. Exhausted as she was from attending Temple University and working two jobs, Lenorra always had a smile for the neighborhood kids.

And she still found time for a social life. She dated, went to proms and fell in love when she was 19 and a freshman. Thonny Prum was 25, a friend of her older brother's, and a quiet guy. "When they fell in love, it was very, very deep. She'd do anything for him, and he'd do anything for her," says Leendavy.

Tragedy From Guns and Racism

On the afternoon of Sunday, June 30, Thonny was stuck at his job at a video store, and Lenorra brought him some cookies. She had no way of knowing that earlier in the afternoon, two boys in the store had gotten into a fight over whose turn it was at a video game. The scuffle had turned rough, and Thonny had thrown everyone out. The police had come and taken a report, and the mother of a kid who'd been punched paid Thonny an angry visit, threatening to send over the boy's older brother.

What happened next, police say, is that the brother, 20-year-old Damon Sparrow, walked into the store and started blasting away with guns in both hands. His target? Anyone who looked Asian. Lenorra, who hadn't even been in the store at the time of the fight, was shot once just below her stomach. A neighbor, 18-year-old Huy Hean, who'd come into the store for the first time that afternoon, fatally took seven bullets. Thonny rushed out of the back of the store and put his arms around Lenorra, where she lay by the video games. "Honey, I got shot," she whispered.

Lenorra's older brother had been shot the year before in a holdup and escaped with little injury, so when the family was told Lenorra had been shot, they didn't panic. Not until a doctor came to break the news.

Hundreds of people—friends from the city and immigrants from all over the country who knew of the family's folk-dancing fame—came to a memorial service outside the video store. Newspapers ran front-page stories; the mayor came to offer his sympathy. None of it made the family understand why this talented, beautiful girl who had survived so much should lose her life so pointlessly. "Why us?" asks Leendavy. "We're the family who tried anything to get an education, to make a living, to make a difference in the community.

"My sister was an innocent victim who brought so much happiness. . . . Why us?"

Guns Can Prevent Violence

by John R. Lott Jr.

About the author: *John R. Lott Jr., author of* More Guns, Less Crime, *is the John M. Olin Law and Economics Fellow at the University of Chicago School of Law.*

America may indeed be obsessed with guns, but much of what passes as fact simply isn't true. The news media's focus on only tragic outcomes, while ignoring tragic events that were avoided, may be responsible for some misimpressions. Horrific events like the 1998 shooting in Jonesboro, Arkansas receive massive news coverage, as they should, but the 2.5 million times each year that people use guns defensively are never discussed—including cases where public shootings are stopped before they happen. Dramatic stories of mothers using guns to prevent their children from being kidnapped by carjackers seldom even make the local news.

Unfortunately, these misimpressions have real costs for people's safety. Many myths needlessly frighten people and prevent them from defending themselves most effectively.

Myth No. 1: When one is attacked, passive behavior is the safest approach.

The Department of Justice's National Crime Victimization Survey reports that the probability of serious injury from an attack is 2.5 times greater for women offering no resistance than for women resisting with a gun. Men also benefit from using a gun, but the benefits are smaller: offering no resistance is 1.4 times more likely to result in serious injury than resisting with a gun.

Micro and Macro Myths

Myth No. 2: Friends or relatives are the most likely killers.

The myth is usually based on two claims: 1) 58 percent of murder victims are killed by either relatives or acquaintances and 2) anyone could be a murderer.

With the broad definition of "acquaintances" used in the FBI's Uniform Crime Reports, most victims are indeed classified as knowing their killer. However, what is not made clear is that acquaintance murder primarily includes drug buyers killing drug pushers, cabdrivers killed by first-time customers,

Reprinted from John R. Lott Jr., "The Cold, Hard Facts About Guns," *Chicago Tribune*, May 8, 1998, by permission of the author.

gang members killing other gang members, prostitutes killed by their clients, and so on. Only one city, Chicago, reports a precise breakdown on the nature of acquaintance killings: between 1990 and 1995 just 17 percent of murder victims were either family members, friends, neighbors and/or roommates.

Murderers also are not your average citizen. For example, about 90 percent of adult murderers have already had a criminal record as an adult. Murderers are overwhelmingly young males with low IQs and who have difficult times getting along with others. Furthermore, unfortunately, murder is disproportionately committed against blacks and by blacks.

Myth No. 3: The United States has such a high murder rate because Americans own so many guns.

There is no international evidence backing this up. The Swiss, New Zealanders and Finns all own guns as frequently as Americans, yet in 1995 Switzerland had a murder rate 40 percent lower than Germany's, and New Zealand had one lower than Australia's. Finland and Sweden have very different gun ownership rates, but very similar murder rates. Israel, with a higher gun ownership rate than the U.S., has a murder rate 40 percent below Canada's. When one studies all countries rather than just a select few, as is usually done, there is absolutely no relationship between gun ownership and murder.

Myths of Gun Ownership

Myth No. 4: If law-abiding citizens are allowed to carry concealed handguns, people will end up shooting each other after traffic accidents as well as accidentally shooting police officers.

Millions of people currently hold concealed handgun permits, and some states have issued them for as long as 60 years. Yet, only one permit holder has ever been arrested for using a concealed handgun after a traffic accident and that case was ruled as self-defense. The type of person willing to go through the permitting process is extremely law-abiding. In Florida, almost 444,000 licenses were granted from 1987 to 1997, but only 84 people have lost their licenses for felonies involving firearms. Most violations that lead to permits being revoked involve accidentally carrying a gun into restricted areas, like airports or schools. In Virginia, not a single permit holder has committed a violent crime. Similarly encouraging results have been reported for Kentucky, Nevada, North Carolina, South Carolina, Texas and Tennessee (the only other states where information is available).

"The 2.5 million times each year that people use guns defensively are never discussed—including cases where public shootings are stopped before they happen."

Myth No. 5: The family gun is more likely to kill you or someone you know than to kill in self-defense.

The studies yielding such numbers never actually inquired as to whose gun was used in the killing. Instead, if a household owned a gun and if a person in that household or someone they knew was shot to death while in the home, the gun in the household was blamed. In fact, virtually all the killings in these studies were committed by guns brought in by an intruder. No more than four percent of the gun deaths can be attributed to the homeowner's gun. The very fact that most people were killed by intruders also surely raises questions about why they owned guns in the first place and whether they had sufficient protection.

> *"When one studies all countries rather than just a select few, as is usually done, there is absolutely no relationship between gun ownership and murder."*

How many attacks have been deterred from ever occurring by the potential victims owning a gun? My own research finds that more concealed handguns, and increased gun ownership generally, unambiguously deter murders, robbery, and aggravated assaults. This is also in line with the well-known fact that criminals prefer attacking victims that they consider weak.

These are only some of the myths about guns and crime that drive the public policy debate. We must not lose sight of the ultimate question: Will allowing law-abiding citizens to own guns save lives? The evidence strongly indicates that it does.

Guns Should Not Be Blamed for Violence

by Don Feder

About the author: *Don Feder is a syndicated conservative columnist for the* Boston Herald. *He has also written articles for the* National Review, Human Events, *and* Reason.

Blame the guns. Don't blame the wretched little monsters who murdered four children and a pregnant teacher because one of them had just been dumped by a girlfriend; blame the guns.

Don't blame a culture where many parents spend more time watching televised sports events than with their kids, blame the guns. Don't blame an entertainment industry that rarely makes a movie without severed body parts, blame the guns.

Blaming guns is easy. Unlike baby-faced killers, it's difficult to feel much sympathy for metallic objects. For those who don't believe in individual responsibility and are loath to acknowledge the existence of evil, guns are an appealing target.

A Heap of Excuses

The smoke had hardly cleared from the grounds of the Jonesboro, Ark., middle school, when the cry went up. "It is foolhardy to think that we can reduce gun violence among young people without reducing their easy access to weapons," wrote NRA-aphobe Osha Gray Davidson in the New York *Times*.

I don't own a gun. There is no NRA sticker on my SUV. I don't hunt or shoot. And I don't buy it.

There are roughly 200 million guns in private hands in this country, almost one for every American. So tell me, Osha Gray Davidson, how do we deny murderous punks access to same?

We have tried waiting periods, background checks, licensing, bans on semiautomatics, and even outright prohibition. None of it has succeeded in keeping guns out of the hands of hardened criminals, raving nutcases or juvenile killers.

Reprinted by permission of Don Feder and Creators Syndicate from "Arkansas Violence: Blaming Guns Is Easy," *Human Events*, April 24, 1998.

Chapter 1

A Surplus of Metal

Bottom line: Gun control works with people who obey laws. People with murderous impulses, adults or kids, will always find a way to get guns.

How is it that in New York City, where ownership is legally restricted at every turn, pre-teens regularly come to school packing? During the 1991–92 school year alone, there were 56 shooting incidents in and around the city's schools. In one, a 14-year-old armed with a 38-caliber Smith & Wesson walked up to two classmates and shot them dead.

Nor is New York the exception. Chicago, Detroit and Los Angeles all have their student pistoleers. This problem is so pervasive that many inner-city schools have set up metal detectors to keep out weapons.

Efforts to further restrict firearms punish the innocent. Guns are used in crimes. They are also used to prevent crimes.

John R. Lott of the University of Chicago Law School and author of the book *More Guns, Less Crime* estimates that guns are used to thwart crime 2.5 million times each year. Florida State University criminologist Gary Kleck says that for every murder committed with a gun, 75 lives are saved.

> *"Blaming guns is easy. Unlike baby-faced killers, it's difficult to feel much sympathy for metallic objects."*

Further evidence comes from a Policy Analysis of the Cato Institute, which examined the 24 states that have passed "concealed-carry" laws (allowing the law-abiding to go about armed) since 1987—in other words, dare I say it, easing access to firearms. On average, their murder rates are down 7.7%, while rapes and aggravated assaults have declined 5.2% and 7.7%, respectively.

Another school shooting incident occurred in Pearl, Miss., in 1997. Two students were murdered. Others might have died, had not an assistant principal retrieved a gun from his car and disarmed the killer.

Set a True Example

It is interesting and revealing that, generally, those who exploit mass murders to push gun-control panaceas are opposed to the death sentence, opposed to three-strikes-and-you're-out laws, opposed to mandatory minimum sentences, resist efforts to reform the juvenile justice system (to treat underage predators like the animals they are) and endorse the ACLU's interpretation of the Bill of Rights as a get-out-of-jail-free card.

Blaming guns allows them to avoid reality and still feel that they're doing something about crime. The problem isn't easy access to guns, but easy access to oxygen. Certain people shouldn't be breathing.

Fortunately, limiting their access to air is easier than trying to control 200 million guns. We can start by cutting off the air supply of Arkansas' kid-killers.

The Public's Fear of Violent Crime Is Excessive

by Beth Shuster

About the author: *Beth Shuster, a staff writer for the* Los Angeles Times, *frequently writes about urban life and contemporary culture.*

They are on the news almost nightly: carjackers, sexual predators, workplace gunmen, follow-home, takeover and home invasion robbers, killers enraged on the road.

By the numbers, there are fewer and fewer of them. Yet fear of them has held steady. That fear has overwhelmed reality, causing many Americans to feel more threatened by crime even as the nation has become a safer place in which to live.

The reasons for that disparity are complex, and sometimes shockingly deliberate. Police stoke fear in part because they take crime seriously, but also to prime their budgets; politicians feel deeply about the issue, but also manipulate it to win votes. News organizations amplify fear by ratcheting up their crime coverage, even as crime declines, because it helps ratings. Security companies, theft detection manufacturers and others tap into deeply held fears and end up turning a profit.

Merging to Keep Crime

In some respects, the merger of profit and political advantage has turned the crime business into the domestic equivalent of what President Dwight Eisenhower once described as the "military-industrial complex." In that incarnation, the fear of Soviet adventurism was real and the enemy a dangerous one. But in their desire to combat it, military contractors, politicians and Pentagon brass congealed into a self-sustaining system.

In the new version, prison guard unions, burglar alarm companies and others, in effect, cooperate with politicians and police to perpetuate public fear of a domestic enemy, in this case crime. It too presents real dangers, but even as those dangers have waned, fear has persisted.

Competition for bigger and better weapons against crime proceeds at a frantic pace. Burglar- and car-alarm sales are rising. Security services are in hot demand. Gated communities spring up across the country. Self-defense classes are jammed. Pepper spray canisters hang from key chains.

Fearing Fear Itself

Crime rates notwithstanding, who today feels safer?

"The fear of crime is highly irrational and reflects a very deep culture of ignorance of risk factors and safety," said Eric Sterling, president of the Criminal Justice Policy Foundation in Washington. "We're a nation of 230 million people. Much of the country is perfectly safe. Crime, particularly violent crime, is very highly concentrated . . . and yet that feeling of fear lasts."

The effect of such persistent fear is subtle but profound. It can color political choices, favoring the efforts of politicians who promise to fight crime and hurting those who argue for social solutions. It can contribute to vigilance, and to tighter community links through such programs as Neighborhood Watch. But it can also lead to empty streets, barred doors and suspicion.

Where the fear of crime has ebbed perceptibly, such as in New York City, the sense of newfound freedom of movement has helped spark an urban renaissance. But elsewhere, where fear persists out of proportion to crime, the potential benefits of that kind of turnaround are elusive.

Violent Crime on the Decline

There is no single reason for declining crime rates. Theories abound as to whether stiffer penalties and more aggressive policing have led to the drop or whether sociological and demographic forces should get more credit. Some argue that soaring prison populations have taken criminals off the streets and that drugs and violence have killed many more. Others point to a drop in the number of young people, traditionally the most crime-prone group, and shifting drug preferences.

Whatever the reason, violent crime—defined by the FBI as murder, manslaughter, rape, robbery and aggravated assault—fell more than 5% last year in the U.S., from 1.68 million offenses to 1.59 million. That drop was the latest of the 1990s, during which crime has steadily tapered off, particularly in the largest cities.

> *"Fear has overwhelmed reality, causing many Americans to feel more threatened by crime even as the nation has become a safer place in which to live."*

In California, the statistics show similar reductions. 1997's crime decline marked the culmination of the biggest sustained four-year drop in state history. In 1998, crime in California is at its lowest level since 1967.

And, violent crime also made marked declines. In the first half of 1998, according to Los Angeles Police Department data, homicides were down 34% in the city—from 271 to 180. Overall violent crime dropped 13% in the first half of 1998.

Homicides in 1997 dropped to the lowest level in 20 years. In 1997, there were 590 slayings in the city; at the beginning of the decade, more than 1,000 Los Angeles residents' lives each year ended at the hands of killers.

Fear Still Reigns

But at the same time, Gallup polls have begun to discern a marked increase in concerns about violence.

Tallying responses to the question, "What is the most important problem facing the country today?" the Gallup Organization found in 1996 that crime and violence had begun to surpass such other critical issues as international tensions, unemployment and high taxes.

To be sure, the poll's crime responses could also reflect the diminution in this decade of some of the nation's more troubling crises, such as the Cold War and the recession. People who are jobless, for example, could be more inclined to rate unemployment as their most pressing concern until they find jobs, when crime becomes a higher priority.

But a Los Angeles Times poll taken in 1997 also found high numbers of people whose sense of security had been sorely shaken. The poll found that nearly three-fourths of residents surveyed believed crime in their

> *"The fear of crime is highly irrational and reflects a very deep culture of ignorance of risk factors and safety."*

neighborhoods to be about the same as it was in 1993 or worse. Seventy-seven percent said they felt less safe or about as safe as they did in 1993.

Nationally, an ABC News poll conducted in 1997 found that 51% of respondents were more afraid of crime than they were in 1993; only 7% were less worried about crime. And the Justice Department, in its regular reports, has found no decline whatsoever in the fear expressed by Americans throughout the 1990s.

Violence Lingers in Public's Mind

Criminologists note that, to some extent, a sense of security will lag behind reality because fear preys on memory.

Even long after crimes occur, the names, even faces, of victims linger. Twelve-year-old Polly Klaas is kidnapped from her Petaluma bedroom, then raped and murdered. Three-year-old Stephanie Kuhen is shot to death in a Cypress Park alley. South-Central teacher Alfredo Perez is shot in the head in a school library by a gangster's stray bullet. Six-year-old beauty queen JonBenet Ramsey dies of strangulation, and her parents are not ruled out as suspects in the crime, which occurs in the tidy town of Boulder, Colo.

"While memory fades over time, it gets kicked up every time you hear about a new crime that allows you to identify with the victim," said Alfred Blumstein, a criminology professor at Carnegie Mellon University's Heinz School of Public Policy and Management. "Polly Klaas could have been any of our daughters, and that murder stirs up all of our concerns for our daughters."

Police Keep Sense of Threat Alive

And those memories allow the institutions invested in crime to benefit from fear.

For example, although police departments often take credit for falling crime, they rarely serve to calm the public. Indeed, they often take the opposite tack, warning of danger even as crime subsides.

"Our business is crime," said former LAPD acting Police Chief Bayan Lewis. "Our business is not to go to Neighborhood Watch meetings and say, 'Don't worry about it anymore.' Our business is to maintain a strong Neighborhood Watch, encourage people to get to know their local community police officers."

Although that may serve the political interests of police, it also helps to distort the reality of declining crime.

> *"Criminologists note that, to some extent, a sense of security will lag behind reality because fear preys on memory."*

"It's a two-edged sword," Lewis said. "We have convinced the public to support three-strikes laws [lengthening prison sentences], to make judges tough on criminals. . . . Now we can't say, 'OK, great, we don't need all that now.' You have to be cautious about that."

Los Angeles Police Chief Bernard C. Parks, who has boasted about crime declines and asked to be judged on his ability to fight crime, surprised top city officials when he announced that he will need at least 1,000 more officers over the next five years [1998 to 2003]. The reason: an ever-present threat of crime.

In addition, police officials such as Parks and Lewis say it's not prudent to cut back on tough sentencing or a national police buildup, because law enforcement authorities believe they are largely responsible for declining crime. If police told people they could relax about crime, the argument goes, violence would rebound, and the public would increasingly be in real danger.

Investing in Fear Pays Off

If playing on fears is what it took to convince the public to invest in more police, then it has not been without a return. Experts generally agree that the increase in police has made some impact on crime, particularly in cities such as New York.

In that city, where overall crime dropped nearly half from levels of 1993, business and tourism are booming—in large part because there is a perception that the city is safer.

"The reduction in crime has improved New York's quality of life, bolstered job growth and increased investment throughout the city," said Bernadette O'Leary, a spokeswoman for the New York City Economic Development Corp. "I think the crime decline has been very significant in the city's revival."

Tourism in the city has set records each year since 1995, and investors are sinking money into developments and businesses. In August 1998, developers announced plans for a $66-million retail and entertainment complex. Not in Times Square. In Harlem.

"Big business isn't afraid to invest in the city anymore," said Colleen Roche, New York Mayor Rudolph Giuliani's spokeswoman. "It's not just that crime is down, but [that] the whole quality of life is better."

Giuliani's emphasis, a tougher version of a program touted by Mayor Richard Riordan for Los Angeles, has been to rid the city of aggressive panhandlers, even the so-called squeegee-men who would run up to cars and begin washing windshields for change.

"The extra dollars for the increased police presence and the no-nonsense attitude on prosecution has made people feel safer and made more people want to come to the city," said Mark Jaffe, executive director of the Greater New York Chamber of Commerce. "That's the word on the street."

Public Is Still a Hard Sell

In New York as well as Los Angeles, some say declining drug sales in neighborhoods have led to fewer violent confrontations on city streets. Gang members are receiving stiffer penalties, as are other criminals, taking them off the streets and reducing their opportunities to claim new victims.

Los Angeles City Atty. James K. Hahn points to those efforts and others as part of the reasons for the declining crime rates. But he also sees a "skeptical public" that is hard-pressed to believe these efforts are working.

"If police told people they could relax about crime, the argument goes, violence would rebound, and the public would increasingly be in real danger."

"Trying to sell this big drop in crime is not an easy task," Hahn said. "That message seems to be in direct conflict with everything else they're hearing."

Although prosecutors and police believe they are helping to improve communities and allay fears, some observers warn that anti-crime efforts can actually breed fear even as they thwart crime.

"There are constantly new categories of violence," said Barry Glassner, a USC sociology professor who is writing a book about the culture of fear. "For a while, it was carjacking. . . . Now, it's road rage. . . . The effect of it is that the public hears a lot about what they think is this new pressing problem. You wouldn't have panicked three months ago, but there's more of a reason to panic now."

Chapter 1

Crime Always Safe as a Campaign Issue

If police and prosecutors heighten fear for their own reasons, politicians bring another level of anxiety.

Crime frequently becomes a campaign issue as politicians routinely tap into the public's fear. In 1993, Riordan won the mayor's office in part based on his slogan, "Tough enough to turn L.A. around," and his campaign's vivid imagery of a decaying, dangerous Hollywood. Riordan's literature did not mention that the city already was experiencing a drop in crime.

Similar techniques are used nationally by both Democrats and Republicans. In 1988, George Bush hammered Michael Dukakis for releasing criminals into the community. In 1992, Bill Clinton won office in part based on his pledge to put 100,000 more police officers on the nation's streets.

"Crime is always safe," said Joe Cerrell, a Los Angeles political consultant. "It's good for the political routine, for the political roadshow. I put this right up there with motherhood and apple pie: the fear of crime. Who's going to say we don't need a few damn more cops?"

Sterling, of the Criminal Justice Policy Foundation, agreed, saying that politicians who pronounce their tough attitude toward crime are rarely attacked by opponents or, more important, voters.

"This is one area where they will offend no constituents, no special interest," Sterling said. "If I'm running

> *"Crime frequently becomes a campaign issue as politicians routinely tap into the public's fear."*

for office and I want to show how tough I am, I point to crime. The rhetoric simply serves political objectives."

But why not let a candidate boast about crime *drops*, about increasing numbers of officers on the streets? About safer neighborhoods and schools?

The answer: That message is not as sexy and has much less impact.

And that is nowhere more true than on television, where the adage "If it bleeds, it leads" has become the catch phrase for national and local news.

TV News Creates Reality

Indeed, some experts and media critics point to television as the main reason for the public's rising fear of crime. To be sure, they also criticize tabloids for sensationalizing crime—such as the JonBenet case and others—but they say television appears to have broader impact.

On national and local TV news broadcasts, crime stories have soared. From 1990 to 1995—a period when the FBI reported a 13% drop in the homicide rate—network news coverage of murder increased a whopping 336%, and that did not even include coverage of the O.J. Simpson case, according to the Center for Media and Public Affairs, a Washington-based nonpartisan, nonprofit group that monitors the media.

"I think this is the best example I've seen of media images driving public perception in the face of contradictory facts," said Bob Lichter, president of the group. "The reality is going one way, the media images are going another and the public perception follows the images rather than the reality."

> *"Some experts and media critics point to television as the main reason for the public's rising fear of crime."*

Lichter's study of crime stories on the news found some other startling results: Crime was the leading television news topic in the 1990s, far outpacing international and national news—even presidential campaign coverage. During 1995, for example, the three networks aired 2,574 crime stories, more than triple the total three years earlier.

"It's one thing to see an interview with an unemployed worker and another to see a blood-splattered crime scene," Lichter said. *"That* holds your attention."

Television news executives, who are somewhat weary of the criticism and defensive about their crime coverage, say the current trend is to add more balance to their broadcasts. But they readily acknowledge that a "good" crime story with video does grab viewers, and that means higher ratings.

"Do I think there are too many crime stories on television? Yes," said Pat Casey, managing editor at KCBS-Channel 2 in Los Angeles. "But it's not nearly what it was or what it could be. . . . Every story needs to be judged on its merits. I think that's our responsibility."

Local television stations have ever more vivid ways of covering crime. With the rise of freelancers who shoot nighttime crime video and then sell it to the stations, as well as the use of news helicopters, stations could rely solely on crime news for their broadcasts if they wished.

"In Los Angeles, the thing you need to watch is stringer tape [the nighttime video] and helicopters," Casey said, adding that the station has cut in half the number of freelance video pieces it buys. "In any afternoon in Los Angeles, you could find death and destruction to fly over."

Crime Generates More Research

The fear of crime also has spawned whole new areas of research for criminologists, sociologists and others. At Florida State University, Ted Chiricos, a professor in the criminology and criminal justice school, said he has conducted several large-scale surveys on that issue.

In his study, the impact of local television crime news on residents' fear levels was significant, regardless of whether the residents lived in high-crime areas.

"People living in places with lower crime rates and people with high crime rates all had the same levels of fear," Chiricos said. "Local news is definitely related to higher levels of fear."

The Times Poll, which surveyed 1,143 city residents with a margin of error of

3 percentage points in either direction, found similar results. In that poll, 80% of city residents believed that media reports of violent crimes increased their personal fear of crime, with more than half saying it increases fear "a lot."

The same poll found that a majority of the residents—58%—did not know anyone who had been shot, stabbed or seriously wounded in Los Angeles.

But crimes, particularly violent ones such as assaults or rapes, leave a legacy of fear in victims. For those people, declining crime statistics are nearly meaningless. Once the crime occurs, victims often say, it shatters whatever sense of security they once had.

As a result, the message put out by some police and politicians confirms victims' perceptions of crime.

The Crime Prevention Business Is Booming

Fear not only helps police and politicians, it also is good for business.

The Correctional Corp. of America, a publicly held company that builds private prisons, has looked at California with relish: The state needs to build prisons to accommodate the 25,000 more inmates expected by 2000. The prison guards union, the California Correctional Peace Officers Assn., has become one of the most powerful lobbies in Sacramento—in part because it donates huge sums to political campaigns.

The security industry is booming. Americans spent an estimated $14 billion on professionally installed electronic security products and services in 1997, and more than one in five homes in the United States and Canada had electronic alarm systems by the end of 1997.

> *"Some security, alarm and lock companies regularly promote products by manipulating crime data so crime appears to be worse."*

Experts say these companies, not unlike campaigning politicians, use the public's fear of crime to sell the latest home- and car-alarm systems and other protective devices.

Aside from their television and print ads—which can be graphic in depicting lone motorists securing their cars—some security, alarm and lock companies regularly promote products by manipulating crime data so crime appears to be worse.

For example, at the end of a release issued by a lock company, officials said that "in the time it has taken you to read this article, another nine property thefts have occurred. . . . Theft is a crime of opportunity; eliminating the opportunity eliminates your chance of becoming a victim."

One security alarm company sent out notices listing burglars' "likes and dislikes," including these: "Burglars prefer homes near highways and homes with privacy fences and large shrubs. . . . Their favorite time to operate is during the day, when no one is home. Deterrents for burglars include security systems and dogs."

Fear Does Not Dissipate

Those who work in the industry defend their practices.

"I think we are part of the solution," said Dave Saddler, a spokesman for the National Burglar and Fire Alarm Assn. in Bethesda, Md. "The steps people are taking to protect their communities themselves are working. I think it's the random nature of crime—that it can happen any time, anywhere—that keeps people afraid."

Perhaps, as some suggest, reasons to be fearful are so prevalent that residents can't help but be afraid.

"If I'm watching a cop show at 10 and then the news comes on at 11 with the latest murder, it all just blends together," said Sterling of the Criminal Justice Policy Foundation. "That's reality, and I see it every night. It's counterintuitive to think of the actual crime rates.

"The data is boring, it's numbers and it's irrelevant," he said. "*This* is what I'm seeing: another atrocious crime being committed. And that is still attention-grabbing."

America's Gun Violence Problem Is Exaggerated

by Ted Drane

About the author: *Ted Drane writes for* SSAA, *a monthly gun advocacy journal published by the Sporting Shooters Association of Australia.*

The United States of America is usually put forward as the extreme case of private possession of firearms causing high crime and murder rates. "We don't want it to get like it is in America" is a predictable cry amongst politicians and the media.

The USA is linked to the gun and portrayed as the murder center of the world despite the fact that Mexico, its nearest neighbor to the south, has very strict gun laws and also a much higher murder rate. The reality is that many parts of the USA have very low murder rates and many of these have both liberal gun laws and high lawful firearm ownership.

The Hidden Numbers

For example, official FBI statistics for 1993 show that the entire state of Vermont had only 12 murders; Wyoming had 16, North Dakota 11, South Dakota 18, and New Hampshire 20.

When expressed in the more usual way, this is 2.1 per 100,000 of population for Vermont, 3.5 for Wyoming, 1.72 for North Dakota, 2.6 for South Dakota, and 1.8 for New Hampshire. These figures are all considerably lower than Australia's Northern Territory, which runs at about 11 per 100,000 with very tight gun laws, and yet all five of these American states have almost no restrictions on gun ownership, including the carrying of concealed handguns.

If gun ownership is responsible for crime, then clearly this could not be so, and people in the Australian media need to have this put before them at every opportunity.

However, the USA figures overall do show that it has a murder rate of roughly 10 per 100,000, which is five times that of Australia's overall. So what

Reprinted from "Institute of Legislative Action," by Ted Drane, *SSAA*, March 1997, by permission of the Sporting Shooters Association of Australia.

is it that puts up the figures, and allows gun prohibitionists to complain that Australia mustn't ever be like it is—or appears to be—in America?

Making Comparisons

In figures available the state of Washington (not to be confused with Washington DC, the capital) had 264 murders in a population under five million, or 5.2 per 100,000; Florida had 1,223, or 8.9 per 100,000, and New York had 2,415, which is 13.3 per 100,000. Here is where the figures rapidly rise. We see that when the statistics are pulled out for individual cities and centers of urban activity, then the picture changes rapidly.

But let us go on to compare these figures with some European cities which have no popular reputation for violence. For example, Amsterdam has a murder rate of 38 per 100,000, Stockholm has 15.9, Helsinki has 15.3 and even Copenhagen has 10.5.

In other words, the murder rate in Florida, where the traveller risks death, according to the Australian media, is considerably lower than that of several Scandinavian nations.

As an aside, the murder rate in Jerusalem, where the people are armed to the teeth, is 3.1.

Looked at another way, some US states have a murder rate one tenth of that of Stockholm and one twentieth that of Amsterdam (remember Holland's tight gun laws) and neither of these cities is usually portrayed as particularly violent. Certainly tourists are not known to avoid them, yet tourists have been avoiding Florida. No doubt the media can take the credit for this distorted view.

Since Florida passed a law that requires the issuing of a concealed handgun carry permit to any resident who is a qualified applicant (that is, without criminal record or mental illness), the violent crime rate throughout the state has decreased at a rate faster than the national average. . . . Florida will also grant a carry permit to any qualified interstate visitor, a policy that may explain the increase in attacks on foreign tourists, the only group in Florida known with certainty to be unarmed.

This should not be interpreted as a belief by the Institute of Legislative Action that everybody ought to be armed. However, it is still a fact which the Australian media and high-profile politicians must be confronted with. They claim lawful gun ownership brings crime; they are wrong.

In fact, in the US a person is 34 times more likely to die in a car accident than to be killed in a firearms-related accident. There are approximately 48,000 annual motor vehicle deaths and 1400 annual firearm-related accidental deaths.

Gun Prohibitionists Alter Truths

The matter of accidents with firearms has also become a big money-spinner for gun prohibitionists in the USA, and some of the figures which are bandied around are remarkable.

One such, a recent report by the Children's Defense Fund, claimed that 50,000 children have been killed by firearms in the 1990s.

This is the kind of statement that tugs at the heartstrings, but its reality is different: it is true if and only if persons up to 24 years of age are classed as children. Many "researchers" who ought to be neutral but who are plainly not, and particularly some health advocacy workers, . . . present figures this way because of the massive increase in crime amongst young adults in the inner city areas. This is an effective way of bulking up the figures.

> *"The USA is linked to the gun and portrayed as the murder center of the world despite the fact that Mexico, its nearest neighbor to the south, has . . . a much higher murder rate."*

Here is where we come to the significant developments in homicide rates in America.

Since 1991 the murder rate for black males, ages 15–24, has increased by a factor of three. Since there has not been any significant increase in firearms during this period, there must be another cause for the increase in violence. Could it conceivably be the rise in the crack cocaine trade combined with lenient sentences for younger offenders which has encouraged an increase in crime amongst the younger age-groups of black males?

Of course, this is a very politically dangerous thing to say. In fact, it may be so much so that it is safer for authorities in many countries to let it keep happening, and not bring out the truth—safer for the authorities, of course, because they do not have to live in those places.

Guns Are Not the Problem

However, outlawing firearms because some children are killed by them is illogical. In the USA in 1990, 890 children (that is to say, a genuine 14 years and under) were killed either by criminals or law enforcement officials. Of these 890 children, 283 were killed with firearms.

Another 236 died as a result of firearm accidents for a total of 519 firearms-related deaths (there were no reported firearms suicides in this age group).

In the same year, a total of 15,367 children died, so the percentage of children who died from firearms is 3.3% of the total. To put this percentage in perspective, of those children who died in 1990, 20.7% (3182 children) died in motor vehicle accidents, 7.5% (1148 children) drowned and 6.3% (972 children) died in fires. It is certainly not our intention to trivialize these deaths, but it is still fair to say that no one would suggest that cars, swimming pools and matches should be banned or registered because they can kill children, yet all these present far bigger dangers than firearms across all the USA.

As in Australia, the rate of firearm-related accidental deaths in the USA has been declining at an average of 2.6% annually averaged over the 1950s to the 1990s for all age groups, no doubt spurred along by ever-increasing education programs run by the National Rifle Association. This is the same NRA that is so often vilified by the media, which in fact has no idea about what the NRA actually says and does, but prefers to run with its own film-induced perception of the group instead.

(We can say that in particular, the now-departed Federal Justice Minister Duncan Kerr was quite happy to criticize the policies of the NRA, but to our knowledge no NRA official ever reported him getting in touch to find out what they actually are, despite our offers of assistance if he wanted to do so.)

Gun Ownership Restrictions Are Useless

In the USA, the chances of being murdered vary enormously depending on race, with the murder rate for blacks (usually by other blacks) being higher than that for Hispanics, which again is much higher than for whites.

Washington D.C. has the highest murder rate in the country but has very restrictive gun ownership laws.

Gun control advocates assert that guns are simply bought in neighboring areas to circumvent the restrictions but are at a loss to explain why crime rates are much lower in some areas than in others.

If guns can be transported then why not crime? Why are there widely different crime rates in the USA?

Gun prohibitionists see such truths as we have presented here not as posing questions to be answered, but as offering information that needs to be covered up in order to allow them to keep putting the case which they believe in so passionately—despite the facts.

It remains clear that there are parts of America which are undoubtedly violent, but they are not violent because of legal gun ownership there or anywhere else. There are also parts with similar gun ownership which are very peaceful.

Chapter 2

Does Gun Control Reduce Crime?

Chapter Preface

More than three decades following the 1968 Gun Control Act, which banned gun ownership by minors and adults with felony records, the debate on gun control continues, often with heated words and plenty of legislative action from both sides of the debate. With approximately 20,000 federal, state, and local gun laws in the United States, the gun control arena seems at times its own industry. Many argue that even more gun control laws are needed to curtail the trend of increased gun use and violence.

The Center to Prevent Handgun Violence states, "We believe we can save lives by regulating the sale of firearms and we believe there's more than adequate proof of that." Citing examples of crimes thwarted by gun restrictions, gun control groups point out that laws have deterred crime by making it harder for potential criminals to obtain guns and easier for law enforcement to keep track of where guns proliferate. Other studies have shown that a large number of shooting deaths often occur in states with lax gun restrictions.

The National Rifle Association (NRA), however, holds that "no empirical study of the effectiveness of gun laws has shown any positive effect on crime." Instead, notes the NRA and other gun lobbying groups, studies have shown that the deterrent effect of guns, not laws, were responsible for preventing crime. With their successful push for "right-to-carry" laws in more than thirty states, gun lobbyists point to research indicating that responsible gun ownership is an effective strategy for self-defense as well as a proven method for preventing crime.

In another study, Gary Kleck, a professor of criminology at Florida State University, argued that gun control laws have not reduced crimes and that guns are used legally 2.5 million times a year in self-defense. Kleck's findings did not make him a champion of the NRA, however, since he also concluded that background checks and a number of gun control laws were still necessary for overall safety. Kleck concludes that in pushing political agendas, both sides of the debate have lost sight of the citizen's best interest.

The validity of gun control studies, the relationship between gun control and crime reduction, and the circumstances surrounding gun use during crimes are some of the issues debated in the following chapter.

Enforcing Gun Control Laws Can Reduce Murders

by Jeffrey A. Roth

About the author: *Jeffrey A. Roth is a research director for the Law and Public Policy area of Abt Associates, Inc. He served as study director for the Panel on the Understanding and Control of Violent Behavior.*

Approximately 60 percent of all murder victims in the United States in 1989 (about 12,000 people) were killed with firearms. According to estimates, firearm attacks injured another 70,000 victims, some of whom were left permanently disabled. In 1985, the cost of shootings—either by others, through self-inflicted wounds, or in accidents—was estimated to be more than $14 billion nationwide for medical care, long-term disability, and premature death. Among firearms, handguns are the murder weapon of choice. While handguns make up only about one-third of all firearms owned in the United States, they account for 80 percent of all murders committed with firearms.

Young People Are Victims

Teenagers and young adults face especially high risks of being murdered with a firearm. Figures for 1990 from the National Center for Health Statistics indicated that 82 percent of all murder victims aged 15 to 19 and 76 percent of victims aged 20 to 24 were killed with guns. The risk was particularly high for black males in those age ranges. The firearm murder rate was 105.3 per 100,000 black males aged 15 to 19, compared to 9.7 for white males in the same age group. This 11:1 ratio of black to white rates reflects a perplexing increase since 1985, when the firearm murder rate for black males aged 15 to 19 was 37.4 per 100,000. Among 20- to 24-year-old black males, the rate increased from 63.1 to 140.7. For several years before 1985, the rates for black males in these age groups had been decreasing. The increases have not been

Excerpted from Jeffrey A. Roth, "Firearms and Violence," *NIJ Research in Brief,* February 1994. *Endnotes in the original have been omitted in this reprint.*

paralleled for females, whites, or older black males, nor have they been matched in non-gun murder rates or even firearm suicide rates for young black males. (The latter are higher among whites than among blacks but have risen for both races.)

For these reasons, the Panel on the Understanding and Control of Violent Behavior devoted substantial attention to issues surrounding firearms and violence, relying on a commissioned background paper, critical commentary on a draft of that paper, and its own review of published research literature. This report summarizes the panel's conclusions.

> *"While handguns make up only about one-third of all firearms owned in the United States, they account for 80 percent of all murders committed with firearms."*

Any firearm murder follows a particular chain of events: One person acquires a firearm; two or more people come within reach of the firearm; a dispute escalates into an attack, the weapon is fired; it causes an injury; and the injury is serious enough to cause death. While that sequence probably seems obvious, thinking about gun murders as a chain of events draws attention to a series of risks that should be measured and questions that should be considered in designing strategies to reduce murders or other violent events that involve guns.

Some potentially useful distinctions should be made at the outset:

1. Availability of guns refers to the overall number of guns in society and the ease of obtaining them.
2. Possession of a gun simply means ownership, regardless of how the weapon is stored, carried, or used.
3. Access to a gun as a weapon of violence means its immediate availability at the site of a violent event and depends on how the gun is stored or carried.
4. Allocation of guns refers to the distribution of gun possession among people who have and people who have not demonstrated high potentials for violent behavior.
5. Lethality of guns or other weapons means the likelihood that a person injured by the weapon will die as a result.

Each of these distinctions raises specific issues about the relationship of guns to violence.

Relating Guns to Violence

Speculation about the relationship between gun availability and violence levels takes two directions. On one hand, greater availability of guns may deter some potential perpetrators of violent crimes out of fear that the intended victim may be armed. On the other hand, greater availability of guns may encourage people who are contemplating committing a violent crime to carry it out but first to arm themselves to overcome their fear of retaliation. Greater gun availability may also increase violence levels if guns kept at home or in cars are stolen during burglaries, enter illegal markets, and encourage criminals to attack victims they would pass up without being armed. Guns kept in homes may also be used in family arguments that might have ended nonviolently if guns were not available.

How are these conflicting speculations resolved in actual practice? The best way to answer this question would be to measure violent crime levels before and after an intervention that substantially reduced gun availability. However, opportunities to evaluate the effects of such interventions have arisen in only a few jurisdictions.

Different Approaches, Varying Results

Because evaluation opportunities have been rare, researchers have used four less powerful approaches to study how gun availability affects violence and its consequences. The findings, while somewhat tentative and not entirely consistent, suggest that greater gun availability increases murder rates and influences the choice of weapon in violent crimes, but does not affect overall levels of nonfatal violence.

The first research approach asks how differences in violence across American cities are related to variations in gun availability, controlling for other relevant factors. These studies generally find small positive correlations between measures of gun availability and both felony gun use and felony murder. However, they find no consistent relationship between gun availability and overall rates of violent crime.

> *"Greater availability of guns may encourage people who are contemplating committing a violent crime to carry it out but first to arm themselves to overcome their fear of retaliation."*

The second approach used was a comparison of two jurisdictions. The neighboring cities of Seattle and Vancouver have similar economic profiles and were found to have similar rates of burglary and assault. However, Seattle, with its less restrictive gun possession laws, had a 60 percent higher homicide rate and a 400 percent higher firearm homicide rate than Vancouver. It is not clear whether the differences in gun laws accounted for all the variation between the two cities in homicide rates, or whether differences in culture were also contributing factors.

Uncovering the Layers of Approaches

The third approach relies on cross-national statistical comparisons. These studies have generally reached one of the conclusions found in studies of American cities: a small positive correlation between gun availability and homicide rates. The finding is difficult to interpret, however, in view of differences by country in culture and in gun regulations. For example, murder rates are low in Switzerland, where militia requirements make possession of long guns by males nearly universal. This seems to suggest there is no positive correlation between gun availability and murder rates. But this interpretation is clouded because in Switzerland access to guns is limited: militia members are required to keep their guns locked up and to account for every bullet.

The fourth approach relies on analyses of trends over time. Studies using this method have found no correlations between gun availability and rates of violent crime. But trends are subject to a variety of influences, which may mask a relationship that would emerge in the aftermath of some new law or other intervention that substantially reduced gun availability. Evaluation findings about such interventions are discussed later in this report, but more such evaluations are needed to obtain better answers to this question.

Gun Possession For Violent Crimes

Although available data on how guns are obtained are fragmented, outdated, and subject to sampling bias, they suggest that illegal or unregulated transactions are the primary sources of guns used in violence. For example, only 29 percent of 113 guns used in felonies committed in Boston during 1975 and 1976 were bought directly from federally licensed dealers (27 of the 29 percent were obtained by legally eligible purchasers). Between the manufacturer and the criminal user, 20 percent of the guns passed through a chain of unregulated private transfers, while 40 percent were stolen. Most of the illegal suppliers found in this sample were small-scale independent operators who sold only a few guns per month, rather than large organizations or licensed dealers working largely off the books.

Other data were available on how incarcerated felons in 10 States obtained the guns they used in committing crime. The figures revealed that in 1982 only 16 percent of those who used guns in criminal activities reported buying them from licensed dealers. Twice as many (32 percent) reported stealing the gun, and the rest borrowed or bought it from friends or acquaintances. Thefts and illegal purchases were not surprisingly most common among the incarcerated felons who said they acquired their guns primarily to commit crimes. . . .

"Between the manufacturer and the criminal user, 20 percent of the guns passed through a chain of unregulated private transfers, while 40 percent were stolen."

Researchers have studied how the presence of a gun affects the consequences of two types of violent crime—personal robbery and assault. Both types of crime may begin with a threat to use violence. Studies have examined how the likelihood of three outcomes of the threat—escalation to an actual attack, to injury, and to death—changes if the robber or assaulter posing the threat is armed with a gun.

A study of personal robberies revealed that escalation from threat to attack is less likely if the robber is armed with a gun than if he or she is unarmed. A similar pattern was found in assaults. Perhaps the reason is that robbers armed with guns are less nervous, or victims confronted with guns are too frightened to resist, or both. Either effect could reduce the risk of escalation from threat to attack.

> *"Studies have generally concluded that death was at least twice as likely in gun assaults as in knife assaults."*

One implication of the lower escalation rate when guns are used is that robbery and assault victims are less likely to be injured when the perpetrator has a gun. When data reported through the National Crime Victimization Survey (NCVS) between 1973 and 1982 are combined, they reveal that among victims who survive attacks, the chance of injury was 14 percent when the offender was armed with a gun. It was higher when a gun was not used—25 percent when the offender was armed with a knife, 30 percent when unarmed, and 45 percent when armed with another weapon.

Death Often Results from Guns

The overall fatality rate in gun robberies is an estimated 4 per 1,000—about 3 times the rate for knife robberies, 10 times the rate for robberies with other weapons, and 20 times the rate for robberies by unarmed offenders. For assaults, a crime which includes threats, the most widely cited estimate of the fatality rate is derived from a 1968 analysis of assaults and homicides committed in Chicago. The study, prepared for the National Commission on the Causes and Prevention of Violence, reported that gun attacks kill 12.2 percent of their intended victims. This is about 5 times as often as in attacks with knives, the second most deadly weapon used in violent crimes. Studies have generally concluded that death was at least twice as likely in gun assaults as in knife assaults.

While researchers who have looked at the question generally concur that victims injured by guns are more likely to die than victims injured by other weapons, an important question remains: how much of this greater lethality reflects properties of the gun, and how much reflects greater determination to kill by those who choose guns over other weapons for their violent acts? The question is significant for public policy because even the removal of all guns from society would not prevent homicides if the greater lethality of gun injuries were due entirely to violent gun users' greater determination. They would simply achieve their goal using other weapons.

Motivation Is Explored

The relative importance of weapon type and user determination in affecting the deadliness of gun attacks has not been definitively established because researchers cannot directly measure user determination. Indirect measures indicate that firearms are sometimes fired at people without a premeditated intent to kill. The question is how often? If the motivations of gun murderers and knife murderers systematically differed, then systematic differences in the surrounding circumstances would be expected. In fact, however, the gun and knife murders in the 1968 Chicago sample occurred under similar circumstances—largely arguments in which alcohol and temporary rage, not single-minded intent, were most likely to have influenced the killer's behavior. More than 80 percent of gun victims in the sample received only a single wound, a finding which suggests that killers and assaulters who used guns failed to use the full capabilities of their guns to achieve the goal of killing. The interpretation of these statistics has been questioned on methodological grounds, however; and, in any event, the interactions among circumstances, motivation, and weapon choice in murder may well have changed since 1968.

Weapons of Choice

The study of personal robberies, discussed above, suggests at least one reason other than lethal intentions why some robbers use guns: to enable them to attack certain types of victims, such as businesses and groups of teenage males, who would otherwise be relatively invulnerable. Guns are used more often to rob these types of victims than to rob women and the elderly, who are considered more vulnerable. Serial killers are considered the most intent of all killers, but they have rarely used guns. People who killed in violent family fights seem unlikely to have carefully considered their weapon choices; more likely, they resorted to the nearest available weapon, including hands or feet. Even among incarcerated felons, those interviewed in the 10-State survey cited above, 76 percent of those who fired guns in criminal situations claimed to have had no prior intention of doing so.

> *"Firearm sales and uses are subject to Federal, State, and local regulations that are intended to reduce gun-related criminal activity."*

These observations and findings strongly suggest that properties of weapons, rather than intentions of attackers, account for at least some of the difference in lethality between guns and other weapons. However, the apportionment is not precise, and questions have been raised about the methodologies used in the studies. Measuring more precisely how much of the lethality difference arises from different intentions rather than from the choice of a gun remains a problem for future research.

The Validity of Self-Defense Through Guns

Self-defense is commonly cited as a reason to own a gun. This is the explanation given by 20 percent of all gun owners and 40 percent of all handgun owners contacted for a household survey conducted in 1979. Just how often potential victims of violence defend themselves with guns is unclear, in part because "self-defense" is a vague term. Among a sample of prisoners, 48 percent of those who fired their guns while committing crimes claimed they did so in self-defense. At a minimum, victims use guns to attack or threaten the perpetrators in about 1 percent of robberies and assaults—about 70,000 times per year—according to NCVS data for recent years. These victims were less likely to report being injured than those who either defended themselves by other means or took no self-protective measures at all. Thus, while 33 percent of all surviving robbery victims were injured, only 25 percent of those who offered no resistance and 17 percent of those who defended themselves with guns were injured. For surviving assault victims, the corresponding injury rates were, respectively, 30 percent, 27 percent, and 12 percent.

For two reasons, these statistics are an insufficient basis for the personal decision whether or not to obtain a gun for self-protection. First, the decision involves a trade-off between the risks of gun accidents and violent victimization. Second, it is not entirely clear that the relatively few robberies and assaults in which victims defended themselves with guns are typical of these types of crimes and that the lower injury rates resulted from the self-defense action rather than some other factor. Perhaps offenders lost the advantage of surprise, which allowed victims not only to deploy their guns but also to take other evasive action. More detailed analysis of gun self-defense cases is needed to measure both the frequency and consequences of different self-defense actions using guns.

Policy Implications

Firearm sales and uses are subject to Federal, State, and local regulations that are intended to reduce gun-related criminal activity. The Federal Gun Control Act of 1968 is intended to control the allocation of guns by requiring that dealers obtain Federal licenses; by prohibiting them from selling guns through the mail or across State lines to anyone except other licensed dealers; and by barring sales to high-risk-category individuals such as minors, felons, and drug users. According to the U.S. General Accounting Office, resources available to enforce the Act declined during the 1980's, and the news media have reported instances of convicted felons and active drug dealers obtaining Federal dealers' licenses that have permitted them to purchase guns in large quantities.

> *"Some States have attempted to reduce the lethality of available weapons by banning sales of certain categories of weapons used in violent crimes."*

Changing the allocation of guns from high-risk to low-risk individuals is one of four strategies that have been attempted to reduce gun-related violent crimes. To reduce high-risk uses of guns, some States have enacted "place and manner" laws to prevent carrying or concealing guns in public, or to enhance sentences for felonies in which guns are used. Other legal strategies are intended to reduce the availability of guns through restrictive licensing that permits only selected categories of people (such as police and private security officers) to possess guns. Legally required waiting periods for gun purchases are intended both to facilitate verification that purchasers belong to the permit-

> *"The 1977 District of Columbia Firearms Control Act . . . reduced gun robberies, assaults, and homicides for several years."*

ted categories and to reduce "impulse buying" by people who may have temporary violent intentions.

Some States have attempted to reduce the lethality of available weapons by banning sales of certain categories of weapons used in violent crimes. These categories include concealable "Saturday night specials" or high-capacity "assault weapons," both of which have proven difficult to define in practice.

Two Main Influences

The high lethality of gun injuries and the heavy involvement of guns in murder have prompted an intense public debate and a search for strategies to reduce gun homicides. Legal, technological, and public education approaches may all have roles to play. However, the effectiveness of any of these strategies in reducing gun murders depends on the strength of two influences that counteract each other:

- The behavioral response—the extent to which people behave in ways that reduce the level or severity of gun violence because of newly available protective technology, public education campaigns, or the threat of legal punishment.
- Substitution effects—the extent to which the desired behavioral responses are offset by high-risk behaviors such as use of more lethal guns, disarming of gun combination locks by gun thieves, or the assignment by drug organizations of juveniles to gun-using roles because they are subject to lighter penalties than adults.

Valuable Strategies

Because the strength of these two effects cannot be predicted in advance, evaluation is needed to identify the effects of any of the four types of strategies/interventions. Most of them have not been evaluated, and some of the evaluations have produced unclear results. However, studies of the four strategies have yielded some valuable information:

- Strategy 1: Alter gun uses. Both "place and manner" laws and sentence enhancements for felony gun use have been shown to be effective in States (Michigan and Pennsylvania) where they have been evaluated. But neither legal approaches (such as making owners or manufacturers liable for damages caused by the gun) nor technological approaches that make guns and their illegal uses more visible have been evaluated. Some public education initiatives have been evaluated, but the findings have been called into question because of measurement problems.

- Strategy 2: Change gun allocation. An evaluation of the effect of the Federal Gun Control Act of 1968 was conducted in two States where restrictions against instate purchases should make interstate trafficking the major source of guns used in crime. The evaluation did not find that the Act reduced gun use in assaults or homicides. However, a later evaluation of a crackdown to enforce the Federal law in the District of Columbia did show a 6-month reduction in gun homicides. Neither technological innovations, such as built-in combination locks that permit only the legal owner to fire the gun, nor law enforcement approaches, such as disruption of illegal gun markets or mandatory minimum sentences for gun theft, have been evaluated.
- Strategy 3: Reduce gun lethality. Neither legal nor technical restrictions that would reduce gun lethality have been evaluated.
- Strategy 4: Reduce gun availability. The results of several evaluations indicated that the 1977 District of Columbia Firearms Control Act, which prohibited handgun ownership by virtually all private citizens, reduced gun robberies, assaults, and homicides for several years. More intrusive legal restrictions on imports, manufacture, or ownership have not been evaluated.

Findings of Significance

The following evaluation findings are especially significant:

- The Massachusetts 1974 Bartley-Fox Amendment, which prescribed a 1-year sentence for unlicensed public carrying of firearms, decreased gun assaults, gun robberies, and gun homicides during the 2-year period in which it was evaluated.
- Several State mandatory add-ons to felony sentences for use of a gun have reduced gun homicides, but whether they have discouraged gun use in robberies and assaults is not clear.
- The decrease in Washington, D.C., gun homicides following passage of the 1977 D.C. Firearms Control Act appears to have been maintained until the mid-1980s when,

> *"Evaluations of firearm laws suggest that enforcement is critical to their effectiveness."*

according to a recent study, the rise of crack markets was accompanied by a substantial increase in gun homicides.
- The 1968 Federal Gun Control Act, which prohibited Federally licensed gun dealers from selling guns to certain designated "dangerous" categories of people, failed to reduce firearm injuries or deaths, apparently because of lax enforcement.

Evaluations of firearm laws suggest that enforcement is critical to their effectiveness. Therefore, while public debate continues over the wisdom of enacting new gun laws, the Panel concluded that priority should be given to three aspects of enforcing existing laws:

- Disrupting illegal gun markets by means of undercover buys, sting operations, and other tactics at the wholesale and retail levels.
- Reducing juveniles' access to guns through better enforcement of the Federal ban on gun dealers' sales to minors and through disruption of the illegal or unregulated channels through which juveniles obtain guns.
- Close police-community cooperation in setting priorities and enforcing gun laws, as a means of reducing the fears that lead to gun ownership for self-defense.

Long-term efforts are needed to design and implement these and other enforcement tactics so they are both effective and acceptable to the local community; to test them in carefully controlled evaluations; to refine them as indicated by the evaluation findings; and to replicate the evaluations in different community settings.

Supporting Gun Control Legislation Would Reduce Crime

by *Glamour*

About the author: Glamour *is a monthly magazine devoted to topics concerning women. Each month features an editorial focus on a contemporary issue.*

An armed society is a polite society. Is this a bad Jay Leno joke? No, it's a slogan coined by Tom Washington, [former] president of the National Rifle Association (NRA). In other words, we'll all mind our manners if we're afraid of being blown away by just about anyone we encounter. As the political battle over gun control resumes, this bizarre motto has become a rallying cry for those who wish to put more guns and ammo in the hands of any and all Americans.

More than any other population group, women reject the notion that public safety comes from the barrel of a gun. Before Congress passed the landmark 1994 ban on semiautomatic assault weapons, a nationwide Gallup Poll showed that 74 percent of men but fully 80 percent of women favored this legislation.

Pro-gun Frenzy

But pro-gun forces are determined, tenacious and indifferent to public opinion. In January 1995 it appeared that Congress—which since the 1994 election includes an unprecedented number of "gun friendly" representatives whose campaigns received heavy financial support from the NRA—would move quickly to repeal the assault weapons ban. In other moves, legislators in 19 states introduced measures to weaken laws restricting the possession of concealed weapons (mainly handguns).

For example, in Michigan, pro-gunners want concealed weapon permits granted automatically to anyone who has not been declared mentally incompetent or convicted of a felony in the past eight years. For example, authorities would be unable to deny a permit to a man who had repeatedly been reported to police for wife or child abuse—unless he had been convicted of a felony or was under a current restraining order.

This pro-gun juggernaut seemed unstoppable—until it was derailed by the bombing of a federal building in Oklahoma City and the arrest of suspects affiliated with armed extremist militias.

Lobbying for Loose Guns

Since then, women and men across the country, including law-abiding gun owners like former president George Bush, are thinking twice about identifying themselves with the gun lobby. In May 1995, Bush resigned his longtime NRA membership to protest the language of a fund-raising letter that described federal agents as "jack-booted thugs."

Nonetheless, gun lobbyists were back at work in the halls of Congress. Though they may not have been able to achieve the repeal of existing federal gun-control laws, . . . they weakened one measure—part of the antiterrorism bill introduced after the Oklahoma City bombing—that would have banned "cop killer" bullets, which are capable of piercing police body armor. Pro-gunners also pushed for the relaxation of concealed-weapons laws in at least five states—Michigan, Massachusetts, Wisconsin, Ohio and South Carolina. Texas passed such a law.

Empower the Victims

At the state as well as the national level, women have a particular interest in handgun control because we are the primary targets (along with children) of domestic abuse. According to Police Chief Ron Deziel of Dearborn, Michigan, an outspoken opponent of wider access to concealed weapons, all law enforcement agencies acknowledge the connection between guns in the home and domestic violence. "It's just too easy for a quarrel to turn deadly when a gun is handy," he says. "If I punch you in the face, you'll still be alive tomorrow. Guns make for irrevocable acts."

"Because lawmakers pay more attention to groups than individuals, women must urge their professional and community organizations to take a more active role on behalf of gun control."

Because lawmakers pay more attention to groups than individuals, women must urge their professional and community organizations to take a more active role on behalf of gun control. Many all-female groups—from those representing women lawyers, police officers, educators and medical personnel to those specifically organized to tackle such issues as domestic violence—can speak to legislators with particular authority. Women can also influence general organizations like their local PTAs to take a public anti-gun stance.

Chapter 2

The Need for Involvement

Above all, it's important for us to pay close attention to the fine print in state and national legislation. In the cop-killer bullet debate, for instance, pro-gun forces replaced the antiterrorism bill's outright ban with a mushy provision calling for a six-month study.

One big problem is that preventing restrictions on arms and ammo is a full-time passion for the pro-gunners, but many ordinary citizens don't wake up until a battle is already lost.

"Our phones were ringing off the hook the day a more permissive handgun law went into effect in Virginia," recalls Joseph Sudbay of Handgun Control Inc., a national gun-control lobbying organization based in Washington, D.C. "There'd been a lot of publicity, but average citizens only react when they see lines of people waiting for licenses."

We must be certain to tell our lawmakers exactly what we think *before* they cast their votes. Maybe the NRA sees guns and armor-piercing bullets as the way to a politer society—but we don't.

Controlling Legal Gun Ownership Does Not Reduce Crime

by John R. Lott Jr.

About the author: *John R. Lott Jr. is a professor at the University of Chicago Law School. He is the author of* More Guns, Less Crime.

Editor's Note: The author wishes to note that the statistics in this article are now dated.

For the Democratic Party, whose 1996 convention showcased gun-control advocates, the solution to violent crime is clear—more regulation of guns. Convention speeches by James and Sarah Brady were filled with moving stories of their personal suffering.

While the impacts described on both sides of the issue do exist, the crucial question underlying all gun-control laws is: What is their net effect? Are more lives lost or saved? Do they deter crime or encourage it? Anecdotal evidence obviously cannot resolve this debate. To provide a more systematic answer, I recently completed a study of one type of gun-control law—laws on concealed handguns, also known as "shall-issue" laws. Thirty-one states give their citizens the right to carry concealed handguns if they do not have a criminal record or a history of significant mental illness. My study, with David Mustard, a graduate student in economics at the University of Chicago, analyzed the FBI's crime statistics for all 3,054 American counties from 1977 to 1992.

Our findings are dramatic. Our most conservative estimates show that by adopting shall-issue laws, states reduced murders by 8.5%, rapes by 5%, aggravated assaults by 7% and robbery by 3%. If those states that did not permit concealed handguns in 1992 had permitted them back then, citizens would have been spared approximately 1,570 murders, 4,177 rapes, 60,000 aggravated assaults and 12,000 robberies. To put it even more simply: Criminals, we found, respond rationally to deterrence threats.

The benefits of concealed handguns are not limited to just those who carry them or use them in self-defense. The very fact that these weapons are concealed keeps criminals uncertain as to whether a potential victim will be able to defend himself with lethal force. The possibility that anyone might be carrying a gun makes attacking everyone less attractive; unarmed citizens in effect "free-ride" on their pistol-packing fellows.

Violent Crimes Fall

Our study further found that while some criminals avoid potentially violent crimes after concealed-handgun laws are passed, they do not necessarily give up the criminal life altogether. Some switch to crimes in which the risk of confronting an armed victim is much lower. Indeed, the downside of concealed-weapons laws is that while violent crime rates fall, property offenses like larceny (e.g., stealing from unattended automobiles or vending machines) and auto theft rise. This is certainly a substitution that the country can live with.

"The possibility that anyone might be carrying a gun makes attacking everyone less attractive; unarmed citizens in effect 'free-ride' on their pistol-packing fellows."

Our study also provided some surprising information. While support for strict gun-control laws usually has been strongest in large cities, where crime rates are highest, that's precisely where right-to-carry laws have produced the largest drops in violent crimes. For example, in counties with populations of more than 200,000 people, concealed-handgun laws produced an average drop in murder rates of more than 13%. The half of the counties with the highest rape rates saw that crime drop by more than 7%.

Women Are Empowered

Concealed handguns also appear to help women more than men. Murder rates decline when either sex carries more guns, but the effect is especially pronounced when women are considered separately. An additional woman carrying a concealed handgun reduces the murder rate for women by about three to four times more than an additional armed man reduces the murder rate for men. Victims of violent crime are generally physically weaker than the criminals who prey on them. Allowing a woman to defend herself with a concealed handgun makes a much larger difference in her ability to defend herself than the change created by providing a man with a handgun. Guns are the great equalizer between the weak and the vicious.

At the Democratic convention, President Bill Clinton played up his proposed expansion of the 1994 Brady law, which by making it harder for men convicted of domestic violence to obtain guns is designed to reduce crime against women. Our study is the first to provide direct empirical evidence of the Brady Law's effect on crime rates—and we found just the opposite result: The law's implementation is associated with *more* aggravated assaults and rapes. Mrs. Brady's exaggerated estimates of the number of felons denied access to guns in her speech are a poor measure of the law's impact on crime rates.

Owners Are Responsible

We also collected data on whether owners of concealed handguns are more likely to use them in committing violent crimes. The rarity of these incidents is reflected in Florida's statistics: More than 300,000 concealed-handgun licenses were issued between Oct. 1, 1987, and Dec. 31, 1995, but only five violent crimes involving permitted pistols were committed in this period, and none of these resulted in fatalities.

What about minor disputes such as traffic accidents? Are legal owners of concealed handguns more likely to use them in such situations? In 31 states, some of which have had concealed weapons laws for decades, there is only one recorded incident (1996 in Texas) in which a concealed handgun was used in a shooting following an accident. Even in that one case, a grand jury found that the shooting was in self-defense: The shooter was being beaten by the other driver.

And what about accidental deaths? The number of accidental handgun deaths each year is fewer than 200. Our estimates imply that if the states without "shall issue" laws were to adopt them, the increase in accidental handgun deaths would be at most nine more deaths per year. This is small indeed when compared to the at least 1,570 murders that would be avoided.

Solid Evidence

While no single study is likely to end the debate on concealed handguns, ours provides the first systematic national evidence. By contrast, the largest prior study examined only 170 cities within a single year. The nearly 50,000 observations in our data set allow us to control for a range of factors that have never been accounted for in any previous study of crime, let alone any previous gun-control study. Among other variables, our regressions control for arrest and conviction rates, prison sentences, changes in handgun laws such as waiting periods and the imposition of additional penalties for using a gun to commit a crime, income, poverty, unemployment, and demographic changes.

> *"Preventing law-abiding citizens from carrying handguns does not end violence, but merely makes them more vulnerable to attack."*

Preventing law-abiding citizens from carrying handguns does not end violence, but merely makes them more vulnerable to attack. The very size and strength of our results should at least give pause to those who oppose concealed handguns. The opportunity to reduce the murder rate by simply relaxing a regulation ought to be difficult to ignore.

Increased Gun Control Would Result in More Burglaries

by David Kopel

About the author: *David Kopel is the research director for the Independence Institute in Golden, Colorado. He is the author of* No More Wacos: What's Wrong with Federal Law Enforcement and How to Fix It.

Guns in the right hands make all good people safer—including people who don't own guns. The higher the number of responsible people who have guns ready to be used for self-defense, the safer the public is. The tremendous degree to which widespread gun ownership makes American homes safer from home invaders is one of the great unreported stories of the American gun-control debate.

The United States suffers from a very high rate of violent crime, compared to most other industrial democracies. Despite improvement, the American crime rate is high for crimes that often involve guns (such as murder), and for crimes that rarely involve guns (such as rape, in which only seven percent of criminals use guns).

Home Sweet Home?

Yet, happily, American homes are comparatively safe from burglary. They are especially safe from "home invasion" or "hot" burglaries—that is, burglaries in which the victim is present during the burglary. As an introductory criminology textbook explains, "Burglars do not want contact with occupants; they depend on stealth for success." The textbook is correct; only 13 percent of residential burglaries in the United States are attempted against occupied homes. But this happy fact of life, so taken for granted in the United States, is not a universal.

In Canada, for example, a Toronto study found that 48 percent of burglaries were against occupied homes, and 21 percent involved a confrontation with the victim. In Edmonton, about half of all burglaries are "hot." A 1982 British sur-

Reprinted from David Kopel, "Burglary and the Armed Homestead," *Chronicles*, January 1998, by permission of the author.

vey found 59 percent of attempted burglaries involved an occupied home.

Why should American criminals, who have proven that they engage in murder, rape, and robbery at a higher rate than their counterparts in other nations, display such a curious reluctance to perpetrate burglaries against occupied residences? Could part of the answer be that they are afraid of getting shot?

Studying the Burglar

In a survey of felony convicts in state prisons, 73 percent of the convicts who had committed a burglary or violent crime agreed "one reason burglars avoid houses when people are at home is that they fear being shot." Another study found that over 90 percent of burglars said that they would not even attempt a burglary in a house that they thought might be occupied.

Most scholarly studies rely on burglars who are currently incarcerated. One important study broke this mold: *Burglars on the Job* by Richard T. Wright and Scott Decker. This was a 1994 survey in St. Louis of 105 currently active burglars. The authors observed, "One of the most serious risks faced by residential burglars is the possibility of being injured or killed by occupants of a target. Many of the offenders we spoke to reported that this was far and away their greatest fear."

> *"The tremendous degree to which widespread gun ownership makes American homes safer from home invaders is one of the great unreported stories of the American gun-control debate."*

The fear of armed victims is not limited to the home. Unlike most other nations, America allows its citizens to be armed for protection not only in their home but in their place of business. A 1996 study of 310 armed robbers, by Athena Research in Seattle, reported that many robbers are afraid of armed victims more than anything else. The fear of armed victims is why armed robbers often avoid "mom and pop" stores where the victim may be armed. Instead, robbers concentrate on chain stores, where corporate policy frequently forbids employees to be armed.

Examining Experiments

Real-world experiments yield results consistent with burglars' reports of their desire to avoid confrontations with armed victims. In the 1960's, gun control advocates in New York City handed out window decals, so that homeowners could proclaim that their home did not contain a gun. The decals quickly became a magnet for burglars, and the decal program was abandoned. The converse of the New York City "victimize this house" program are the real-world experiments in which cities have forcefully reminded potential burglars of the dangers of armed victims.

In Orlando in 1967, the police responded to a rape epidemic by initiating a highly publicized program training women in firearms use. While rape increased in the nation and in Florida over the next year, the rape rate fell 88 percent in Orlando, and burglary dropped 22 percent. The same year, rising rates of store robberies prompted a similar (but smaller-scale) program in Kansas City, Missouri, to train store owners in gun use. The next year, while the robbery rate in Missouri and the United States continued to rise significantly, the rate fell in the Kansas City metro area. The trend of increasing burglary in the area also came to an abrupt end, contrary to state and national patterns.

In 1982, the town of Kennesaw, Georgia, horrified the national media

> *"Unlike most other nations, America allows its citizens to be armed for protection not only in their home but in their place of business."*

by passing an ordinance requiring every home to have a gun. (Exceptions were made for conscientious objectors, people with criminal records, and various other categories.) In the seven months before the ordinance, there had been 45 residential burglaries. In the seven months after the ordinance, there were only five—an 89 percent decline. Over the next five years, the residential burglary rate in Kennesaw was 85 percent below the rate before the enactment of the ordinance.

Armed and Ready

The ordinance may not have actually changed gun ownership patterns much in Kennesaw; the mayor estimated that even before the ordinance, about five of every six Kennesaw homes contained a gun. But the publicity surrounding the Kennesaw law may have served as a very powerful warning to persons contemplating a residential burglary in the town: any homeowner confronted during a burglary would almost certainly be armed.

Not just in Kennesaw, but throughout the United States, the armed victim is a serious danger to burglars. One of 31 burglars has been shot during a burglary. Thus, American burglary patterns are heavily influenced by the perpetrators' fears of confronting an armed victim. Most burglars report that they avoid late-night burglaries because "That's the way to get shot."

Opponents of gun ownership for home defense insist that—despite what burglars say again and again—the fear of armed victims has little to do with burglary patterns. Instead, burglars are claimed to be nonconfrontational by nature, wanting to avoid seeing any victim, armed or not. But this assertion fails to explain why burglars in Great Britain or Canada are so much less shy than their American cousins. Besides, burglars are *not* nonconfrontational by nature. A multistate study of felony prisoners found that 62 percent of burglars had also perpetrated robberies. (A burglary is an entry into a building to commit a felony, and does not necessarily involve a confrontation; a robbery is the taking of property from a victim through force or the threat of force.)

The St. Louis study of currently active burglars observed: "Most offenders in our sample . . . showed little concern for the well-being of their victims. In fact, several of them said they were prepared to use violence against anyone who got in their way during the commission of an offense." As one St. Louis burglar told Wright and Decker: "When [the victims] come in there, they better have some boxin' gloves on cause . . . I'm gon hurt you, I ain't lyin'."

When burglars do encounter victims who cannot protect themselves, the results can be terrifying. In 30 percent of the cases in which a burglar does confront a victim, the victim is assaulted or threatened. In ten percent of these cases, the assaults turn into rapes. Florida State University criminologist Gary Kleck, in *Point Blank: Guns and Violence in America*, explains the implications of these statistics:

> Suppose that the percentage of "hot" burglaries rose from current American levels (around 12 or 13%) to the Canadian level (around 45%). Knowing how often a hot burglary turns into an assault, we can predict that an increase in hot burglaries to Canadian levels would result in 545,713 more assaults every year. This by itself would raise the American violent crime rate 9.4%.

Guns Benefit the Community

While the gun prohibition lobby portrays gun owners as atavistic and selfish, gun ownership for home protection is considerably more beneficial to the entire community than many other anti-burglary measures.

Burglars (or convenience-store robbers) do not know which of their potential victims may be armed. Until a confrontation with a homeowner, the potential burglar generally has no idea whether any given homeowner has a gun. Thus, burglars must (and most do) take care to avoid entering any home where a victim might be present. Because about half of all American homes contain a gun, burglars tend to avoid all occupied American homes. People who don't own guns—even people who belong to gun-prohibition organizations—enjoy free-rider safety benefits from America's armed homes.

In contrast to guns, burglar alarms appear to have no net community benefit. Burglar alarms have been shown to reduce burglaries for homes in which they are installed; but the presence of many burglar alarms in a neighborhood does not appear to decrease or increase the burglary rate for unalarmed homes.

False alarms—which account for 94 to 98 of all burglar alarm activations—impose very large public safety costs through misappropriation of limited police resources. False-alarm signals travel over 911 lines, and may crowd out genuine emergencies. Guns, of course, lie inert until someone decides to use them; they do not go off because a cat jumped into a beam of light.

> *"When burglars do encounter victims who cannot protect themselves, the results can be terrifying."*

Gun prohibitionists make all sorts of claims about the risks of "a gun in the home," and these claims have some validity if the gun happens to be in the home of a violent felon, or an alcoholic, or a person with suicidal tendencies. But in responsible hands, guns are no danger at all, since the gun will only shoot in the direction in which it is pointed, and will not fire unless the trigger is pulled.

In any case, whatever risks a gun in the home may present are borne almost entirely by the people in that home. The non-gunowners in the community get the benefit of safety from home-invasion burglars, while assuming no risks at all. (The only significant external danger of a gun in the home is if the gun is stolen by a criminal, a risk that also applies to any other device that could be stolen and used by a criminal, such as a car or a crowbar, or any valuables which could be sold and the profits used to buy crime tools.) And, of course, guns stay quiet and unobtrusive until needed. They do not bark all night and wake up the neighborhood, like dogs often do. Nor do guns rush into the street to attack and sometimes kill innocent people, as some guard dogs do. Guns in the right hands do nothing at all, until they are needed. Firearms, which are typically stored deep inside a home, do not make a neighborhood look ugly. But window bars give a neighborhood the appearance of a prison, and some window bars can trap the occupants of a home during a fire.

> *"If it is reasonable for people to reduce the risks of burglary by buying insurance, it is far more reasonable for people to reduce the risks of burglary by purchasing a gun for home protection."*

Better than Insurance

Most people consider it rational for householders to have burglary insurance. Yet insurance premiums must (for the insurance company to stay in business) be set at a level at which the cost of the premiums exceeds the probable payout by the insurance company over the long run. Insurance is, by definition, a losing bet. If it is reasonable for people to reduce the risks of burglary by buying insurance, it is far more reasonable for people to reduce the risks of burglary by purchasing a gun for home protection. Over a ten-year period, the cost of insurance premiums far exceeds the cost of a good gun. Moreover, the gun, unlike the insurance premium, can actually prevent a victim from being injured.

Unfortunately, the antigun lobby is morally opposed to gun ownership for defensive purposes. As Sarah Brady explains, "To me, the only reason for guns in civilian hands is for sporting purposes." This view is antithetical to legislation enacted in Colorado and other states which makes explicit the common-law right to use deadly force against violent home invaders. Thus, the antigun lobbies push for laws like Canada's, which effectively abolishes home defense. In Canada, "safe storage" laws require that guns be stored unloaded or locked up, thus making them difficult to deploy in a sudden emergency. The antigun lobbies and their numerous media allies are also running a propaganda campaign against guns in the home—a campaign which tries to convince ordinary Americans that they are just as prone to criminal violence as are convicted felons and substance abusers. But as long as tens of millions of Americans continue to exercise their constitutional right to own a gun to protect their homes and families, then all Americans will continue to enjoy lower risks of assault and greater safety in their homes, thanks to the widespread community benefits of guns in the right hands.

Domestic Violence Gun Control Laws Hinder Crime Reduction

by James Bovard

About the author: *James Bovard, a freelance writer, is author of* Lost Rights: The Destruction of American Liberty.

"Rank and file police officers have never had a better friend in the White House than Bill Clinton," announced national Fraternal Order of Police President Gil Gallegos when his group endorsed the president on Sept. 15, 1996. A few weeks later, Mr. Clinton signed a gun-control act that is wreaking havoc on America's police and also decimates the constitutional rights of millions of other Americans.

Most police organizations have enthusiastically supported every gun-control gambit Mr. Clinton has put forward. That may be because such legislation almost always contained an exemption for the policemen themselves while they were on duty. No more. On Sept. 28, 1996, as part of a massive appropriations bill, Congress passed the Lautenberg Act, which may greatly increase the number of Americans prohibited by federal law from owning firearms. For the first time, thanks to an amendment by Rep. Bob Barr (R., Ga.), law enforcement officials are not exempt from the nation's gun control laws.

Long Sentences

The Lautenberg Act prohibits from owning a gun or possessing any ammunition anyone who has ever been convicted of a misdemeanor involving the use or attempted use of physical force, or the threatened use of a deadly weapon against a spouse, child, intimate partner or other cohabitant. (People with any felony conviction have been prohibited from owning guns since 1968.) Any person with such a misdemeanor on his record who is found in possession of a gun, or even of a single bullet, can face a $250,000 fine and 10 years in prison—longer than the average convicted murderer serves in this country.

Gerald Arenberg, executive director of the National Association of Chiefs of Police, observed that the act "has thrown the whole world into confusion for cops." A recent survey by the Frater-nal Order of Police found that 82% of its members believed that domes-tic violence is a problem for police families, but only 27% believed that police officers would answer ques-tions about such violence. Victor Kappeler, director of the Criminal Justice Graduate Program at Eastern Kentucky University, estimated that if ac-curate reporting of such police domestic violence occurred, and if all such as-saults were fully prosecuted, 10% of the nation's law enforcement officials (70,000 individuals) could be found guilty and thus banned from possessing a firearm under the law. This is far more police than Mr. Clinton has actually managed to put on the street with his vaunted "100,000 new cops" program.

> *"State laws on 'domestic violence' are totally inconsistent; some states even define 'trespassing' as an act of domestic violence."*

In Columbus, Ohio, five police officers have been stripped of their duties and weapons under this legislation. Similarly, in Minneapolis, six police officers—including the supervisor of the homicide team—are on paid leave pending re-sults of an investigation by the police department. The National Association of Police Organizations is calling for Congress to amend the law to exempt police. Beth Weaver, a spokesman for the group, complained: "What we are concerned about is that law enforcement officers are the only group of workers in the country who stand to lose their jobs because of this regulation." Perhaps the po-lice need to be exempt from the law in order to have sufficient personnel to take away other people's guns.

Considering the Ramifications

With the Lautenberg Act, Congress has cast a far wider anti-gun net than most Americans realize. State laws on "domestic violence" are totally inconsis-tent; some states even define "trespassing" as an act of domestic violence. Early in the administration, Hillary Clinton was widely rumored to have thrown a lamp at her husband; if she did, she is guilty of domestic violence, and thus could be forever prohibited from owning an Uzi. In some states, a husband who mimicked Jackie Gleason and shook his fist in the air towards his wife snarling, "One of these days, Alice!" could be permanently stripped of his right to own firearms. University of Maryland Prof. Lawrence Sherman noted, "When you touch people for the purpose of inflicting pain or fear of pain—many states will define that in their case law as an assault. Many of the arrests [from domestic violence] are based on such things as shoves"—rather than knock-down punches or chairs broken over people's heads.

The 1996 law could provide vigilante prosecutors the power to seize the guns of parents who are not following Dr. Spock's child-rearing recommendations. According to Chris Klicka, director of the National Center for Home Education, "There is a move across the country by child rights groups to outlaw corporal punishment. In a few instances, families have been found guilty of abusing their children as a result of spanking—not that their children were hurt or anything."

Bogus charges of domestic violence are routinely used as tactics in divorce proceedings, and many people who plea-bargained 20 years ago on such a charge and paid a small court fine (instead of spending $5,000 in legal fees to defend themselves) will be surprised to discover that they have lost one of their constitutional rights. "Many domestic violence charges are false—perhaps as many as one-third where child custody or divorce issues are involved," says Peter Proctor, a forensic expert in Houston.

Women Lose Greatly

Sen. Frank Lautenberg (D., N.J.) described his bill on the Senate floor on Aug. 2: "My amendment stands for the simple proposition that if you beat your wife . . . you should not have a gun." But women are not exempt from the law, and even though they may need guns more than physically stronger men, they are increasingly likely to be stripped of the means of self-defense by its provisions. Many localities require police to make arrests when answering domestic violence calls, and some Virginia counties have seen a tripling of domestic abuse charges against women since 1994.

Disarming women can have deadly consequences. Polly Pryzbyl, a Cheektowaga, N.Y., woman, was murdered by her husband in August 1994 after police took away her guns. A few days earlier, she had separated from her husband and taken her children with her to her mother's house. Her husband came to her mother's house and threatened her; she brandished a pistol to force her husband to back off. Police arrived and seized her gun. A week later, she and her mother went to her husband's house to pick up clothing for the children; her husband stepped out of the house and gunned them both down.

What Epidemic?

The presumption behind the Lautenberg law is that men must be disarmed in order to reduce an epidemic of wife killing. However, according to FBI statistics, the rate of women killed by husbands or boyfriends since the mid-1970s has fallen almost 20%. It's true that some jurisdictions have been criminally negligent in prosecuting and incarcerating people (almost entirely men) who repeatedly use severe physical force against their spouses. The solution is to jail the bad guys, not wave a legislative magic wand and presume that everyone with a misdemeanor is a time bomb, just waiting to empty his six-shooter into his spouse.

Congress held no hearings on the Lautenberg Act before it was enacted and most congressmen will likely be surprised at the police backlash against the law. Prof. Sherman, of the University of Maryland, estimated that 100,000 to 150,000 Americans are convicted of domestic violence each year. Thanks to the Lautenberg Act, there are probably at least one million new felons in this nation—people with misdemeanor convictions who retain their firearms because they are unaware of their duty to disarm themselves.

The act should be repealed, and local prosecutors should stop letting real wife-beaters dance away with a slap on the wrist.

Chapter 3

Is Gun Control Constitutional?

The Second Amendment and Gun Control: An Overview

by Wendy Kaminer

About the author: *Wendy Kaminer is a lawyer, social critic, and contributing editor to the* Atlantic Monthly. *She is the author of* It's All the Rage: Crime and Culture.

I've been invited to the shooting range to "observe and try out the right to bear arms in action," along with about twenty other participants in a two-day seminar on guns and the Constitution, sponsored by Academics for the Second Amendment. Funded partly by the National Rifle Association, Academics for the Second Amendment isn't exactly a collection of academic gun nuts—most of its more than 500 members aren't academics, and its president, Joseph Olson, an NRA board member and a professor at Hamline Law School, in Minnesota, seems a rational, open-minded man. But the organization is engaged in a genteel lobbying effort to popularize what many liberals consider the gun nut's view of the Second Amendment: that it confers an individual right to bear arms, not just the right to bear arms in a well-regulated militia.

Since it was founded, in 1992, Academics for the Second Amendment has held four by-invitation-only seminars for academics who share its beliefs about the Second Amendment—or might be persuaded to adopt them. In 1994 I asked permission to attend a seminar but was turned down; in 1995 I received an unsolicited invitation, apparently in response to an article in which I had questioned the effectiveness of traditional approaches to gun control.

Seminar for Gun Advocacy

Don Kates, who is a San Francisco lawyer, a gun aficionado, and the author of numerous articles on guns and the Constitution, leads the seminar energetically, taking only a little time out to show us pictures of his parrot. His ap-

Abridged from Wendy Kaminer, "Second Thoughts on the Second Amendment," *The Atlantic Monthly*, March 1996. Reprinted by permission of the author.

proach is scattershot, or spray and pray. Ranging over legal, moral, and practical arguments for private gun ownership, he discusses self-defense and the deterrent effect of an armed citizenry; the correlation between guns and crime; difficulties of enforcing gun controls; bigotry against gun owners; and, finally, constitutional rights. Comments by participants are sometimes sensible and occasionally insane: one man proclaims that mothers should give guns to children who attend dangerous public schools.

"What would you do if you had a fourteen-year-old kid who felt he needed a gun for self-defense?" he asks me repeatedly.

"I'd take him out of school before giving him a gun."

> *"Opposition to gun prohibitions focuses on attempts to disarm more or less sane, law-abiding adults."*

But even among gun advocates there is relatively little support for the rights of juveniles to own guns, or opposition to bans on juvenile ownership. Opposition to gun prohibitions focuses on attempts to disarm more or less sane, law-abiding adults, who are deemed to be endowed with both natural and constitutional rights to self-defense against criminals and despots.

Who Is Right About Crime?

Like moral and legal claims about gun owners' rights, the practical consequences of widespread gun ownership are highly debatable. No one can say with any certainty whether it increases violence or decreases crime. Don Kates speculates that magically reducing the approximately 200 million firearms in circulation to five million would have virtually no reductive effect on the crime rate: according to a 1983 National Institute of Justice-funded study by James D. Wright, Peter H. Rossi, and Kathleen Daly, about one percent of privately owned firearms are involved in criminal activity, suggesting that eliminating 99 percent of the nation's guns would not ameliorate crime.

Or would it? Philip Cook, an economist at Duke University and a leading researcher on gun violence, considers Kates's speculation about the uselessness of reducing the number of guns "patently absurd." We can't predict which guns will be used in crimes, he says, even if a relatively small number are used feloniously overall. Reducing the availability of guns would raise their price and therefore reduce their accessibility, to adult felons as well as juveniles. And even if a drastic reduction in the number of guns wouldn't necessarily decrease crime, it would decrease fatalities. Guns are particularly lethal, Cook has stressed: the "fraction of serious gun assaults that result in the victim's death is much higher than that of assaults with other weapons." Since not all gun homicides reflect a clearly formulated intent to kill, Cook reasons, access to guns can increase the lethality of assaults. A decrease in the use of guns, however, might lead to an increase in nonfatal injuries. Robberies committed with guns tend to involve less violence than other robberies because the victims are less likely to resist. (Cook speculates that victims who do resist robbers armed with guns are more likely to be killed.)

Empirical Evidence Is Needed

Debates about gun ownership and gun control are driven more by values and ideology than by pragmatism—and hardly at all by the existing empirical research, which is complex and inconclusive. Wright, Rossi, and Daly reported that there is not even any "suggestive evidence" showing that "gun ownership . . . as a whole is, per se, an important cause of criminal violence." The evidence that guns deter criminal violence is equally insubstantial, they added, as is evidence that additional gun controls would reduce crime. Many are already in place and rarely, if ever, enforced; or they make no sense. In 1983 Wright, Rossi, and Daly concluded that the "benefits of stricter gun controls . . . are at best uncertain, and at worst close to nil."

As for legal debates about the existence of constitutional rights, empirical data is irrelevant, or at best peripheral. But the paucity of proof that gun controls lessen crime is particularly galling to people who believe that they have a fundamental right to bear arms. In theory, at least, we restrict constitutional rights only when the costs of exercising them seem unbearably high. In fact we argue continually about what those costs are: Does violence in the media cause violence in real life? Did the release of the Pentagon Papers endanger the national security?

> *"Debates about gun ownership and gun control are driven more by values and ideology than by pragmatism."*

Does hate speech constitute discrimination? In the debate about firearms, however, we can't even agree on the principles that should govern restrictions on guns, because we can't agree about the right to own them.

No Definite Answers

How could we, given the importance of the competing values at stake—public safety and the right of self-defense—and the opacity of the constitutional text? The awkwardly drafted Second Amendment doesn't quite make itself clear: "A well regulated Militia, being necessary to the security of a free State, the right of the people to keep and bear Arms, shall not be infringed." Is the reference to a militia a limitation on the right to bear arms or merely an explanation of an armed citizenry's role in a government by consent? There is little dispute that one purpose of the Second Amendment was to ensure that the people would be able to resist a central government should it ever devolve into despotism. But there is little agreement about what that capacity for resistance was meant to entail—armed citizens acting under the auspices of state militias or armed citizens able to organize and act on their own. And there is virtually no consensus about the constitutional right to own a gun in the interests of individual self-defense against crime, rather than communal defense against tyranny. Is defense of the state, and of the common good, the *raison d'être* of the Second Amendment or merely one use of it?

The Supreme Court has never answered these fundamental questions about the constitutional uses of guns. It has paid scant attention to the Second Amendment, providing little guidance in the gun-control debate. Two frequently cited late-nineteenth-century cases relating to the Second Amendment were more about federalism than about the right to bear arms. *Presser v. Illinois*, decided in 1886, involved a challenge to a state law prohibiting private citizens from organizing their own military units and parades. The Court held that the Second Amendment was a limitation on federal, not state, power, reflecting the prevailing view (now discredited) that the Bill of Rights in general applied only to the federal government, not to the states. (A hundred years ago the Court did not apply the First Amendment to the states either.) *Presser* followed *U.S. v. Cruikshank*, which held that the federal government could not protect people from private infringement of their rights to assemble and bear arms. *Cruikshank*, decided in 1876, invalidated the federal convictions of participants in the lynching of two black men. This ruling, essentially concerned with limiting federal police power, is virtually irrelevant to Second Amendment debates today, although it has been cited to support the proposition that an oppressed minority has a compelling need (or a natural right) to bear arms in self-defense.

Two Suitable Interpretations

The most significant Supreme Court decision on the Second Amendment was *U.S. v. Miller* (1939), a less-than-definitive holding now cited approvingly by both sides in the gun-control debate. *Miller* involved a prosecution under the 1934 National Firearms Act. Jack Miller and his accomplice had been convicted of transporting an unregistered shotgun of less than regulation length across state lines. In striking down their Second Amendment claim and upholding their conviction, the Court noted that no evidence had been presented that a shotgun was in fact a militia weapon, providing no factual basis for a Second Amendment claim. This ruling implies that the Second Amendment could protect the right to bear arms suitable for a militia.

"In the debate about firearms . . . we can't even agree on the principles that should govern restrictions on guns, because we can't agree about the right to own them."

Advocates of gun control or prohibition like the Miller case because it makes the right to bear arms dependent on at least the possibility of service in a militia. They cite the Court's declaration that the Second Amendment was obviously intended to "assure the continuation and render possible the effectiveness" of state militias; they place less emphasis on the Court's apparent willingness to permit private citizens to possess military weapons. Citing *Miller*, a dealer at a gun show told me that the Second Amendment protects the ownership of only such devices as machine guns, Stingers, and grenade throwers. But advocates of gun ownership don't generally emphasize this awkward implication of *U.S. v. Miller* any more than their opponents do: it could lead to prohibitions on handguns. They like the *Miller* decision because it delves into the history of the Second Amendment and stresses that for the framers, the militia "comprised all males physically capable of acting in concert for the common defense."

The Force of a Militia

This view of the militia as an inchoate citizens' army, not a standing body of professionals, is central to the claim that the Second Amendment protects the rights of individual civilians, not simply the right of states to organize and arm militias. And, in fact, fear and loathing of standing armies did underlie the Second Amendment, which was at least partly intended to ensure that states would be able to call up citizens in defense against a tyrannical central government. (Like the Bill of Rights in general, the Second Amendment was partly a response to concerns about federal abuses of power.) James Madison, the author of the Second Amendment, invoked in *The Federalist Papers* the potential force of a citizen militia as a guarantee against a federal military coup.

> *"There is virtually no consensus about the constitutional right to own a gun in the interests of individual self-defense against crime, rather than communal defense against tyranny."*

> Let a regular army, fully equal to the resources of the country, be formed; and let it be entirely at the devotion of the federal government: still it would not be going too far to say that the State governments with the people on their side would be able to repel the danger. . . . To [the regular army] would be opposed a militia amounting to near half a million of citizens with arms in their hands, officered by men chosen from among themselves, fighting for their common liberties and united and conducted by governments possessing their affection and confidence. It may well be doubted whether a militia thus circumstanced could ever be conquered by such a proportion of regular troops. Those who are best acquainted with the late successful resistance of this country against the British arms will be most inclined to deny the possibility of it. Besides the advantage of being armed, which the Americans possess over the people of almost every other nation, the existence of subordinate governments, to which the people are attached and by which the militia officers are appointed, forms a barrier against the enterprises of ambition, more insurmountable than any which a simple government of any form can admit of.

This passage is enthusiastically cited by advocates of the right to bear arms, because it supports their notion of the militia as the body of people, privately armed; but it's also cited by their opponents, because it suggests that the militia is activated and "conducted" by the states, and it stresses that citizens are "attached" to their local governments. The militia envisioned by Madison is not simply a "collection of unorganized, privately armed citizens," Dennis Henigan, a handgun-control advocate, has argued.

Private or Public Interests?

That Madison's reflections on the militia and the Supreme Court's holding in *U.S. v. Miller* can be cited with some accuracy by both sides in the debate testifies to the hybrid nature of Second Amendment rights. The Second Amendment presumes (as did the framers) that private citizens will possess private arms; Madison referred offhandedly to "the advantage of being armed, which the Americans possess." But Madison also implied that the right to bear arms is based in the obligation of citizens to band together as a militia to defend the common good, as opposed to the prerogative of citizens to take up arms individually in pursuit of self-interest and happiness.

The tension at the heart of the Second Amendment, which makes it so difficult to construe, is the tension between republicanism and liberal individualism. (To put it very simply, republicanism calls for the subordination of individual interests to the public good; liberalism focuses on protecting individuals against popular conceptions of the good.) A growing body of scholarly literature on the Second Amendment locates the right to bear arms in republican theories of governance. In a 1989 article in the *Yale Law Journal* that helped animate the Second Amendment debate, the University of Texas law professor Sanford Levinson argued that the Second Amendment confers an individual right to bear arms so that, in the republican tradition, armed citizens might rise up against an oppressive state. Wendy Brown, a professor of women's studies at the University of California at Santa Cruz, and David C. Williams, a law professor at Cornell University, have questioned the validity of a republican right to bear arms in a society that lacks the republican virtue of being willing to put communal interests first. Pro-gun activists don't generally acknowledge the challenge posed by republicanism to the individualist culture that many gun owners inhabit. They embrace republican justifications for gun ownership, stressing the use of arms in defending the community, at the same time that they stress the importance of guns in protecting individual autonomy.

> *"The Second Amendment . . . was at least partly intended to ensure that states would be able to call up citizens in defense against a tyrannical central government."*

Advocates of the right to bear arms often insist that the Second Amendment is rooted in both collective and individual rights of self-defense—against political oppression and crime—without recognizing how those rights conflict. The republican right to resist oppression is the right of the majority, or the people, not the right of a small religious cult in Waco, Texas, or of a few survivalist tax protesters in Idaho. The members of these groups have individual rights against the government, state and federal. (Both the American Civil Liberties Union and the NRA protested the government's actions in Waco and its attack on the survivalist Randy Weaver and his family.) But refuseniks and refugees from society are not republicans. They do not constitute the citizen militia envisioned by the framers, any more than they stand for the American community; indeed, they stand against it—withdrawing from the body politic, asserting their rights to alienation and anomie or membership in exclusionary alternative communities of their own. Republicanism can't logically be invoked in the service of libertarianism. It elevates civic virtue over individualism, consensus over dissent.

> *"The tension at the heart of the Second Amendment . . . is the tension between republicanism and liberal individualism."*

Nor can social-contract theory be readily invoked in support of a right to arm yourself in a war against street crime, despite the claims of some gun-ownership advocates. The right or power to engage in punishment or retribution is precisely what is given up when you enter an ordered civil society. The loss of self-help remedies is the price of the social contract. "God hath certainly appointed Government to restrain the partiality and violence of Men," John Locke wrote. A person may always defend his or her life when threatened, but only when there is no chance to appeal to the law. If a man points his sword at me and demands my purse, Locke explained, I may kill him. But if he steals my purse by stealth and then raises a sword to defend it, I may not use force to get it back. "My Life not being in danger, I may have the *benefit of appealing* to the Law, and have Reparation . . . that way."

A Matter of Perspective

Locke was drawing a line between self-defense and vigilantism which many gun owners would no doubt respect. Others would point to the inability of the criminal-justice system to avenge crimes and provide reparation to victims, and thus they would assert a right to engage in self-help. Social-contract theory, however, might suggest that if the government is no longer able to provide order, or justice, the remedy is not vigilantism but revolution; the utter failure of law enforcement is a fundamental breach of trust. And, in fact, there are large pockets of disaffected citizens who do not trust the government to protect them or to provide impartial justice, and who might be persuaded to rise up against it, as evidenced by the disorder that followed the 1992 acquittal of police officers who assaulted Rodney King. Was Los Angeles the scene of a riot or of an uprising?

Injustice, and the sense of oppression it spawns, are often matters of perspective—particularly today, when claims of political victimization abound and there is little consensus on the demands of public welfare. We use the term "oppression" promiscuously, to describe any instance of discrimination. In this climate of grievance and hyperbole, many acts of violence are politicized. How do we decide whether an insurrection is just? Don Kates observes that the Second Amendment doesn't exactly confer the right to resist. He says, "It gives you a right to win."

A Right of Self-Protection

The prospect of armed resistance, however, is probably irrelevant to much public support for gun ownership, which reflects a fear of crime more than a fear or loathing of government. People don't buy guns in order to overthrow or even to thwart the government; in the belief that the police can't protect them, people buy guns to protect themselves and their families. Recognizing this, the NRA appeals to fear of crime, particularly crime against women. ("Choose to refuse to be a victim," NRA ads proclaim, showing a woman and her daughter alone in a desolate parking lot at night.) And it has countered demands for tougher gun controls not with radical individualist appeals for insurrection but with statist appeals for tougher anti-crime laws, notably stringent mandatory-minimum sentences and parole reform. There is considerable precedent for the NRA's appeal to state authority: founded after the Civil War, with the mission of teaching soldiers to shoot straight, in its early years the NRA was closely tied to the military and dependent on government largesse; until the mid-1990s it drew considerable moral support from the police. Today, however, statist anti-crime campaigns are mainly matters of politics for the NRA and for gun advocates in general; laws mandating tough sentences for the criminal use of firearms defuse demands for firearm controls. Personal liberty—meaning the liberty to own guns and use them against the government if necessary—is these people's passion.

> *"Advocates of the right to bear arms often insist that the Second Amendment is rooted in both collective and individual rights of self-defense."*

Gun advocates are apt to be extravagantly libertarian when the right to own guns is at stake. At heart many are insurrectionists—at least, they need to feel prepared. Nothing arouses their anger more, I've found, than challenges to the belief that private gun ownership is an essential check on political oppression.

Hitting a Sore Spot

During the two-day seminar held by Academics for the Second Amendment, we argue equanimously about nearly everything—crime control, constitutional rights, and the fairness and feasibility of gun controls—until I question whether, 200 years after the Revolution, citizens armed with rifles and handguns can effectively resist the federal government. I ask, If Nixon had staged a military coup in 1974—assuming he had military support—instead of resigning the presidency, could the NRA and the nation's unaffiliated gun owners have stopped him? For the first time in two days Don Kates flares up in anger, and the room is incandescent.

"Give me one example from history of a successful government oppression of an armed populace," he demands. The FBI raid on David Koresh's compound in Waco, Texas, doesn't count, he says, because Koresh's group was a small, isolated minority. The Civil War doesn't count either. (I can't remember why.) Neither do uprisings in Malaysia and the Philippines.

People like me think it is possible to oppose the government only with nuclear weapons, Kates rages, because we're stupid; we don't understand military strategy and the effectiveness of guerrilla warfare, and we underestimate the hesitancy of troops to engage their fellow citizens in armed conflict. Millions of Americans armed only with pistols and long guns could turn a bloodless coup into a prolonged civil war.

Perhaps. I am almost persuaded that Kates might have a point, until he brings up the Holocaust.

A Twist in History

Gun advocates sometimes point out that the Holocaust was preceded by gun-control laws that disarmed the Jews and made it easy to round them up. (In a 1994 article in *Guns and Ammo*, Jay Simkin, the president of Jews for the Preservation of Firearms Ownership, argued that gun control causes genocide. Simkin wrote that today "genocides can be prevented if civilians worldwide own military-type rifles and plenty of ammunition.") Kates doesn't go nearly this far, but he does point out that genocides are difficult to predict. At the turn of the century, he says, I would not have predicted the Holocaust, and today I can't predict what holocausts may occur in the next fifteen or fifty years. I give up. "If millions are slaughtered in the next fifty years because of gun-control laws," I declare, "let their deaths be on my head."

"It's very interesting that you say that," Kates concludes, a bit triumphantly.

Kates apologizes later for his outburst, and in a subsequent phone conversation he acknowledges that "the Holocaust was not an event where guns would have mattered; the force was overwhelming." But he adds that guns might have mattered to individual Jews who could have saved themselves had they been armed, even if the Jewish community couldn't have saved itself collectively. And guns might matter to a Croatian woman who shoots a Serbian soldier breaking into her house, he suggests; if there were a Second Amendment in Bosnia, it would protect her.

> *"People don't buy guns in order to overthrow or even to thwart the government, . . . people buy guns to protect themselves."*

Chapter 3

Fear of a Central Government

Zealots in the pro-gun camp (Kates is not among them) seem to identify with the woman defending her home to the extent that they fear attack by the federal government. "Using a national epidemic of crime and violence as their justification, media pundits and collectivist politicians are aggressively campaigning to disarm private citizens and strengthen federal law enforcement powers," proclaims a special edition of *The New American*, a magazine on sale at gun shows. After gun control, the editors suggest, the greatest threat to individual liberty is the Clinton plan for providing local police departments with federal assistance. "Is it possible that some of those who are advocating a disarmed populace and a centralized police system have totalitarian designs in mind? It is worth noting that this is exactly what happened in many countries during this century."

> *"Personal liberty—meaning the liberty to own guns and use them against the government if necessary—is [gun advocates'] passion."*

This can be dismissed as ravings on the fringe, but it captures in crazed form the hostility toward a powerful central government which inspired the adoption of the Second Amendment right to bear arms 200 years ago and fuels support for it today. Advocates of First Amendment rights, who believe firmly that free speech is both a moral imperative and an instrument of democratic governance, should understand the passion of Second Amendment claims.

They should be sympathetic as well to the more dispassionate constitutional arguments of gun owners. Civil libertarians who believe that the Bill of Rights in general protects individuals have a hard time explaining why the Second Amendment protects only groups. They have a hard time reconciling their opposition to prohibitions of problematic behavior, such as drug abuse, with their support for the prohibition of guns. (Liberals tend to demonize guns and gun owners the way conservatives tend to demonize drugs and pornography and the people who use them.) In asserting that the Second Amendment provides no individual right to bear arms or that the right provided is anachronistic and not worth its cost, civil libertarians place themselves in the awkward position of denying the existence of a constitutional right because they don't value its exercise.

The Argument Circles

The civil-libertarian principles at issue in the gun debate are made clear by the arguments of First Amendment and Second Amendment advocates, which are strikingly similar—as are the arguments their opponents use. Pornography rapes, some feminists say. Words oppress, according to advocates of censoring hate speech. "Words Kill," declared a Planned Parenthood ad following the abortion-clinic shootings in Brookline, Massachusetts, [in 1995]. And all you can say in response is "Words don't kill people; people kill people." To an anti-libertarian, the literature sold at gun shows may seem as dangerous as the guns; at a recent gun show I bought Incendiaries, an army manual on unconventional warfare; Exotic Weapons: An Access Book; Gunrunning for Fun and Profit; and Vigilante Handbook, which tells me how to harass, torture, and assassinate people. Should any of this material be censored? If it were, it would be sold on the black market; and the remedy for bad speech is good speech, First Amendment devotees point out. According to Second Amendment supporters, gun-control laws affect only law-abiding gun owners, and the best defense against armed criminals is armed victims; the remedy for the bad use of guns in violent crime is the good use of guns in self-defense.

Of course, guns do seem a bit more dangerous than books, and apart from a few anti-pornography feminists, most of us would rather be accosted by a man with a video than a man with a gun. But none of our constitutional rights are absolute. Recognizing that the Second Amendment confers an individual right to bear arms would not immunize guns from regulation; it would require that the government establish a necessity, not just a desire, to regulate. The majority of gun owners, Don Kates suggests, would be amenable to gun controls, such as waiting periods and even licensing and training requirements, if they didn't perceive them as preludes to prohibition. The irony of the Second Amendment debate is that acknowledging an individual right to bear arms might facilitate gun control more than denying it ever could.

"Civil libertarians who believe that the Bill of Rights in general protects individuals have a hard time explaining why the Second Amendment protects only groups."

But it will not facilitate civic engagement or the community that Americans are exhorted to seek. The civil-libertarian defense of Second Amendment rights is not a republican one. It does not derive the individual right to bear arms from republican notions of the militia; instead it relies on traditional liberal views of personal autonomy. It is a communitarian nightmare. If the war against crime has replaced the Cold War in popular culture, a private storehouse of guns has replaced the fallout shelter in the psyche of Americans who feel besieged. Increasingly barricaded, mistrustful of their neighbors, they've sacrificed virtue to fear.

Gun Control Is Constitutional

by Melissa Huelsman

About the author: *Melissa Huelsman is a contributing writer for the South-western University* Law Review, *a quarterly journal that publishes scholarly articles and commentary on the law.*

More than 38,000 people died from gunshot wounds in 1991. The U.S. homicide rate is 8.4 per 100,000 people, which is twice that of France and Germany, four times the rate in Great Britain and seven times higher than Japan's figures. The weapon of choice in 70% of homicides in 1993 was firearms and the number of violent crimes committed using firearms increased by 55% from 1987 through 1992, according to Bureau of Justice Statistics. Firearm homicides are increasing in all areas, with increases of over 23% between 1987 and 1989 in inner-city and suburban neighborhoods and an 8% increase in rural areas, according to a National Center of Health Statistics study. The Bureau of Alcohol, Tobacco and Firearms estimates that there are 222 million firearms circulating in the U.S. (compared to a population of approximately 260 million).

The statistics related above probably do not shock or surprise anyone. We hear these sorts of figures recited virtually every day by the media. We are all aware, especially since we are living and/or attending school in one of the largest urban centers in the world, of the impact that violent crimes has on our everyday behavior and lives, and in the precautions we now must take to (hopefully) prevent us from becoming part of the statistics. Yet the debate about gun control rages on with advocates on both sides fanning the flames of an already explosive issue by implying that anyone who supports "the other side" is either a fanatic of some sort, a supporter of criminals, unpatriotic or willing to submit to a "new world order" without a fight.

The Second Amendment Is Qualified

Much of the debate on gun control centers around interpretation of the Second Amendment and whether it protects collective rights of gun ownership or

Reprinted from Melissa Huelsman, "Gun Control," from www.humboldt1.com/~dsampson/guncontrl.htm, by permission of the author.

individual rights. Both sides argue that historical information regarding the Founding Fathers' feelings and beliefs on the subject, and the compromise language they reached, supports their interpretation of the Amendment. However, review of the language itself seems to indicate that the arms specified were intended to be kept as part of a "well regulated militia," since the Amendment has the sort of qualifying language that is not present in the wording of the other individual rights Amendments. Historical records indicate that the Founding Fathers considered language specifying that arms be kept for self-defense and other purposes, but opted not to use such language. Certainly at the time the Second Amendment was drafted guns were

> *"Gun control opponents cry out that their alleged individual right to gun ownership is more important than our collective rights to attempt to protect our citizens from firearm violence."*

much more of an integral and necessary part of everyday life than they are today and still the Founding Fathers did not include such specific language. Nevertheless, it seems to me that even if we as a country adopt the individual rights interpretation of the Second Amendment, the Amendment does not prohibit the government from restricting or regulating that right for our collective safety, much as it does the rest of the individual rights Amendments.

Restricting Individual Rights Is Necessary

In all of the argument over the interpretation of the Second Amendment, we seem to have lost track of the fact that people are dying every day from firearm wounds. Six states, including California, saw firearms surpass motor vehicles as the leading cause of death by injury in 1993 and it is likely, based upon a number of on-going studies, that the numbers will continue to increase in those states, as well as in others. The government regulates an individual's operation of a car on our nation's roads and highways because we have decided that in the interest of safety for all, it is better to restrict the rights of a small percentage of individuals who are more likely to cause harm to others. However, when the government wants to act in the same fashion with respect to gun ownership, the NRA leadership and other gun control opponents cry out that their alleged individual right to gun ownership is more important than our collective rights to attempt to protect our citizens from firearm violence. There is no logical argument to support the belief that this is the only Amendment in our Bill of Rights that is not subject to restriction or regulation by the government. There certainly is no other language anywhere else in the Bill of Rights that sets the Second Amendment apart in this manner.

Besides regulation of motor vehicle operation, our government restricts a great number of "individual rights" in order to protect society as a whole. There is no right to yell "Fire!" in a crowded theater or to libel a person, even though the First Amendment holds that "no law" shall be made to abridge free speech. The Fourth Amendment has been interpreted to require that searches shall be executed with warrants issued pursuant to probable cause, but the Supreme Court continues to broaden the scope of situations in which warrantless searches are permitted. These restrictions on individual rights, set forth in the Bill of Rights, have been accepted by the majority of people because they are consistent with the widely accepted principle that individual rights must yield, at some point, to the interests of the community. There is no rational reason why gun control should not be accepted in the same fashion as being designed to merely restrict and regulate an activity that is inherently dangerous.

Gun Control Is Not Complete Control

Although some gun control advocates envision a day when there will be no right to possess any firearms in the U.S., I do not advocate that position nor do I think that it is reflective, in any way, of America's attitude toward gun control. Gun control opponents argue that because some gun control advocates support a complete ban, the enactment of any gun control regulations is the first step on a "slippery slope" to a complete ban and therefore no controls should be put in place. This is erroneous because the majority of gun control advocates support only restrictions and regulations, not a complete ban on gun ownership. The fact that extremists exist within the movement should not preclude all attempts at control. Until a complete ban on all firearms is promulgated and submitted to Congress for consideration, there is no reason to assume that regulations will inevitably lead to a complete ban, just as we do not assume that the mere existence of a tort action for libel will inevitably lead to a complete ban on all forms of free speech.

> *"Individual rights must yield, at some point, to the interests of the community."*

Numerous studies have demonstrated that the majority of Americans support some form of gun control (figures vary from 69% to 89%). They also show that these same Americans do not believe that all rights to gun ownership should be terminated. Considering the vehement manner with which the current gun control debate is being waged, it is highly doubtful that an absolute ban on gun ownership will ever occur in America. However, I do believe that if the media and the public would set aside their emotional attachments to one side or the other, and ignore the personal attacks, then the nation could engage in a rational evaluation of gun control measures. In evaluating the probable effect of these specific measures on our citizenry without using slippery slope theories, the public could balance the measurement of supposed harms that would be suffered by law-abiding gun owners if gun control rules were in place, against the potential benefits. Since we have never had a nationwide restriction on guns, we do not know what the outcome will be. We cannot look at state or city bans on guns for information because guns can still be brought into these restricted areas easily from other states or cities. The reality is that we do not know what the outcome will be, but given the increasing violence in America, shouldn't we give gun control a chance?

Society Is Obligated

Many gun control opponents contend that because criminals do not usually buy guns from stores or certified sellers, a control measure will leave criminals with all the advantages. However, gun control should prevent any legal sales to criminals or others who are prevented from buying guns by law. There are many things that are illegal to possess and criminals possess them nevertheless. The mere fact that criminals may circumvent a law, is no reason not to impose it. A waiting period with a background check will prevent such sales and the time spent waiting might prevent some heat-of-the-moment homicides or suicides. . . .

Finally, I see no reason why parents should not be responsible both criminally and civilly for acts committed with their guns by their children. It is their responsibility as parents to be sure that something as potentially dangerous as a gun be secured and unavailable for use by their children. If we as a society are going to hold something as lethal as guns out to the masses, then we need to recognize our concurrent obligation to do whatever we can to prevent needless injuries and deaths that result from acting on our right to possess guns. Until Americans face up to their responsibility to their neighbors and balance that responsibility against their right to self-preservation, the gun control debate will rage on and Americans will continue to die needlessly.

The Second Amendment Does Not Guarantee the Right to Own a Gun

by Join Together

About the author: *Join Together supports community-based efforts to reduce, prevent, and treat substance abuse and gun violence. Their web site, Join Together Online, provides news and information related to gun violence.*

On June 23, 1998, the *Boston Globe* ran an editorial in which the newspaper evaluated a bill on the control of assault weapons in Massachusetts as a "fair compromise" between forces on both sides of the issue. But in its analysis and documentation, the venerable daily veered onto some shaky constitutional terrain. The *Globe* stated that while the bill would protect citizens from firearms abuse, it would also "fully protect citizens' Second Amendment rights to bear arms."

It's no surprise if the phrasing bears the ring of familiarity—after all, the constitutional reference is a virtual mantra to the gun lobby—but the truth is far less black and white. In fact, the legal and historical interpretations of the Second Amendment are widely disparate and inconclusive. While some scholars argue that the amendment does indeed provide gun-ownership rights to individuals, others contend that the amendment was crafted as a guarantee that states have the rights to arm their own militias to defend against a national army. While the debate about the origins of the Second Amendment may never end, one fact is indisputable: Federal courts do not recognize any constitutional right to bear arms. In fact, no federal court has ever invalidated any gun-control law on Second Amendment grounds.

A Common Lack of Understanding

Thus, in one sense, it is surprising to read the *Globe*'s assertion that the Second Amendment guarantees "citizens' right to bear arms," when the nation's top courts say it doesn't. As Harvard Law Professor Laurence Tribe has stated,

From Join Together, "Second Amendment and 'Rights': The Media Often Get It Wrong," *Join Together Online*, August 19, 1998. Reprinted by permission of Join Together.

"The Second Amendment's preamble makes it clear that it is not designed to create an individual right to bear arms outside of the context of a state-run militia." And as law professor Andy Herz wrote in a Boston University *Law Review* article that was adapted by the Long Island newspaper *Newsday* in 1995, "The gun lobby's constitutional claim is a gross misrepresentation of the Second Amendment's practical meaning in modern-day America. The courts have clearly ruled that there is no 'right' for all Americans to bear arms. There may be legitimate reasons to own guns, but there is no constitutional trump card. Yet the American public has been misled to believe in a broad 'right' to bear arms, and the parameters of our gun control debate have been artificially narrowed by a phantom constitutional barrier."

Therefore, perhaps the phrasing in the *Globe* editorial is not so surprising. After all, because the belief that the Second Amendment guarantees individual rights to own guns is commonly held, why should editorial writers and journalists be any different? The fact is, journalistic instances of this misperception abound. Following are several recent examples:

Examples of Misperception

- The Jan. 10, 1998 *Buffalo News*, in reporting on Philadelphia Mayor Edward Rendell's effort to sue gun manufacturers for creating a public nuisance in his city, stated, "A public-nuisance approach might avoid a clash with the Constitution's Second Amendment, which protects the right to bear arms."
- The July 26, 1998 Allentown, Pa., *Morning Call* editorialized in favor of several pending gun-related bills before Pennsylvania lawmakers, including one that would require trigger locks, because (among other reasons) they "infringe on no one's Second Amendment rights."
- The July 26, 1998 *Arizona Republic* ran an editorial about the killings of two Capitol police officers in Washington, D.C. with a defense of gun ownership and criticism of "imprudent tramplings upon Americans' Second Amendment rights."
- The June 15, 1998 *Des Moines Register* featured a fawning profile of Des Moines Police Chief Kayne Robinson, who is first vice president of the National Rifle Association. In it, Robinson says, "We regard a criminal with a firearm as the biggest enemy of the

> *"Federal courts do not recognize any constitutional right to bear arms. In fact, no federal court has ever invalidated any gun-control law on Second Amendment grounds."*

Second Amendment." The reporter follows this quote with an explanation for his readers: "The Second Amendment gives the people the right to keep and bear arms."

This is not to suggest that the media as a whole have been duped by the gun lobby. On the contrary, a number of writers and newspapers have focused their attention on the Second Amendment recently and come away with different conclusions.

"The Second Amendment is always cited," *Cincinnati Post* columnist Nick Clooney wrote in the April 1, 1998 issue following the Jonesboro, Ark., school-yard shooting. "Read it. The Second Amendment no more sanctions un-fettered use of guns than the First Amendment sanctions the yelling of 'Fire!' in a crowded building, then calling it free speech. Guns do not protect us from our government. They kill our children."

> *"The American public has been misled to believe in a broad 'right' to bear arms."*

The *San Francisco Chronicle* writer Joan Ryan's May 3 article, "The Boy Who Pulled the Trigger," concluded, "As the NRA knows, the Second Amendment doesn't guarantee private citizens the right to own guns. No federal court has ever made a ruling about gun ownership based on the Second Amendment. So gun control isn't about a Constitutional right but simple common sense and safety."

The *St. Louis Post-Dispatch*'s M.W. Guzy examined the gun lobby's perpetual referencing of the Second Amendment as a historical basis for gun ownership and learned that gun control was a lively issue in the Old West, with such historically admirable straight shooters as Wyatt Earp favoring it. Guzy points out that none other than the famous Gunfight at the OK Corral was fought over gun control because an ordinance in Tombstone prohibited firearms within the city limits, and when the Clantons refused to surrender their weapons, Earp and his deputies came after them. "From early on, the need to regulate when and where guns could be carried was recognized," Guzy wrote. ". . . (E)ven in a frontier town, city fathers realized that guns imperiled civil order."

Guns still imperil civil order. And so do the false assertions that gun ownership enjoys constitutional privilege.

Supreme Court Decisions Support the Constitutionality of Gun Control

by Roger Simon

About the author: *Roger Simon, a nationally syndicated columnist, is author of* Show Time: The American Political Circus and the Race for the White House.

If Charlton Heston wants to talk about what it takes to split the Red Sea, I am prepared to listen.

He did a fine job as Moses in "The Ten Commandments," and everybody (except the Egyptians) came through the waters just fine.

But Heston was in Washington, D.C. to talk about guns and the Constitution, and on these two subjects, he is—forgive the pun—all wet.

Heston is a vice president of the National Rifle Association, and the NRA is running huge ads in newspapers throughout the country that begin: "I believe the Second Amendment is America's first freedom, the one right that protects all the others."

(Before I say anything else, I would like to encourage everyone to place huge ads in newspapers as often as possible. Once a week would not be too often.)

The ad goes on to say what Heston said in his speech at the National Press Club: that even though freedom of speech, press, religion, free assembly, etc., are important, they are not as important as the Second Amendment.

"Either you believe that, or you don't, and you must decide," the ad, which contains an enormous picture of Heston, says. "Because today, the Second Amendment is in grave peril."

No Real Information

Doesn't this whet your appetite just a little? Don't you figure that someplace in this ad a basic question will be answered? A question that goes: Just what the heck is the Second Amendment anyway?

Reprinted from Roger Simon, "Charlton Heston and the Second Amendment," *Liberal Opinion Weekly*, September 29, 1997, by permission of Roger Simon and Creators Syndicate.

We all know it's probably not the one about Prohibition or the quartering of troops in private homes, but since it is so important, don't you think the NRA would quote it?

No, it won't. And in September 1997, I saw Heston on TV, where he made his same argument, and once again, he never told people what the Second Amendment says.

Heston will tell people it has something to do with guns and how you need a gun to defend the other amendments. Some villains may want to take our rights away, and we will need guns to stop them, Heston says, though he does not say who those villains are.

One villain that Heston will identify is the "conniving" news media. "Again and again, I hear gun owners say how can we believe anything the anti-gun media says when they can't even get the facts right?" Heston said in his speech.

Quoting the Facts

So let me do something that Heston and the NRA will not do in their ads. I will quote from the Constitution word for word. I will reprint below the entire Second Amendment, which does not take up much space since it is only 26 words long:

"A well-regulated militia, being necessary to the security of a free State, the right of the people to keep and bear arms, shall not be infringed."

Why don't the NRA and Heston like to quote the amendment they say they are defending? Why do they keep the wording such a secret?

Because, as the wording clearly indicates, individual citizens do not have a constitutional right to bear arms. Only a "well-regulated militia" does.

Who says so? The Supreme Court of the United States says so. And it has said so over and over.

Want proof?

Try this: Heston was giving his speech in Washington, D.C., a city that bans the ownership of handguns.

Now if the Second Amendment really guaranteed a constitutional

> *"Individual citizens do not have a constitutional right to bear arms. Only a 'well-regulated militia' does."*

right to bear arms, Washington could not ban handguns. Nor could Skokie, Ill., or Morton Grove, Ill., or a number of other cities around the country.

And if the Second Amendment really did what the NRA and Heston says it does, the Congress could not have banned the sale of assault weapons either.

Supreme Decisions

So who is right? Well, I think the Supreme Court is right. It says the Second Amendment protects the rights of the states to maintain independent militias.

The court rejects the notion that you have a "right" to own a machine gun, bazooka, mortar, handgun or cop-killer bullets.

There are several Supreme Court cases that demonstrate this (none of which the National Rifle Association likes to talk about). Take a 1939 decision, *United States vs. Miller*. In that case, the Supreme Court upheld the federal law making it a crime to transport sawed-off shotguns across state lines.

> *"[The Supreme Court] says the Second Amendment protects the rights of the states to maintain independent militias."*

The court said that there was no relationship between the claim of a Second Amendment "right" to own a sawed-off shotgun and "the preservation or efficiency of a well-regulated militia."

The Second Amendment, in other words, is about militias, not individuals.

Heston, however, says he is now undertaking a "three-year crusade to invest a hundred million dollars toward restoring the Second Amendment to its rightful, honorable, principal place as America's first freedom."

Which is fine with me.

But before Heston and the NRA undertake this gigantic crusade to restore the Second Amendment, maybe they ought to take a few minutes to actually read it.

It could save them a lot of dough.

Gun Control Is Not Constitutional

by Stephen P. Halbrook

About the author: *Stephen Halbrook, a legal expert who focuses on Second Amendment issues, is the author of* That Every Man Be Armed: The Evolution of a Constitutional Right.

The two most politically incorrect parts of the Bill of Rights are the Second and Tenth Amendments. The Second Amendment provides that "the right of the people to keep and bear arms shall not be infringed." The terrible Tenth adds that "the powers not delegated to the United States by the Constitution" are "reserved to the States respectively, or to the people."

Nothing in the Constitution delegates power to Congress to prohibit firearms, and firearms prohibitions obviously infringe on the right to keep and bear arms. These constitutional guarantees are hated by those who would increase federal power beyond any bounds and would use that power to disarm the populace.

As demonstrated in my book *That Every Man Be Armed: The Evolution of a Constitutional Right,* America's Founding Fathers sought to protect the right of individuals to possess and carry firearms both for self-defense and resistance to tyranny. In its 1857 *Dred Scott* decision, the Supreme Court noted that if African Americans were citizens, they could "keep and carry arms wherever they went." And in its 1990 *Verdugo-Urquidez* decision, the Court found that "the people" as used in the First, Second, and Fourth Amendments means the same; i.e., the persons forming our national community. However, the Court has never issued a definitive ruling on the Second Amendment.

Challenging the Law's Mistake

The Brady Act, with its waiting period and requirement that police permission be obtained for handgun purchase, infringes on the right to keep and bear arms. However, just as the Supreme Court never developed a body of case law on the First Amendment right to free speech before World War I, the Supreme Court to date has avoided significant construction of the Second Amendment.

Abridged from Stephen P. Halbrook, "Restoring the Second and Tenth Amendments," *LEAA Advocate*, Summer/Fall 1997. Reprinted by permission of the author and the Law Enforcement Alliance of America.

The Brady Act commands local law enforcement officers to ascertain the legality of handgun transactions, including whatever research in state and local recordkeeping systems are available and in a national system designated by the Attorney General. This contradicts the 1992 Supreme Court decision in *New York v. United States* that, under the Tenth Amendment, Congress may not require the states to enact or administer a federal regulatory program.

I have the honor of representing several sheriffs who had the courage to challenge the constitutionality of the Brady Act. These sheriffs enforce the state criminal laws in their counties—the laws against murder, robbery, rape, burglary, and a host of other crimes. The Brady Act orders them off the street to shuffle paper—they must investigate law-abiding constituents who wish to purchase handguns from licensed dealers. . . .

Informing the Citizen

If the Tenth Amendment has been making a comeback, the Second Amendment remains the orphan of the Bill of Rights. Certain elements of the judiciary have sought to relegate the Second Amendment to oblivion. With a straight face, they declare that "the people" really means the National Guard, that a "right" really means a state power, that "keep and bear" do not mean possess and carry, that "arms" do not include ugly firearms, and that nothing constitutes an "infringement."

The Bill of Rights was intended not only to tell rulers the limits of their powers, but also to inform the citizens of their rights so that they will

> *"Nothing in the Constitution delegates power to Congress to prohibit firearms, and firearms prohibitions obviously infringe on the right to keep and bear arms."*

know when they are violated. The ordinary citizen knows that he or she has, under the Second Amendment, a right to have a rifle, pistol, or shotgun. Moreover, as the history of the Second Amendment's adoption has been researched more, all knowledgeable legal scholars on the subject agree that an individual right to have arms is guaranteed.

Guarding Against Oppression

That Every Man Be Armed traces recognition of this right to ancient Greece. The philosopher Aristotle commented that if the rulers are armed and the farmers disarmed, the former oppress the latter. True citizenship means having the right to be armed. The tradition of the armed citizen continued in ancient Rome, but this tradition gave way to loss of rights as tyrants turned the Republic into an evil Empire.

The concept of the armed populace as a guard against oppression has been linked in the modern age with constitutional republicanism. In England, the Glorious Revolution of 1689 did away with absolute royal power and allowed only a limited monarchy. The English Bill of Rights denounced the disarming of the people and declared the right of subjects to be armed.

A century later, the American colonists felt that the Crown was losing sight of their rights as Englishmen. In 1768, patriots denounced the Redcoats' plans to disarm the inhabitants and to violate the right of trial by a jury of peers. By 1774, British troops were conducting searches for and seizures of firearms from Boston's citizens. and King George III imposed a ban on importation of firearms into America.

Issues of Independence

The War for Independence was sparked in 1775 when General Gage attempted to seize arms from militiamen at Lexington and Concord, and then required all the citizens of Boston to turn in all firearms for "safekeeping." Once the firearms had been turned in, they were seized by Gage and never returned.

The newly independent states adopted various bills of rights. Pennsylvania and Vermont recognized the "right of the people to bear arms for defense of themselves and the state," North Carolina declared "the right to bear arms for defense of the state," and Massachusetts declared "the right to keep and bear arms for the common defense." Virginia and other states founded the defense of a free society on "a well regulated militia, composed of the body of the people, trained to arms."

An Assertion of Rights

When the federal Constitution was proposed in 1787, it included no bill of rights. In the *Federalist Papers,* James Madison contended that "the ultimate authority . . . resides in the people alone." If the federal government became tyrannical, its standing army "would be opposed [by] a militia amounting to near half a million citizens with arms in their hands." Alluding to "the advantage of being armed, which the Americans possess over the people of almost every other nation," Madison continued: "Notwithstanding the military establishments in the several kingdoms of Europe, which are carried as far as the public resources will bear, the governments are afraid to trust the people with arms."

> *"The Bill of Rights was intended not only to tell rulers the limits of their powers, but also to inform the citizens of their rights so that they will know when they are violated."*

Demanding a bill of rights, Richard Henry Lee wrote that "to preserve liberty, it is essential that the whole body of the people always possess arms, and be taught alike, especially when young, how to use them." Samuel Adams implored "that the said Constitution be never construed to authorize Congress to infringe the just liberty of the press . . . or to prevent the people of the United States, who are peaceable citizens, from keeping their own arms."

Several states demanded a bill of rights expressing such guarantees.

Accordingly, in the first Congress under the new Constitution, James Madison proposed a bill of rights, including the following: "The right of the people to keep and bear arms shall not be infringed; a well armed, and well regulated militia being the best security of a free country." Tench Coxe, a strong supporter of the Constitution, explained: "As civil rulers, not having their duty to the people duly before them, may attempt to tyrannize, and as the military forces which must be occasionally raised to defend our country, might pervert their power to the injury of their fellow citizens, the people are confirmed . . . in their right to keep and bear their private arms."

The People Will Not Forget

No one ever doubted that the Second Amendment, like the rest of the Bill of Rights, protected individuals. Only by excluding them from being part of "the peoples" could blacks be prohibited from possession of firearms under the slave codes. After the Civil War abolished slavery, the Fourteenth Amendment to the Constitution was adopted in part to guarantee the right of all people, including blacks, to keep and bear arms for self defense. Reconstruction history includes many instances of freed slaves defending themselves from attacks and oppression by state militias and Ku Klux Klan terrorism.

In order to uphold twentieth-century firearms prohibitions, the doctrine was invented that "the right of the people to keep and bear arms" really means "the power of states to maintain the National Guard." If any of the Framers of the Bill of Rights had that idea, it was the best-kept secret of the eighteenth-century, for no evidence of it exists. This contrived attempt to abrogate a constitutional right found its way into some judicial decisions after enactment of the Gun Control Act of 1968.

Justice Scalia has just published a book interpreting "the Second Amendment as a guarantee that the federal government will not interfere with the individual's right to bear arms for self-defense." Now that particular kinds of firearms have been banned, it remains to be seen whether the Supreme Court will ever give life to this orphan of the Bill of Rights. Regardless of what the Court will do, it is certain that the American people will not forget or abandon this fundamental right.

A Threatened Second Amendment Threatens Freedom

by Charlton Heston

About the author: *Charlton Heston is a well-known actor who has starred in many motion pictures. He is a vice president and spokesman for the National Rifle Association.*

Today I want to talk to you about guns: Why we have them, why the Bill of Rights guarantees that we can have them, and why my right to have a gun is more important than your right to rail against it in the press.

I believe every good journalist needs to know why the Second Amendment must be considered more essential than the First Amendment. This may be a bitter pill to swallow, but the right to keep and bear arms is not archaic. It's not an outdated, dusty idea some old dead white guys dreamed up in fear of the Redcoats. No, it is just as essential to liberty today as it was in 1776. These words may not play well at the Press club, but it's still the gospel down at the corner bar and grill.

And your efforts to undermine the Second Amendment, to deride it and degrade it, to readily accept diluting it and eagerly promote redefining it, threaten not only the physical well-being of millions of Americans but also the core concept of individual liberty our founding fathers struggled to perfect and protect.

The Most Important Right

So now you know what doubtless does not surprise you. I believe strongly in the right of every law-abiding citizen to keep and bear arms, for what I think are good reasons.

The original amendments we refer to as the Bill of Rights contain 10 of what the constitutional framers termed unalienable rights. These rights are ranked in random order and are linked by their essential equality. The Bill of Rights came

Reprinted from Charlton Heston, "Second Amendment More Essential Than First," *Gun News Digest*, Winter 1997–1998, by permission of the author.

to us with blinders on. It doesn't recognize color, or class, or wealth. It protects not just the rights of actors, or editors, or reporters, but extends even to those we love to hate.

That's why the most heinous criminals have rights until they are convicted of a crime. The beauty of the Constitution can be found in the way it takes human nature into consideration. We are not a docile species capable of co-existing within a perfect society under everlasting benevolent rule. We are what we are. Egotistical, corruptible, vengeful, sometimes even a bit power mad. The Bill of Rights recognizes this and builds the barricades that need to be in place to protect the individual.

The Extent of Freedom

You, of course, remain zealous in your belief that a free nation must have a free press and free speech to battle injustice, unmask corruption and provide a voice for those in need of a fair and impartial forum.

I agree wholeheartedly . . . a free press is vital to a free society. But I wonder how many of you will agree with me that the right to keep and bear arms is not just equally vital, but the most vital to protect all the other rights we enjoy?

I say that the Second Amendment is, in order of importance, the first amendment. It is America's First Freedom, the one right that protects all the others. Among freedom of speech, of the press, of religion, of assembly, of redress of grievances, it is the first among equals. It alone offers the absolute capacity to live without fear. The right to keep and bear arms is the one right that allows "rights" to exist at all.

> *"Efforts to undermine the Second Amendment . . . threaten . . . the core concept of individual liberty our founding fathers struggled to perfect and protect."*

Either you believe that, or you don't, and you must decide.

Because there is no such thing as a free nation where police and military are allowed the force of arms but individual citizens are not. That's a "big brother knows best" theater of the absurd that has never boded well for the peasant class, the working class, or even for reporters.

History Provides Proof

Yes, our Constitution provides the doorway for your news and commentary to pass through free and unfettered. But that doorway to freedom is framed by the muskets that stood between a vision of liberty and absolute anarchy at a place called Concord Bridge. Our revolution began when the British sent Redcoats door to door to confiscate the peoples' guns. They didn't succeed: The muskets went out the back door with their owners.

Emerson said it best: "By the rude bridge that arched the flood, Their flag to

April's breeze unfurled, Here once the embattled farmers stood, And fired the shot heard round the world."

King George called us "rabble in arms." But with God's grace, George Washington and many brave men gave us our country. Soon after, God's grace and a few great men gave us our Constitution. It's been said that the creation of the United States is the greatest political act in history . . . I'll sign that.

In the next two centuries, though, freedom did not flourish. The next revolution, the French, collapsed in the bloody terror, then Napoleon's tyranny. There's been no shortage of dictators since, in many countries. Hitler, Mussolini, Stalin, Mao, Idi Amin, Castro, Pol Pot. All these monsters began by confiscating private arms, then literally soaking the earth with the blood of tens and tens of millions of their people. Ah, the joys of gun control.

Pointing Out Hypocrisy

Now, I doubt any of you would prefer a rolled up newspaper as a weapon against a dictator or a criminal intruder. Yet in essence that is what you have asked our loved ones to do, through an ill-contrived and totally naive campaign against the Second Amendment.

Besides, how can we entrust to you the Second Amendment, when you are so stingy with your own First Amendment?

I say this because of the way . . . you have treated your own—those journalists you consider the least among you. How quick you've been to finger the paparazzi with blame and to eye the tabloids with disdain. How eager you've been to draw a line where there is none, to demand some distinction within the First Amendment that sneers "they are not one of us." How readily you let your lesser brethren take the fall, as if their rights were not as worthy, and their purpose not as pure, and their freedom not as sacred as yours.

So now, as politicians consider new laws to shackle and gag paparazzi, who among you will speak up? Who here will stand and defend them? If you won't, I will. Because you do not define the First Amendment. It defines you. And it is bigger than you—big enough to embrace all of you, plus all those you would exclude. That's how freedom works.

It also demands you do your homework. Again and again I hear gunowners say, how can we believe anything the anti-gun media say when they can't even get the facts right? For too long you have swallowed manufactured statistics and fabricated technical support from anti-gun organizations that wouldn't know a semi-auto from a sharp stick. And it shows. You fall for it every time.

"[The Second Amendment] is America's First Freedom, the one right that protects all the others."

That's why you have very little credibility among 70 million gunowners and 20 million hunters and millions of veterans who learned the hard way which end the bullet comes out. And while you attacked the amendment that defends your homes and protects your spouses and children, you have denied those of us who defend all the Bill of Rights a fair hearing or the courtesy of an honest debate.

If the NRA attempts to challenge your assertions, we are ignored. And if we try to buy advertising time or space to answer your charges, more often than not we are denied. How's that for First Amendment freedom?

> *"It is time [young people] learned that firearm ownership is constitutional, not criminal."*

Clearly, too many have used freedom of the press as a weapon not only to strangle our free speech, but to erode and ultimately destroy the right to keep and bear arms as well. In doing so you promote your profession to that of constitutional judge and jury, more powerful even than our Supreme Court, more prejudiced than the Inquisition's tribunals. It is a frightening misuse of constitutional privilege, and I pray that you will come to your senses and see that these abuses are curbed.

A Move to Protect Generations

As a veteran of World War II, as freedom marcher who stood with Dr. Martin Luther King long before it was fashionable, and as a grandfather who wants the coming century to be free and full of promise for my grandchildren, I am . . . troubled.

The right to keep and bear arms is threatened by political theatrics, piecemeal lawmaking, talk show psychology, extreme bad taste in the entertainment industry, an ever-widening educational chasm in our schools and a conniving media, that all add up to cultural warfare against the idea that guns ever had, or should now have, an honorable and proud place in our society.

But all of our rights must be delivered into the 21st century as pure and complete as they came to us at the beginning of the 20th century. Traditionally the passing of that torch is from a gnarled old hand down to an eager young one. So now, at 72, I offer my gnarled old hand.

I have accepted a call from the National Rifle Association of America to help protect the Second Amendment. I feel it is my duty to do that. My mission and vision can be summarized in three simple parts.

First, before we enter the 21st century, I expect to see a pro-Second Amendment president in the White House.

Secondly, I expect to build an NRA with the political muscle and clout to keep a pro-Second Amendment Congress in place.

Third, is a promise to the next generation of free Americans. I hope to help raise $100 million for NRA programs and education before the year 2000. At least half of that sum will go to teach American kids what the right to keep and bear arms really means to their culture and country.

We have raised a generation of young people who think that the Bill of Rights comes with their cable TV. Leave them to their channel surfing and they'll remain oblivious to history and heritage that truly matter.

Think about it—what else must young Americans think when the White House proclaims, as it did, that "a firearm in the hands of youth is a crime or an accident waiting to happen?" No—it is time they learned that firearm ownership is constitutional, not criminal. In fact, few pursuits can teach a young person more about responsibility, safety, conservation, their history and their heritage, all at once.

It is time they found out that the politically correct doctrine of today has misled them. And that when they reach legal age, if they do not break our laws, they have a right to choose to own a gun—a handgun, a long gun, a small gun, a large gun, a black gun, a purple gun, a pretty gun, an ugly gun—and to use that gun to defend themselves and their loved ones or to engage in any lawful purpose they desire without apology or explanation to anyone, ever.

This is their first freedom. If you say it's outdated, then you haven't read your own headlines. If you say guns create only carnage, I would answer that you know better. Declining morals, disintegrating families, vacillating political leadership, an eroding criminal justice system and social mores that blur right and wrong are more to blame—certainly more than any legally-owned firearm.

An Urgent Message

I want to rescue the Second Amendment from an opportunistic president, and from a press that apparently can't comprehend that attacks on the Second Amendment set the stage for assaults on the First.

I want to save the Second Amendment from all these nit-picking little wars of attrition—fights over alleged "Saturday Night Specials," plastic guns, cop killer bullets and so many other made-for-prime-time non-issues invented by some press agent over at gun control headquarters that you guys buy time and again.

I simply cannot stand by and watch a right guaranteed by the Constitution of the United States come under attack from those who either can't understand it, don't like the sound of it, or find themselves too philosophically squeamish to see why it remains the first among equals: Because it is the right we turn to when all else fails.

That's why the Second Amendment is America's first freedom.

Please, go forth and tell the truth. There can be no free speech, no freedom of the press, no freedom to protest, no freedom to worship your god, no freedom to speak your mind, no freedom from fear, no freedom for your children and for theirs, for anybody, anywhere, without the Second Amendment freedom to fight for them.

If you don't believe me, just turn on the news tonight. Civilization's veneer is wearing thinner all the time.

Thank you.

Gun Control Denies Citizens' Rights

by George Detweiler

About the author: *George Detweiler writes for the* New American, *a conservative biweekly magazine.*

In these days when being a victim has become trendy and politically correct, the genuine article can still be found. Matt Billington, a 17-year-old junior at Filer, Idaho, High School, is a case in point. Billington lives on a farm in a western state where guns are as important a tool as a hay rake, a tractor, or a plow. Billington uses his father's .22-caliber pistol to hunt squirrels and rockchucks after school on the farm where he works. Rockchucks can be a substantial factor in crop destruction.

But when Billington forgot to remove the pistol from his vehicle before he went to school—in spite of the fact that the gun was unloaded, had not been taken out of the vehicle, and there was no ammunition for it in the vehicle—he was arrested by a school "resource" officer, based on a tip from another student who had undergone a school indoctrination campaign about the "evils" of firearms possession. Billington's father had entrusted the gun to him, but federal law views firearms possession on school property as a menace to a well- (federally) regulated educational system. Thus, a well-behaved American farm kid suddenly faced the triple wrath of federal, state, and local bureaucracies.

A Victim of Federal Control

Billington faced suspension from his entire senior year in high school under a federal law entitled the "Gun Free Schools Act of 1994." Officials readily admit that Billington was never a disciplinary problem, but was an asset to the school. Nevertheless, he became an unfortunate and inadvertent victim of the statist mindset which holds that government can cure anything and the federal government can do it best. That is the explanation proffered to the public by the statists, but the motivation runs deeper, toward other agendas.

While guns have long been a favorite target of federal control, control of per-

Reprinted from George Detweiler, "Schools, Guns, and Tyranny," *The New American*, September 15, 1997, by permission of *The New American*.

sonal liberty is the ultimate goal. In this case, the mechanics are complex. In the statist mindset and in the drone-like devotion of bureaucrats to federal regulations, one kid in school, or a dozen, would make for an easy sacrifice on the altar of liberty destroyed. It is not that Matt Billington's situation was a surprise which caught the enforcers off guard. It was only a matter of time until some youngster made the mistake. The federal act was crafted as a snare for the unwary—especially

> *"While guns have long been a favorite target of federal control, control of personal liberty is the ultimate goal."*

for school kids who have not lived long enough to experience bureaucratic buffeting and bruising and thereby develop the life skills necessary to live in an over-regulated society.

Looking to Past History

The framers of the Constitution were painfully aware of the dangers inherent in any concentration of power in the hands of a single sovereign. They had fought a war for independence to rid themselves of the yoke of King George III. The cornerstone of the newly created government was a division of sovereignty between the federal government and the states. Federal sovereignty was carved out of the sovereignties of the several states, with the states retaining the bulk of power. Madison expressed the idea in *The Federalist,* #45: "The powers delegated by the proposed Constitution to the federal government are few and defined. Those which are to remain in the State governments are numerous and indefinite."

Where the two overlap, the federal government is supreme. The authority to control crime and preserve civil order are matters of state sovereignty and responsibility; the federal government has only a secondary duty and responsibility in this area when a state, acting through its legislature or its governor, seeks federal assistance for protection against domestic violence under Article IV, Section 4, of the Constitution.

Inaccurate Powers

The Gun Free Schools Act of 1994 is not the result of the exercise of any power granted to Congress under the Constitution. Neither is any provision made in the Constitution for federal involvement in education, a topic which has been respected as an exclusively state prerogative until recent decades.

Not only does Congress lack authority to enact the Gun Free Schools Act, the act flies in the face of the Second Amendment, which prohibits such a statute. The Supreme Court and lesser courts have routinely and regularly ignored its plain, clear language in granting to the *people* the right to keep and bear arms, in favor of a strained and unnatural interpretation which finds that the right is only one to arm the National Guard, or a regularly constituted (government sponsored and controlled) militia.

What Rights?

The absurdity of this interpretation is discovered by considering the meaning of the term "right." States and the federal government are sovereigns, which, by their very nature, are power centers; they have powers and duties. They neither have nor need rights. Rights are protections afforded by law to individual citizens against abuses by the sovereigns and by their fellow citizens. When the Second Amendment established the right to keep and bear arms, it was totally unnecessary to apply it to sovereigns and their agents—the militia or the National Guard—because it is a previously established prerogative and power inherent in those state sovereigns. The obvious conclusion is that the right belongs to some other entity: the people—clearly identified in the text of the Second Amendment.

By this point there should be no lingering doubts about the application of the amendment. However, one final point destroys the notion that the Second Amendment applies to agents of the sovereigns. Under Article I, Section 8 of the Constitution, Congress is given the power to "provide for organizing, arming, and disciplining the militia. . . ." If any credibility is given to the prevailing judicial view that the Second Amendment guarantees only the right of the National Guard/militia to keep and bear arms, an absurdity results: The original form of the Constitution empowered Congress to arm the militia, but the militia (under the Supreme Court view) lacked the authority to accept, to keep, and to bear those arms until the Second Amendment was ratified.

Focus on Personal Rights

The history of the drafting of the Constitution supports the conclusion that the Second Amendment is a personal and individual right. When the Constitutional Convention of 1787, which had deliberated in secret, finally made its work public property, the document met mixed reviews as the country polarized into the Federalist and anti-Federalist camps. One of the major concerns which the anti-Federalists shared with many others in the population was the lack of specific guarantees of personal rights and liberties in the text of the proposed Constitution.

The debates raged in the press and in the ratification conventions in the several states. Since ratification was uncertain, prominent Federalists promised that if the document were ratified, the first Congress would propose amendments to guarantee personal liberties. These amendments were popularly known as the Bill of Rights, and the Second Amendment is among them. Never was there any discussion during the consideration of these amendments of a need to provide additional powers to any level of government, nor to allow the militia to keep and bear the arms which the federal government was already authorized to provide to them.

> *"Rights are protections afforded by law to individual citizens against abuses by the sovereigns and by their fellow citizens."*

The whole focus of the debates was on personal, individual liberties.

How, then, does the Supreme Court reach an interpretation of the Second Amendment which is clearly at odds with the written text of the provision? The answer is that the High Court does not really seek to apply the clear meaning of the Constitution. Rather, it reads the document in the light of the personal preferences and prejudices of the members of the Court. Its interpretation sticks because Congress has not used its power under Article III, Section 2 to limit the High Court's appellate jurisdiction.

> *"The existence of the right of the public to keep and bear arms in the constitutions of the states can provide a measure of protection."*

The Gun Free Schools Act of 1994 has no constitutional foundations to support it. Its predecessor, the Gun-Free School Zones Act of 1990, was an attempt to criminalize anyone (not just a student) possessing a firearm within 1,000 feet of a school. This was too much even for the present Supreme Court, which found it unconstitutional in a split decision. The decision was not based on the Second Amendment (which the Court refuses to enforce), but on the Constitution's commerce clause (the constitutional power of Congress to regulate interstate commerce). The Court found that the power of Congress to regulate interstate commerce did not extend to the prohibitions of the 1990 act because there was no commerce taking place when a citizen was arrested and tried for possessing a gun within the gun-free zone around a school. The dissenters on the Court, however, opined that there was a basis for using the commerce clause to support creation of the act because students would grow up to leave school, enter the work force, and thereby touch or affect interstate commerce. The amazing thing about the case is that the Supreme Court has for years found just about everything to touch interstate commerce. Since the commerce clause appears not to supply power to Congress to enact the 1994 act, a subterfuge was needed.

Funding and Control

Instead of accepting the Supreme Court's decision that the 1990 act was unconstitutional, Congress decided, in writing the 1994 act, to accomplish the same unconstitutional purpose without using the commerce clause. To do it, a devious process was applied, using the largess of the federal treasury as a carrot and stick enticement, bait on which state and local governments are eager to engorge themselves.

The Gun Free Schools Act of 1994 mandates that each state which receives federal funds for education must have a law requiring local educational agencies to expel from school for one year any student who is determined to have brought a firearm to school. Provision is made for the chief administering officer of the local educational agency to modify the expulsion requirement on a case-by-case basis. The Idaho legislature dutifully enacted a statute which mimics the federal law, and the Filer school district adopted its own policy, a policy which failed to add the language allowing amelioration of the sentence on a case-by-case basis.

Why are states so eager to dance to Congress' tune? The reason is simple: The most addictive substance in modern America is not crack, heroin, alcohol, methamphetamines, or cocaine, but federal funding. The addiction is all the more insidious because state agencies and the general public which receive the funding refuse to admit the addiction. Federal funding has become so pervasive that dependence upon it has erased from the public mind any notion of questioning its constitutionality.

After getting the public and the state and local governments addicted to regular injections from the federal treasury, the federal government can add regulatory control as a condition for continued funding—another small step toward having the states themselves become pawns by doing the fed's bidding while simultaneously destroying their own sovereignty. In the process, states have become political prostitutes, willing to perform any act demanded of them by Congress and the federal agencies, as long as they are permitted to engorge at the federal trough.

Judicial Usurpation

Idaho has a provision in its state constitution which guarantees to its citizens the right to keep and bear arms. While the Idaho Supreme Court has spoken of legislative authority to regulate the right, it has never emasculated the provision as the U.S. Supreme Court has done with the Second Amendment. There is always a danger lurking behind a judicial determination that a right is subject to legislative regulation since it can be regulated to the point of removing the protection which the right was enumerated to guarantee. Still, the existence of the right of the public to keep and bear arms in the constitutions of the states can provide a measure of protection where state law does not conflict with the proper exercise of a federal power.

The *Twin Falls Times-News* quoted the Filer school district attorney as saying of the school board: "If anything, they were angry with the boy, even for his inadvertence. . . . Anybody would have made the mistake, but it was a very serious mistake." Note the mindset: The anger is not at Congress for mandating things which are beyond its prescribed powers, but at a 17-year-old boy with the temerity to contravene, inadvertently, a policy and program which keeps federal money flowing into the school district.

Restrictions on Gun Ownership Are the First Step Toward Confiscation

by Brian Puckett

About the author: *Brian Puckett writes for the* Liberty Pole*, a bi-monthly pub-lication of the Lawyer's Second Amendment Society.*

A "Random Shots" article in the March, 1997, issue of *Handguns* magazine, which correctly urged gunowners to work for widespread public support for gun ownership, closes with: "If we can't do that [gain this support], I have the ominous suspicion that we are going to lose."

Lose? What other portion of the Bill of Rights would we speak so helplessly about "losing?" Freedom of speech? Freedom of religion? Freedom of assembly?

No number of citizens—not even 99.99 percent—may vote away a natural right. They may go through the motions and pass a law, but that law will be null and void. The right to self-defense is not a "political issue." It is *irrevocable*.

Essential Protections

The Second Amendment may not be rescinded. Inclusion of a Bill of Rights was required before certain states would agree to ratify the preceding articles of the Constitution, and therefore it is part and parcel of the original agreement among the 13 states.

Moreover, the Second Amendment is one of the enumerated *basic* human rights contained in the Bill of Rights, not some afterthought. It is as vital and as essential as the other enumerated rights—actually, more so, in a fundamental way: it guarantees the other rights cannot be stripped away. It was recognized that the right of citizens to own proper military firearms is the *only* barrier between freedom and tyranny; this is a lesson as old as history. A lesson that the Swiss have never forgotten, and that we are now re-learning.

Reprinted from Brian Puckett, "The Value of Freedom," *The Liberty Pole*, June 1997, by permission of the author.

A Losing Battle?

We must recognize that we are engaged in a struggle between two opposing philosophies—one in which free men and free women direct their government, and one in which government directs its subjects.

We have, on paper and in theory, already given up the essential elements of our right to bear arms. If, for example, a five-day waiting period is allowable and good, then six days, 10 days, a year, would be better. If a 10-round magazine is reasonable and good, then a five-round magazine is better, and a single-shot gun—or no gun—is best. If banning military-looking semi-autos is reasonable and good, then banning all semi-autos—since the difference is merely cosmetic—is best. The basic premises for the extreme positions have been passed into law. If you doubt gun-controllers' wish for these extreme positions to be put into practice, ask the residents of England and Australia.

The anti-gun activists wish to disarm us completely. They have said so. They will not hesitate to use federal agents, federal marshals, and police officers to effect this—they are doing it now. In effecting this disarmament, they will not hesitate to confiscate our property, to imprison us, or to kill us if we resist—they have done it and will do it again.

Warring Freedoms

Gun ownership is not a political game. It is a life-and-death struggle for our country and ourselves. We may win the struggle via politics and education, and we may not. What is to be done if we do not win this struggle politically is the question.

For our Forefathers, the answer was clear: they would not kneel like slaves before a government that violated their basic beliefs. They fought.

If the political analyses referred to in the *Random Shots* article are correct, then the solidly pro-gun constituency of the U.S. is about one-third of the electorate. That represents

> *"Gun ownership is not a political game. It is a life-and-death struggle for our country and ourselves."*

millions of good citizens with firearms. There is a fair chance that one day we will have to fight—literally fight—to restore our rights and our Constitution.

Should it come to that, I say those who will not fight are either grotesquely misguided, pathetically sheeplike, cowardly, or all of these. They do not deserve the freedom under which they have lived.

Government is dictated by those—good or bad—willing to risk their lives for it; this has always been so. If—should political solutions finally fail—even a modest portion of good gun-owning Americans choose to take up arms to defend their Constitution and their natural rights, they will not lose.

Chapter 4

Is Gun Ownership an Effective Means of Self-Defense?

Gun Ownership and Self-Defense: An Overview

by Fred Guterl

About the author: *Fred Guterl, staff writer for* Discover, *writes about topics in science and medicine.*

Sam Walker was not your average American gun owner. For one thing, he had no interest whatsoever in hunting. And whereas the average gun owner owns at least three guns, Walker owned only one, a .38-caliber revolver, which friends persuaded him to buy for the sole purpose of protecting himself and his family in their suburban Houston home. Walker didn't even particularly like guns. He still hadn't gotten around to acquainting himself with his new weapon when his burglar alarm went off one weekday morning in December 1996. Notified by his security company of the intrusion, Walker rushed home from work, quietly entered the house, took the gun out from the spot where he had left it for safe-keeping, and, hearing a noise, moved stealthily up the stairs and opened a closet door. He saw a movement, a figure, and in a split second fired. The smoothly oiled gun worked perfectly, and Walker's aim was true. A body fell to the floor. It was his 16-year-old daughter. She had cut school that day and had hidden in the closet to avoid her father. It wound up costing her her life.

If Walker's tragic story argues against the benefits to be gained by gun ownership, consider an incident that happened a month later, across the country in New York City. One weekday morning in January, in front of a Brooklyn government building in broad daylight, Eric Immesberger stopped to give a man directions. Suddenly a second man came out from behind a pillar and knocked Immesberger to the ground. The two men then demanded his wallet and started beating him. Now, it just so happens that Immesberger is an investigator for the Brooklyn district attorney, and, more to the point, he was armed with a 9-millimeter semiautomatic handgun. He managed to pull his weapon and shoot one of the robbers in the chest. The other fled. Immesberger was later treated at a hospital for a broken nose.

Reprinted from Fred Guterl, "Gunslinging in America," *Discover*, May 1996, by permission of Discover Syndication.

Which case better represents the reality of owning a gun? It depends, of course, on whom you ask. But one point is indisputable: murder is committed more frequently in the United States than just about anywhere else in the developed world, and guns are its chief instrument. For African American males between the ages of 14 and 25, guns are the leading cause of death. And despite the recent downward blip in the numbers, crimes in the United States are far more likely to lead to death than they are in any other developed country. Every two and a half years, guns kill as many Americans as died

> *"Murder is committed more frequently in the United States than just about anywhere else in the developed world, and guns are its chief instrument."*

in the Vietnam War. The litany of statistics is as deadening as it is depressing. Although few people would argue that cleansing the population of all guns wouldn't go a long way to trimming the firearms fatality rate, the country's 230 million guns, shielded by the Second Amendment, seem likely to remain in circulation for a long time.

Lacking a consensus on gun control, lawmakers have at least tried to put fewer guns in the hands of criminals and more in the hands of law-abiding citizens. The Brady Bill, for instance, seeks to curtail the proliferation of handguns, the weapons of choice for both crime and self-defense, by imposing background checks and a waiting period on new purchases. At the same time, the states are passing laws making it easy for residents to carry concealed handguns. But is arming the citizenry a good way to offset the risk of crime?

Not Enough Proof

In the 1990s researchers have focused unprecedented attention on the problem, and authors of some of the more dramatic studies have managed to amass impressively large stacks of press clippings. But science has not been especially helpful here. So far, nobody has been able to marshal convincing evidence for either side of the debate. "The first point that's obvious in any scientific reading of the field is the extreme paucity of data," says Franklin Zimring, a professor of law at the University of California at Berkeley. "What we have is critically flawed—on both sides." Indeed, the scientific literature on the subject seems to teach very little, except for the tedious fact that it is difficult to say anything rigorously scientific about human behavior—particularly aggression.

What's obvious by now to most scientists is that assessing the risk of owning a gun is nothing like assessing the risk of smoking cigarettes was 30 or 40 years ago. Back then medical researchers convinced themselves quickly of the cause-and-effect relationship between cigarettes and cancer. Although they had no direct, mechanistic proof, the epidemiological evidence proved the case far beyond any reasonable doubt. With guns, such a link has proved elusive, to say the least. Researchers think that about half of American households possess guns, they're fairly sure that about two-thirds of these households have handguns, and they believe the proportion of handguns, within the total number of guns of all types, is rising. Their reasoning rests partly on the assumption that most guns bought these days are intended for self-defense; because of their small size, handguns are the overwhelming choice for this purpose. They also assume that the relative number of handguns owned will be reflected in the relative number of firearms deaths caused by handguns—about 60 percent.

Assessing Risk Is Difficult

Given the magnitude of the violence and the prevalence of the weapons, it is surprising that science has come to the issue of risk only recently. Criminologists have spent several decades exploring the impact of guns on crime and the behavior of criminals, but they have neglected the question of individual risk. When the medical profession got interested in guns in the early 1980s, it made them a public health issue, looking at the risk to the public at large. Emergency room doctors see the associated hazards every day, in the children who die or are wounded by playing with guns, in the successful and unsuccessful teenage suicides, and in countless other gun-related accidents claiming victims of all ages. The doctors concerned themselves not only with unintended firings but also with accidents such as Walker's, in which the gun itself functions properly in only a narrow mechanical sense and the risk is more clearly seen in retrospect. And this public health perspective spurred

"Most guns bought these days are intended for self-defense; because of their small size, handguns are the overwhelming choice for this purpose."

renewed interest in studies that test to what degree the presence of guns increases the likelihood of death to their owners. But this approach, of course, focused on gun ownership as a societal issue; it did not assume the point of view of the individual. Doing so would have treated a gun as a consumer product, like a power drill or a lawn mower or a food processor, that carries with it a certain risk of accidental injury or death that must be weighed against its benefits.

A Possible Answer?

Many of these public health studies attracted a great deal of publicity because they seemed to settle the question of risk once and for all. Arthur Kellermann, an emergency room doctor, is perhaps the most prolific and visible of the medical researchers who have tried to quantify the risk of owning a gun. Although he is a southerner who was raised with guns and who likes target shooting, he has nonetheless become a major source of bumper-sticker statistics for gun-control advocates. He insists that he has proved not only that a gun is a poor deterrent to residential crime but that having one actually increases the chance that somebody in your home will be shot and killed. In particular, his studies conclude that gun-owning households, when compared with gunless ones, are almost three times as likely to be the scene of a homicide and almost five times as likely to be the scene of a suicide. "If having a gun in the home was a good deterrent," Kellermann says, "then we should have seen few guns in the homes of murder victims. But we found the opposite."

Kellermann's work has drawn fire from researchers who suspect that his passion for the issue has blinded him to ambiguities in his data. "Kellermann has decided that guns are bad, and he's out to prove it," says Yale sociologist Albert Reiss. Although in general criminologists don't object to Kellermann's research methods, they part company in their interpretation of his results. His evidence, say critics, is so riddled with uncertainties as to preclude any definitive interpretation.

Method of Study

Upon close inspection, Kellermann's results are much more modest than his dramatic conclusions would indicate. He chose to study guns in the home not only because lots of people buy them for self-defense and keep them in a drawer beside their beds but also because *home* is a well-defined place that simplifies the task of collecting data. Police homicide records specifically include the location of each incident and the weapon used, and it was a straightforward matter for Kellermann to follow up each case by interviewing surviving family members and friends. The problem was in coming up with a suitable control group against which to draw comparisons. Ideally, you want to pair each victim with a control that differs from the victim only in that one was shot and the other wasn't. Kellermann devised a clever methodology for doing so. For each victim, he randomly selected one neighbor after another until he found someone who was the same age, sex, and race. Eventually he assembled "matched pairs" for 388 homicide victims.

When he compared the victims with the control group, however, he found that many more factors differentiated the two groups than their victim status. It turned out that the households in which homicides took place were more likely to contain a family member who abused alcohol or drugs and had a history of domestic violence—these factors contributed to the likelihood of homicide independent of the existence of guns. Kellermann took pains to compensate for these other factors using standard statistical techniques of epidemiology. In essence, he tried to estimate how much each factor, such as alcohol abuse, might have influenced the homicide rate among victims in his study, and then he adjusted his figures accordingly.

> *"Public health studies attracted a great deal of publicity because they seemed to settle the question of risk once and for all."*

What neither Kellermann nor his critics can know for certain is whether this statistical juggling actually uncovers any underlying trends or whether something else is going on that Kellermann hasn't accounted for. Kellermann himself admits the possibility of some kind of "psychological confounding"—that some intangible factor such as aggression, rather than merely the presence of guns, is influencing the results. Critics also point out that the victims in Kellermann's study may have gotten guns because they felt themselves to be threatened in some way, which means they might have suffered higher homicide rates even if they hadn't bothered to arm themselves. "Kellermann has shown that homicide victims are more likely to keep a gun at home, but criminologists have known that for years," says Gary Kleck, of Florida State University in Tallahassee.

> *"[Researchers] are guilty of failing to explain what happens when people carry guns, and how possessing one affects their interactions with criminals."*

Kellermann's even more dramatic figures on suicide in the home are especially problematic, mainly because Kellermann relies on the numbers without offering an explanation. "There's no theory to account for his conclusion," says Zimring. Suicide is also thought to be prone to substitution—that is, although guns are the preferred instrument of suicide in the United States, a person bent on suicide can easily find a substitute if need be. Since Kellermann's study focuses on suicides in the home, it doesn't account for the victim who, lacking a gun, decides instead to jump off a bridge.

The Criminologist Angle

Regardless of their personal feelings on guns, criminologists, who tend to look at violence through the lens of police statistics and surveys, are usually more open than doctors to the possibility that a gun can now and then deter a crime. Trouble is, social scientists are poorly equipped to measure events that do not occur—crimes that are averted because the would-be victim had a gun. As a result, criminologists have resorted to surveys to get at this phenomenon. Kleck conducted a survey to find out how often gun owners actually use their guns in self-defense. His controversial results depict the country's gun owners as holding back a tidal wave of violence and crime. He estimates that 2.5 million times each year, somebody somewhere in America uses a gun in self-defense. This figure has become a mantra of the National Rifle Association (with whom Kleck has no affiliation).

Most other criminologists are critical of Kleck's methods, and almost all of them are incredulous at the results. A big complaint is that he leaves it to his survey respondents to define a "defensive gun use," so he may have captured incidents that most people would consider trivial. "An awful lot of what some people would call self-defense is, like, somebody asks you for a quarter and you tell them to get lost, but as you walk away you keep your hand on your gun," says Philip Cook, a Duke University economist. In addition, many incidents that people report as self-defense may in fact be assaults, in which the respondent takes a more active role than he admits. "In many instances, we may only be talking to one side of an argument," says Zimring.

Definite Answers Are Rare

What this criticism comes down to is that Kleck, like Kellermann and all the other researchers in this field, is guilty of failing to explain what happens when people carry guns, and how possessing one affects their interactions with criminals. As Reiss puts it, "We know very little about how motivation enters into an action." Zimring likens efforts to understand the deterrent effect of guns to "dancing with clouds." Kleck himself admits that "the better the research, the more it tends to support the null hypothesis—that gun ownership and control laws have no net effect on violence."

Even when a seemingly perfect opportunity for a real-life experiment presents itself, as it did recently to criminologist David McDowall, the null hypothesis is often all that a criminologist is left with. In 1993, Florida, Mississippi, and Oregon adopted "shall issue" laws requiring the states to issue a license to almost anybody who wants to carry a concealed handgun. McDowall saw that the effect of these laws would give him a laboratory in which to test the arms-race hypothesis: he could find out whether criminals, knowing their victims are more likely to be armed with handguns, are more likely to use guns themselves. He could also find out whether citizens, when armed, can deter crime.

> *"For the time being . . . there will remain very little one researcher can say about risk that another researcher cannot refute."*

After the 1993 laws were passed, permits to carry concealed handguns rose enormously—in Florida the number of licenses soared from 17,000 before the law was passed in 1987 to 141,000 seven years later. After studying five cities, McDowall found that the rate of firearms homicides increased overall by 26 percent. Although this would seem to support the arms-race hypothesis, the results were inconsistent. Whereas McDowall had expected the effects of the liberalized laws to be greatest in Miami, the biggest city in the study and the one with the highest crime rate, the rise in homicides there was too small to be statistically significant. However, McDowall believes his evidence is strong enough to show that armed citizens do not decrease the number of firearms-related deaths.

Guns Can Be Confounding

Despite the frustrating lack of clarity, researchers are universally optimistic that, with time and the accretion of data, insight into the mechanism of violence will come, and with it, a greater consensus on the real risks of guns. For the time being, however, there will remain very little one researcher can say about risk that another researcher cannot refute. Most favor restricting the availability of guns by mandating background checks and waiting periods, which serve to some degree to keep guns out of the hands of "hotheads" and criminals. There is also a consensus that higher homicide rates have everything to do with the preponderance of guns—an obvious inference when considering, say, crime statistics of London and New York. These two cities have similar crime rates, but the homicide rate from burglaries and robberies in gun-rich New York is vastly higher—54 times higher in 1992, according to Zimring. "America doesn't have a crime problem," he says, "it has a lethal violence problem. It's that thin layer of lethal crime that Americans are afraid of."

Given that purging guns from the population is problematic, would the world be safer if each law-abiding citizen carried a gun? Alessandro Veralli hesitates before answering this question. For most of his adult life, he has carried a concealed handgun almost everywhere he goes, whether it's out to the movies with his wife or to the local hardware store on a Saturday afternoon. Yet Veralli, a Master Firearms Instructor for the New York City Police Department and an NRA life member, admits that as a civilian he has had very little opportunity to use his gun. If he ever found himself a customer at a liquor store that was being held up, in most cases his training and common sense would tell him to lie low rather than start a shoot-out. If he was out with his wife and a thief demanded his wallet, he would probably hand it over. "In a robbery, there's not much you can do except maybe shoot at the guy as he's walking away," he says. "But what if he shoots back? I'd be putting my wife in danger, and for what?" He carries a gun for the hypothetical extreme case when having it might mean the difference between life and death. "Personally I'd hate to get into a bad situation and think that I might have been able to do something if I had had a gun," he says.

But should other citizens carry guns? "I'm tempted to say yes," he says, but then he demurs. "Maybe it makes sense in other parts of the country where they have more space. New York, though, is too crowded. There's something about all these people being confined in a small space. People can fly off the handle over little things. I don't think I'd want to see each and every one of them carrying a gun."

Gun Ownership Provides Effective Self-Defense

by Sarah Thompson

About the author: *Sarah Thompson is a retired physician. She writes an on-line column, "The Righter," which focuses on civil liberties.*

The right of law-abiding citizens to carry concealed firearms for purposes of self-defense has become a hot and controversial topic. Claims have been made citing everything from "the presence of a firearm in the home increases the risk of homicide by 43 times" to "there are up to 2.5 million defensive uses of private firearms per year, with up to 400,000 lives saved as a result." There are people who feel endangered by the presence of a gun nearby and other people who feel vulnerable when not carrying a gun on their person. Some law enforcement agents welcome the increasing numbers of lawfully armed citizens while others view them as a deadly threat. What and where is the truth in all of this disagreement, and what are the implications for public policy?

A Criminal Subculture Is to Blame

Prior to Prohibition, there was virtually no federal gun control, and no concept of guns being "evil". Guns were seen as a threat to society only when they were possessed by blacks, and the history of gun control closely parallels the history of racism in this country. Guns were simply tools, useful for protecting one's livelihood and property, obtaining food for one's family, recreation, and when necessary, self-defense. The gun culture was an accepted and respected part of American life.

However, in a situation similar to the one we face today, Prohibition gave birth to a criminal subculture which depended on violence and guns, terrorizing law abiding citizens. After Prohibition was repealed, these criminal organizations remained. Rather than attacking crime and criminals, the government passed the National Firearms Act in 1934, which put a $200 "transfer tax" (about $4000 in 1996 dollars) on certain guns, particularly machine guns and short barreled shotguns. (For comparison, a short-barreled shotgun cost only about $5!) The Federal Firearms Act followed in 1938, which required firearms dealers to obtain licenses, and started a new federal bureaucracy to "control guns".

The war on guns again escalated after the assassinations of President Kennedy, Senator Robert Kennedy, and the Rev. Martin Luther King in the 1960's. This resulted in the Federal Firearms Act of 1968 which, when compared word for word to the Nazi weapons laws of 1938, is almost identical. In the late 1980's to early 1990's, the attempted assassination of President Reagan and the wounding of his Press Secretary James Brady, and the escalation of violent, firearms-related crimes due to the failed "War on Drugs", have led to an intensification of the "War on Guns". We now have innumerable state and local laws restricting gun ownership, carrying, use, and even appearance, along with federal laws such as the Brady Act and the impending "Brady II".

> *"Guns were simply tools, useful for protecting one's livelihood and property, obtaining food for one's family, recreation, and when necessary, self-defense."*

To enforce these laws, the government needed to get "the people" to support them, to willingly give up their Second Amendment rights and their right to self-defense. To do this, it recruited powerful spokespeople, primarily doctors and the media, to convince people that guns were bad and needed to be banned. Doctors, at least until recently, were highly respected professionals, scientists whose words were above questioning. The same was true of the elite medical journals. Most prestigious of all were the revered doctors and scientists who worked at the huge federal institutes of research. To their enduring shame, some of these doctors were co-opted into helping the government in its "War on Guns".

Opportunistic Doctors

Doctors, of course, are not superhuman and they have weaknesses like everyone. Many well-meaning doctors just didn't analyze correctly what they were seeing, and didn't bother to ask the right questions, since they had been trained to obey medical authorities. For example, doctors who work in emergency rooms see the horrors that misuse of guns can create. They dedicate their lives to saving lives, and watching people, especially young people, die of gunshot wounds is extremely painful. This makes it easy for them to be swayed by emotion and blame the gun instead of the person who misused it. Of course they never see the people who use guns safely and responsibly, and they never see the people whose lives were saved by defensive gun use. It's a very one-sided view.

At the same time, there were other doctors who saw the huge amounts of money being poured into biased gun research and saw the opportunity to get grant money, have their work published, or become famous. All this required was designing research that aided the government's pre-conceived policy of "proving" that guns were bad in order to disarm the populace. In my opinion there is only one term that applies to people who sell their integrity and their credentials for fame and profit.

Thus since 1987 we have been bombarded with medical "experts" proclaiming that guns were the cause of nearly everything wrong in society. The media gave tremendous coverage to these studies, and reinforced them with emotional and melodramatic stories of lives ruined by guns—by inanimate guns, not by criminals, carelessness, or their own stupidity. People, especially people raised in urban areas who had no experience with guns, believed these stories. No doubt you've heard these claims, and maybe even worried that invoking your Second Amendment rights was a bad idea.

Establishing Public Misperception

Many of these studies were funded by the National Center for Injury Prevention and Control (NCIPC), a division of the Centers for Disease Control (CDC)—funded, of course, with OUR tax dollars. That's right. Our government officials, sworn to uphold the Constitution, used our money to try to deprive us of one of our most important Constitutional rights. And the NCIPC didn't even pretend to be objective. Dr. Mark Rosenberg, former director of NCIPC, has been quoted avowing his and the CDC's desire to create a public perception of firearms as "dirty, deadly—and banned".

One common excuse for gun control, designed to sound scientific, is that guns are a public health problem, that guns are "pathogens" (germs) which must be eliminated to eliminate the "disease" of gun violence.

> *"[Biased doctors] never see the people who use guns safely and responsibly, and they never see the people whose lives were saved by defensive gun use."*

This simply is not true. To be true, the presence of a gun would cause the disease (violence) in all those exposed to it, and in its absence, violence should not be found. (Every physician is taught the criteria for determining what is or isn't a pathogen early in medical school, so this is inexcusable.) If all those exposed to firearms attempted homicide, our streets truly would be running with blood. Approximately half of all American households own guns, yet few people are involved with homicide or other gun misuse. There are approximately 230 million guns in the United States, more than enough for each adult and teen, yet only a minuscule number of people commit homicide. And if degree of exposure to guns correlated with homicide rates, our police would be the worst offenders.

Scientific Research?

One often quoted study is the Sloan-Kellerman comparison of Seattle and Vancouver, published in the "New England Journal of Medicine". Their methodology was simplistic and merely compared the homicide rates in the two cities, then assumed the lower rate in Vancouver was due to gun control. Obviously there are nearly infinite differences in any two cities, yet the study did not control for any differences. The difference in homicide rates could just as easily have been due to economic, cultural, or ethnic variables, differences in laws, age differences, substance abuse, or anything else. Based on their data, one could just as well conclude that the difference was due to the number of movie theaters or eating Twinkies. As a final insult to scientific research, the homicide rates before gun control were not evaluated. Homicide actually increased 25% after the institution of the 1977 gun law. . . .

Perhaps the most often quoted myth about the risks of gun ownership is that having a gun in one's home increases one's risk of homicide by a factor of 43. This study, by Kellerman, is full of errors and deceit, and has been widely discredited. Yet the 43 times figure continues to be repeated until it has now achieved the status of "common knowledge". Among the errors, Kellerman did not show that even ONE victim was killed with the gun kept in the home. In fact, at least 49% of the victims were killed by someone who did not live in the home and probably had no access to guns kept there. He assumed that the victim of the crime was the one killed, ignoring the possibility that it was the criminal, not the victim, who was killed. Finally, the study showed that substance abuse, family violence, living alone, and living in a rented home were all greater predictors of homicide than was gun ownership. Curiously, the authors have refused to make their data available to other researchers who wish to evaluate the study. Yet, as I mentioned before, this study was funded with our tax dollars. *[Editor's Note: These data have since been released.]*

Criminologists Provide Relief

Fortunately, these fraudulent researchers at the NCIPC were finally exposed in 1996 by a coalition of physicians and criminologists who testified before the House appropriations committee. As a result, the NCIPC's funding for so-called "gun research" was cut from the budget. Of course there were people doing well-designed, accurate research on guns and violence during this period as well. . . .

But they weren't doctors, they weren't supported by the government, and the media totally ignored them. They were criminologists, sociologists, lawyers, and their studies weren't considered important, especially by the medical establishment.

> *"Perhaps the most often quoted myth about the risks of gun ownership is that having a gun in one's home increases one's risk of homicide by a factor of 43."*

Gary Kleck's book, *Point Blank: Guns and Violence in America*, was published in 1991, and received a prestigious criminology award. Although it was generally ignored by both the media and the medical researchers, it was a turning point. At last there was a comprehensive, unbiased assessment of the issues surrounding guns and violence that was available to lay people and researchers alike.

In 1995 there was another breakthrough when Kleck and Gertz's study "Armed Resistance to Crime: The Prevalence and Nature of Self-Defense with a Gun" was published. This study is the first one devoted specifically to the subject of armed self-defense. Of the nearly 5000 respondents, 222 reported a defensive gun use within the past 12 months and 313 within the past 5 years. By extrapolating to the total population, he estimated there are about 2.2 to 2.5 million defensive gun uses by civilians each year, with 1.5 to 1.9 million involving handguns! 400,000 of these people felt the defensive use of a gun "almost certainly" prevented a murder. This is ten times the total number of firearms deaths from all causes in a year! Clearly the risk of allowing civilians to arm themselves for self-defense pales in comparison to the huge numbers of lives saved.

> *"People who carry concealed handguns protect not only themselves and their families, but the public in general."*

The Lott and Mustard Study

Now, in the words of David Kopel, "All of the research about concealed-carry laws has been eclipsed by a comprehensive study by University of Chicago law professor John Lott, with graduate student David Mustard."

This study goes far beyond any previous study both in its design and in the comprehensive data collected. Most studies of handgun effects on crime or violence use either time series or cross-sectional data. Time series data means that you look at a particular area (for example Salt Lake County) over time, either continuously or at specified times. Such studies are open to error due to the time periods chosen. If someone compared the crime rates in Salt Lake County from 1992 to 1995 (the year the "shall issue" law became effective), there would likely be little difference since few people had had the time to obtain the permits to carry concealed.

Use of Precise Methods

Cross-sectional data refers to comparing two or more different areas at the same time. The accuracy of these studies depends on how well the areas are matched, and how well the differences between them are controlled for in the study. As we saw with the Seattle-Vancouver study, if the cities are not well matched, it is easy to draw, or even create, the wrong conclusions. In addition, the area one chooses to study is important. Cross-sectional data from states are commonly used, since concealed carry laws are generally passed at the state level. But states are not uniform at all; they have large cities, small cities, suburban areas, rural areas, etc. Mixing data from extremely different areas, such as large population centers and rural communities together obscures important information. For example, combining statistics from Salt Lake County (urban) and Kane county (rural) and saying it represents "Utah" actually makes any statistics representing "Utah" quite misleading.

The Lott study solves these problems by using cross-sectional and time series data. They studied every county in the United States continuously from 1977 to 1992, a period of 16 years. Studying counties allowed them to separate urban from rural areas, and a sixteen year study period is long enough to allow for any temporary, but meaningless, shift in statistics. In addition, the Lott study includes such variables as the type of crime committed, probability of arrest, of conviction, and the length of prison sentences, as well as mandatory sentencing guidelines. It also includes variables such as age, sex, race, income, population and population density. This provides a more detailed, "three-dimensional" picture of the effect of concealed carry permits on crime.

The numbers of arrests and types of crimes were provided by the FBI's Uniform Crime Report, while the information on population was collected from the Census Bureau. Additional information was obtained from state and county officials whenever possible. Other factors which could affect the results such as changes in the laws involving the use of firearms, or sentencing enhancement laws were either eliminated as possibilities or controlled for statistically.

Dramatic Results

The results of this study show that violent crimes (murder, rape, aggravated assault) decrease dramatically when "shall issue" laws are passed. At the same time, property crimes (auto theft and larceny) increase slightly. This can be explained by habitual criminals changing their preferred method of crime. It makes sense that criminals would switch from crimes where they must confront the victim and thus may get shot, to crimes of stealth where they are much less likely to confront an armed victim. Certainly a small increase in property crimes is a small price to pay for a large savings in human life and health.

The statistics are dramatic. Whenever concealed carry laws went into effect in a county during this 16 year period, murders fell by 8.5%, rapes by 5%, and aggravated assaults by 7%. If, in 1992, all states had enacted "shall issue" laws, murders in the United States would have decreased by 1,570. There would have been 4,177 fewer rapes and over 60,000 fewer aggravated assaults. This unequivocally supports the wisdom of our Founding Fathers who guaranteed that our right to keep and bear arms "shall not be infringed".

"Because the imbalance between a woman and her attacker is much greater, the benefits of carrying [a gun] are also much greater."

It means that the bleeding heart gun control advocates, the Sarah Brady types weeping about dead children, and our legislators and presidents who support them, are directly responsible for the deaths of over 1500 Americans and the rapes of over 4,000 innocent women every single year!

The anti-gunners are unable to find any scientific flaws or errors of analysis in this study. Instead they have attacked the researchers personally, just as they did to the doctors who dared speak the "politically incorrect" truth. There is no place for name-calling in either scientific research or in setting policy that affects millions of lives.

Anti-gunners might ask if allowing concealed carry would cause an increase in accidental deaths. However, the entire number of accidental deaths in the U.S. in 1992 was 1,409, and only 546 of these occurred in states with concealed carry laws. The total number of accidental handgun deaths per year is less than 200. At most, there would be nine more accidental deaths per year if all states passed concealed carry laws, in contrast to 1,500 lives saved.

> *"Concealed carrying of firearms by citizens with no prior felony record or history of severe mental illness decreases violent crime."*

Anti-gunners use the argument that if concealed carry were enacted, every minor fender-bender or disagreement would turn into a shoot-out. Over 300,000 permits have been issued in Florida since 1986, but only five violent crimes involving permitted pistols were committed as of December 1995, and none of them resulted in a fatality. There is only one recorded instance of a permitted pistol being used in a shooting following a traffic accident, and in that case a grand jury found that the shooting was justified.

Self-Defense Is Highlighted

In 1993, private citizens accidentally killed 30 innocent people who they thought were committing a crime, while police killed 330 innocent people. Given the nature of police work, this is not an entirely fair comparison. However, it clearly shows the public can be trusted with concealed pistols.

Another finding is that people who carry concealed handguns protect not only themselves and their families, but the public in general, even that part of the public that protests most loudly against guns. Since by definition a concealed weapon is hidden, a criminal has no way of knowing if a prospective victim is armed, and is therefore less likely to commit a violent crime against any given person.

This is particularly important for women. Women are the victims of a disproportionate number of violent crimes. A woman who carries a gun has a much greater deterrent effect on crime than does a man. Women are usually smaller and weaker than their attackers, and the presence of a firearm equalizes this imbalance. Because the imbalance between a woman and her attacker is much greater, the benefits of carrying are also much greater. A woman carrying a gun decreases the murder rate for women by 3-4 times the amount a man carrying a gun decreases the murder rate for men.

While numerous studies have attempted to quantify the cost of firearms related deaths and injuries, this is the first paper to study the economic benefits of allowing concealed carry. For the sake of consistency, the authors based their figures on estimates for the cost of various crimes used by a National Institute of Justice study published in 1996. Costs included loss of life, lost productivity, medical bills, property losses, as well as losses related to fear, pain, suffering, and decreased quality of life.

Guns Are Good for the Economy

These figures are based on jury trial awards, which may not be the best way to estimate economic loss. However they are the figures used in anti-gun studies and so the authors chose to use them to more clearly illustrate the economic benefits of gun ownership. The reduction in violent crime caused by concealed weapons permits provides an economic gain of $6.6 billion, compared to a much smaller economic loss of $417 million due to the increase in property crimes. The net gain is still $6.2 billion!

These results may seem like ordinary common sense. Other results seem to go against "common wisdom". For example, it has been traditional to have the most restrictive gun laws in high population, high crime, urban areas such as Los Angeles, New York City, and Washington, D.C. It is common to hear people say that "It's fine for those people who live out in the country to have guns, but people in the city shouldn't have them."

> *"Learning to protect oneself from crime and violence is as important to a woman's health as is learning to detect breast cancer or prevent heart disease."*

But this study shows that the effect of allowing concealed carry is much greater in high population counties and in high crime counties. For example, the murder rate in very large cities drops by 12% when CCW is passed, while it drops by only about 1.6% in an average-sized city. Data for rural areas is unreliable since the murder rates in most rural areas are so low that accurate statistical studies cannot be done. An increase from one murder per year to two would show up as a 100% increase in the murder rate, which is misleading when compared to cities with daily murders. However, consistent with the earlier comments on criminals switching to "safer" methods of crime, the increase in property crimes in urban areas is also greater than the increase in rural areas.

Urban Life May Be Hazardous

Contrary to frequently espoused theories about causes of crime, real per capita income showed only a small, though statistically significant, correlation with both violent crimes and property crimes. It would appear that living in a high population density area may contribute more to crime than does poverty, although this requires more study.

Another finding which deserves comment is that the presence of young, black males increases the rate of property crime by 22% and violent crime by 5%. However, these numbers cannot be accepted completely at face value, nor should they be used to justify racism. The history of gun control in this country reflects the history of racism. The first state and local firearms laws were designed primarily to disarm blacks, and enough damage has already been done. It is necessary to take into account studies showing that young black males are disproportionately arrested and incarcerated for crimes, and that they are disproportionately victims of crimes. In addition, they tend to live in high population areas and have low incomes, both of which are independent factors for increased crime. Finally, in view of recent allegations that the CIA deliberately introduced drugs, guns, and thus crime, into inner city black neighborhoods, more study is necessary before any definite conclusions can be reached. Neither Professor Lott nor I believe that race is a cause of crime. . . .

Excellent Findings

While it is generally a bad idea to base policy on the results of a single study, the Lott and Mustard study is so well designed and well controlled that it is difficult, if not impossible, to argue with their findings. In addition, their results agree with those of previous researchers, most notably Kleck and Gertz.

Two findings stand out above all. Concealed carrying of firearms by citizens with no prior felony record or history of severe mental illness decreases violent crime, providing a large benefit both to the individuals who carry and the public as a whole. Second, arrests by law enforcement officers have a large deterrent effect on crime, while conviction has a lesser, but still important, effect.

The obvious conclusion is that concealed carry provides a very large benefit to society in terms of lives saved, violent assaults and rapes prevented, and economic savings. At the same time misuse of legally concealed weapons and accidental handgun deaths from concealed weapons are almost non-existent. Thus every effort should be made to facilitate concealed carry by law-abiding citizens. "Shall issue" permit laws should be adopted by all those states that have not yet done so. In particular, large, urban areas should actively encourage arming their good citizens and definitely should not prevent or discourage them from carrying concealed weapons.

Regulations such as gun-free zones which serve only to disarm and/or harass gun owners are counterproductive and should be eliminated at local, state and federal levels. The Supreme Court has already found gun-free school zones unconstitutional and the justices should uphold this finding in light of the current administration's repeated attempts to enact this mis-

> *"The self-sufficient, self-protecting gun culture must be restored to its rightful place of respect in society, not demonized as a hotbed of terrorists."*

guided legislation. Concealed carry permits should be accepted on a reciprocal basis by all states, just as driver's licenses are, under the full faith and credit act of the Constitution.

In view of the negligible incidence of negative events resulting from concealed carry, further studies are indicated to determine whether the extensive background checks and training requirements which most states demand are even necessary. It may be that "Vermont-style", i.e. universal concealed carry without need for a permit, is more appropriate and would remove both the financial disincentives to lawful carry as well as decrease the demand on the often overworked staff of state permitting agencies and the FBI. Further, the Constitution guarantees the right to keep and bear arms, and many people (including the author) consider the requirement for a permit, which gives them "permission" to exercise what is already an enumerated right to be both unconstitutional and offensive.

> *"Those who preach gun control have contributed to the deaths of at least six thousand innocent people whose lives they have sworn to protect and whose freedoms they have sworn to uphold."*

Because the beneficial effect of women carrying concealed weapons far outweighs that of men carrying, women should be encouraged to carry, and special classes designed to teach women how to safely use, maintain and carry weapons, along with other self-defense techniques, need to be developed and made widely available. Learning to protect oneself from crime and violence is as important to a woman's health as is learning to detect breast cancer or prevent heart disease. The psychological benefits to women of feeling safe are very significant, but have yet to be studied scientifically.

Guns Can Unite Citizens

In many areas, including the Salt Lake metropolitan area, there is currently much bad feeling between some law enforcement officers who feel citizens who carry pose a "deadly threat" to them and citizens who feel harassed by police. Lott's study shows that this is not only unnecessary, but counterproductive. Armed citizens can protect themselves, their families and others from violent crimes. Police cannot be everywhere simultaneously, and have no duty to protect individuals. Their role is primarily to investigate crimes after the fact and bring perpetrators to justice. By decreasing the number of violent crimes committed, armed citizens actually decrease the police workload and enable them to be more productive and apprehend a greater percentage of criminals which in turn further decreases crime.

Armed citizens and police who are able to cooperate have a synergistic effect on decreasing crime. Both groups need to acknowledge this, accommodate to the changes in the laws, stop competing, and learn to respect and trust each other. Law enforcement agencies, working with citizens' groups, must develop clear written policies for police and armed citizen interactions and disseminate these policies widely. The self-sufficient, self-protecting gun culture must be restored to its rightful place of respect in society, not demonized as a hotbed of terrorists. The Second Amendment right to keep and bear arms must be unequivocally upheld.

Those who wish to disarm the populace of this country must be exposed for the frauds they are and held responsible morally, if not legally, for the deaths and suffering created by their misguided policies. In the four years since 1992, those who preach gun control have contributed to the deaths of at least six thousand innocent people whose lives they have sworn to protect and whose freedoms they have sworn to uphold.

Gun Ownership Displays Responsible Behavior

by Tara Powell

About the author: *Tara Powell is a student at the University of North Carolina at Chapel Hill. She has written for the* Daily Tar Heel, *the student newspaper.*

In my wallet there is a yellow card stating that in October 1989 I passed the hunter's education course in Pasquotank County.

I confess to not having passed with flying colors. Still, it was a hoop I had to jump through to get out of high school, and I did it.

Yes, that's right. My hometown requires that no one leave high school without having learned how guns work and how to aim and fire rifles, shotguns and handguns. Though Elizabeth City has some foolish features, this is one area where the system is to be commended.

Growing up in a family where manhood is measured in antlers, I saw a "dead Bambi" before I was 10. Still, the first time I touched a loaded weapon it was partly in excitement, but mostly in trepidation. In the slick, cold metal that morning, I seemed to hold Danger. I didn't possess it—merely held it in shaking hands.

That changed as I fired the gun clumsily and it kicked, bruising my shoulder. I'd seen plenty of guns fired, but the hole that rifle ripped on the far corner of the target was mine. And I realized that, with practice, I could put that hole anywhere I needed it to go.

The Paradox of Guns

Guns are not Danger, they are Power.

We organize our lives around power—who holds it, why, and how much. Political power, economic power, intellectual power, physical power. . . .

A gun is a form of physical power that represents both mastery and weakness. The fact that man can build a gun to defend or feed himself is strength—a monument to intellectual power, to his ability to master nature's beasts and the beasts in the ranks of his own species.

Reprinted, by permission, from Tara Powell, "Armed Citizens Are Powerful, Responsible Ones," *Daily Tar Heel*, January 7, 1997.

On the other hand, that guns are fired at human beings is a monument to human imperfection. Like any other form of power, a gun is a weapon that irresponsible, insane and evil people can wield against the rest of society.

I am lazy enough (and lucky enough) that I will probably never hunt for my food. But the insanity of the world around me means that I, myself, might be hunted. It could be by a lunatic, by a calculating enemy or perhaps by a government turned totalitarian. It may well be by a robber sneaking in my house with the intention of taking my property. Though the forms of threat vary, I am reminded of my frailty each time I turn down a dark alley or a strange shadow looms by my window late at night.

Empowering Law-Abiding People

We live in a society where we can almost uniformly assume muggers will be armed, and law-abiding citizens not in uniform will be defenseless. This tilts the odds dreadfully in favor of the maniac. Laws that take guns from the populace only take them from those that obey the law—excluding the population we ostensibly wish to prevent from carrying arms!

In 1995, North Carolina passed a law allowing citizens to obtain permits to legally carry concealed weapons. Since that time, over 20,000 Tar Heels have applied for and been granted such permits. These permits return a basic right and a sense of security to the people who go through the necessary rigamarole to obtain them.

> *"A gun is a form of physical power that represents both mastery and weakness."*

The only reported instance I have found of a gun owner licensed under the North Carolina law actually using his weapon was in Wake County. A Raleigh mechanic named Marty Hite stopped a restaurant hold-up by shooting a robber in the leg. In the 28 other states who have similar laws, the effects of concealed-carry permits are under debate. Though some studies correlate the permits with decreases in violent crime, the statistics are hotly disputed.

Be that as it may, it is clear that concealed weapons have not, as some critics supposed they might, turned the state into the "OK Corral."

Gun Ownership: A Civic Duty

I'd like to see us go further. Not only does the U.S. Constitution guarantee citizens the right to bear arms, but bearing them is, in a sense, a social duty. Informed, conscientious citizens (like Mr. Hite) committed to a free society should be able to protect their persons, property and ideals from forces that threaten them.

Are guns a form of power some people are not responsible enough to exercise? Yes. Is it possible for improper use of guns to result in accidents? Yes. Should children, maniacs and criminals be permitted the authorized use of such weapons? Certainly not.

The notion that an educated, responsible adult should not only be capable of carrying, but should, in fact, carry a weapon is one that is long overdue. It is frankly pathetic that in a state of over 7 million people, only 20,000 have accepted their moral and civic duty to take advantage of the 1995 permits.

> *"We should each take it upon ourselves to preserve our social system—to carry weapons and to know how to use them."*

Democracy is based upon the notion that individuals have an entitlement to access to power—to be protected from it and to exercise it to protect themselves. Guns are one of the most obvious and effective forms of exercising power that exists. We should each take it upon ourselves to preserve our social system—to carry weapons and to know how to use them.

Being Armed Means Having Power

An ideal society would be one where there was no need to protect oneself.

The next best society would be an armed one—where every adult was armed with both intellectual and physical power to combat danger, insanity and injustice. Power should rest neither in criminals nor in external authority. Power should reside in the citizenry.

Guns, like other forms of power, make us masters rather than victims—willful agents rather than serfs at the whim of externalities. Only when we are all empowered will the first best society become a possibility.

Eight years ago on a chilly autumn morning, I realized I could exercise power to prevent myself from being a victim. I don't have my handgun yet, but guess what my first paycheck after graduation will buy?

Gun Owners Protect Themselves from Crime

by Stephen Chapman

About the author: *Stephen Chapman, columnist for the* Chicago Tribune, *has written articles for the* Atlantic, Harper's Magazine, *and* Reason.

During 1994's re-election campaign, Texas Gov. Ann Richards knew enough to cultivate the gun-owners vote: She made a show of taking a shotgun into the field on the first day of dove season. Though no game birds ventured her way, she came off better than her Republican opponent, George W. Bush, who mistakenly (and illegally) bagged a killdeer. But Richards had vetoed a bill making it easier to get a concealed-weapon permit, which Bush endorsed. On Election Day, shotgun and all, she got cashiered by the voters.

This issue is not just one of those weird Texas things. The most striking development in gun laws is not 1994's federal ban on "assault weapons." It is the parade of states that have decided to let responsible adults carry handguns. From 1987 to 1995, 10 states have made concealed-weapon permits easy to get, bringing to 19 the number with such a policy. Several more are considering the idea.

Better Off?

Guns, in the wrong hands, facilitate crime. But in the right hands, they can also prevent it, which is why we insist that cops be armed. In this violent society, the wrong people—namely criminals—already wield firearms in abundance. The question is whether we would be better off or worse off if more of the right people—law-abiding, mentally competent citizens who have taken gun-safety courses—were also packing heat.

Whoever killed Nicole Simpson didn't need a gun: He was (or they were) strong enough to dispatch two healthy adults with only a knife. But if she had been carrying one, she might be alive today. Texas has an example that is less hypothetical: a woman who left her pistol in the car when she went into Luby's Cafeteria in Killeen and then had to watch as an armed man killed 22 patrons, including her parents.

Reprinted from Stephen Chapman, "Could More Guns Make Our Streets Safer?" *Conservative Chronicle*, February 8, 1995. Reprinted by permission of Stephen Chapman and Creators Syndicate.

Citing the Wrong Statistics

Advocates of gun control are appalled at the idea of allowing more ordinance on our streets, which they equate with gasoline on a forest fire. Their Exhibit A is Florida, the first state to liberalize its concealed-handgun law. Handgun Control Inc. notes that "between 1987—the year Florida enacted its law—and 1992, the violent crime rate rose 17.8 percent. Florida's 1992 violent crime rate of 1,207.2 per 100,000 people is the highest in the nation for any state."

But Florida had more than its share of mayhem long before this law. Handgun Control doesn't mention that between 1987 and 1992, the violent crime rate for the country as a whole rose by 24 percent—considerably faster than in the Sunshine State. During that period, the national murder rate increased by 12 percent nationally, but the Florida murder rate fell by 21 percent.

Not a Shootout

Handgun Control warns that "more guns lead to more deaths and injuries from gunshots." Not in Florida, they don't. More than 100,000 people have licenses to carry concealed handguns, but the abuses have been rare. By the end of 1993, only 17 licenses had been revoked because the licensee committed a crime with a firearm. The prediction that every traffic dispute would end in a hail of bullets has not come true.

Meanwhile, a few crimes have been thwarted by permit holders. And, as the Independence Institute of Colorado notes, "There was no known incident of a permit holder intervening in an incompetent or dangerous manner, such as shooting an innocent bystander by mistake." The case of Florida suggests that permissive "concealed carry" laws won't necessarily increase crime.

> *"Guns, in the wrong hands, facilitate crime. But in the right hands, they can also prevent it."*

A Risk Worth Taking

But, you may wonder, why take a chance? Two reasons. First, because law-abiding citizens can't count on law-enforcement agencies to preserve their lives and property. A woman who has to come home late to a gang-infested housing project is bound to be safer with a pistol in her pocket, if only because she couldn't possibly be less safe.

Even if she never had to use her weapon, she would gain some peace of mind from knowing she could defend against predators. Likewise for lots of other people who have the bad luck to live or work in the many places where thugs abound.

A second reason is that such permit holders could eventually deter crime, as crooks begin to perceive a heightened risk in their profession. The presence of guns in the home is a major reason why the high-crime United States has a lower burglary rate than England, where guns are largely forbidden and intruders don't have to worry about death from Sudden Perforation Syndrome. For those who worry that America will come to resemble the Wild West, the Independence Institute says we should be so lucky: Homicide was almost unknown in Dodge City and other gun-heavy places.

The fallacy of the gun-control argument is that because guns are dangerous in the hands of people who are criminally inclined or mentally unstable, they are also dangerous in the hands of those who are law-abiding and sane. It may be the height of sanity to suppose that if our police can't protect us from criminals, we should insist on the right to protect ourselves.

Gun Ownership Does Not Increase Personal Safety

by Robin Arquette

About the author: *Robin Arquette, a freelance writer, focuses on women's issues.*

In 1991, I wrote an essay for this page called "I Want to Feel Safe Again," which explained why I had decided to carry a gun. I still believe that a woman stands a better chance of surviving an assault if she is armed. But my gun no longer travels with me wherever I go.

I bought the gun after Kate, my 18-year-old sister, was murdered. In 1989, she was driving home from a girlfriend's house around 10:30, when she was chased by another car and shot twice in the head.

Her murder remains unsolved. After her death, I began to feel afraid. I saw the world as a threatening place and felt that I would be naive to assume that bad things couldn't happen to me. So I bought a gun and learned how to use it.

Next I got a concealed weapons permit and started carrying the gun in my purse. It made me feel in control again. I believed I was acknowledging the reality of a dangerous world and was prepared to defend myself if evil came my way.

Paranoia Ensues

It wasn't long, though, until that feeling began to fade. Instead of comforting me, the gun served as a constant reminder of what a frightening place the world could be. I became hypervigilant, always checking my surroundings and rummaging around in my purse to make sure I could find my gun if I had to. I lived in a constant state of red alert, suspicious and anxious all the time.

Gone was life's joy and wonder, yet I still wasn't ready to give up my protection . . . at least not until the accident. As I was hurrying out the front door, I realized I had forgotten to perform my morning ritual: Before putting my semiautomatic in my purse, I'd empty the bullet from the chamber and put the safety on so it would be safe to carry.

Reprinted from Robin Arquette, "Why I've Stopped Carrying a Gun," *Woman's Day*, April 27, 1997, by permission of the author.

That day, when I pulled back the slide to unload the bullet, my fingers slipped and the gun fired. It sounded like a cannon had gone off in my living room. My ears rang and a pungent cloud of burnt gunpowder stung my eyes. Imagining the worst, I froze. What if the bullet had passed through the wall and hit a child waiting for a school bus? I would never be able to forgive myself.

Trembling, I scrambled around mumbling, "please, no, please, no," as I searched for the spent bullet. I prayed not to hear the scream of an ambulance or the wail of a grief-stricken mother discovering her injured child.

> *"Instead of comforting me, the gun served as a constant reminder of what a frightening place the world could be."*

Finally, I found the bullet, a mangled wad of lead, lying on the floor. I cried with relief.

The accident happened so quickly, a single moment in which I could have shot myself or somebody else. I began to wonder if by protecting myself I was actually putting other people's lives at risk.

Another Hindrance

As frightening as that experience was, I still might not have given up carrying the gun if there hadn't been so many other aggravations.

I was surprised to discover, for instance, that although I owned a concealed weapons permit, not everybody honored it. Rules against firearms were enforced at my workplace, the airport, government buildings, school grounds and television stations.

I learned that every state had its own gun regulations. If I wanted to take my gun along on an interstate car trip, I might end up breaking the law in another state.

Serious Considerations

Children were also a great concern. When my sister, Kerry, and her three children visited my husband and me, she became fearful and anxious and insisted I unload the gun and lock it away. Her worry was justified. After all, kids have an amazing knack for finding and playing with guns no matter how much you warn them.

Overall, it seemed like there were more places I couldn't make use of the gun than I could. So for now I've decided to compromise: I don't take the gun out anymore; it stays home next to my bed. Still, sometimes when I'm walking through a deserted parking garage or driving alone at night, I think about my gun and hope to God I haven't made the wrong decision.

Guns in the House Endanger Innocent Lives

by Jane E. Brody

About the author: *Jane Brody is a nationally syndicated columnist who writes about personal health issues.*

In 1995, a young Las Vegas family was shattered by a 3-year-old girl who found her father's loaded revolver in a desk drawer. Thinking the gun was a toy, she aimed it at her pregnant mother, who was asleep on the sofa, and pulled the trigger. The mother died on her way to the hospital.

In 1997, a 13-year-old Brooklyn boy, whom a neighbor described as a good person who "always did the right thing," was shot and killed while he and his friends were playing with a gun.

In Montgomery, Ala., a 9-year-old boy accidentally shot his 7-year-old brother with a gun he had found in the glove compartment of the family car. The boy died, even though the incident occurred in a hospital parking lot, where the father had left the car and the boys while he ran an errand.

More Guns, More Accidents

These incidents are the tip of a growing iceberg of deaths related to guns in and around people's homes. Nearly half the households in the United States contain firearms and one-fourth have handguns. More than half a million guns are stolen from homes each year. Deaths caused by firearms, most of them handguns, number about 40,000 each year in the United States. More than 1,600 of them are accidents, and the number of nonfatal injuries caused by gun accidents is four to six times as high. Josh Sugarmann, executive director of the Violence Policy Center, a research organization in Washington, points out that "guns are the second most deadly consumer product, after cars, on the market," and that in some states the death rate related to firearms already exceeded that associated with motor vehicles. In an article in *Mother Jones* magazine in January 1994, Mr. Sugarmann noted, "Many consumer products, from lawn darts to the Dalkon Shield, have been banned in the United States, even though they claimed only a fraction of the lives guns do in a day."

Alarmed by the statistics and the many tragic incidents attended to by their members, a number of medical organizations have become staunch advocates of tighter gun regulations and safety precautions. The Emergency Nurses Association in Parkridge, Ill., which has begun a national parent education program called "Gun Safety, It's No Accident," wants all guns in homes stored unloaded and locked up in ways that prevent access by children and other unauthorized people. The Johns Hopkins School of Public Health has a Center for Gun Policy and Research that is pressing for personalization of handguns to prevent all but the authorized users from firing them. The American Academy of Pediatrics, noting the failure of lesser measures to control gun-related tragedies, has suggested amending the constitutional right of citizens to bear arms.

> *"Studies published in medical journals since 1990 have repeatedly documented the fact that guns are more likely to cause than prevent harm to innocent people."*

National polls have shown that about two-thirds of citizens support stricter gun-control laws, and a 1993 poll found that 52 percent of adults favored a Federal ban on ownership of handguns.

Risk vs. Protection

The Johns Hopkins Center, established in 1995 with financing from the Joyce Foundation of Chicago, has pointed out that "while personalized handguns will likely reduce the risks of some gun deaths, reliable studies still teach us that possessing a gun in the home is more perilous than protective." Studies published in medical journals since 1990 have repeatedly documented the fact that guns are more likely to cause than prevent harm to innocent people. The most recent such report, published last month in Archives of Internal Medicine, found that gunshot wounds were the single most common cause of death for women in the home, accounting for 42 percent of suicides and 46 percent of homicides. The researchers, who examined all suicides and murders in the homes of female victims in three metropolitan counties, concluded that the presence of a gun in the home increased their risk of being murdered and committing suicide. Although many people say they own a gun for self-protection, instead of for protecting family members, the gun is more likely to be used against them, most often in the heat of a domestic argument or jealous rage. According to a 1996 report in the journal *Pediatrics*, a publication of the academy, data from "several rigorously conducted studies indicate that home ownership of guns" increased the risk of homicide among teen-agers and young adults more than threefold and the risk of suicide more than tenfold. In these studies, guns were used in nearly three-fifths of the suicides and a third of the homicides that occurred in the victim's home. The availability of a gun greatly increases the likelihood that a suicide attempt will succeed. Since suicidal impulses are usually fleeting, many suicides involving a gun could be prevented if a less-lethal method were used. Nationwide, firearms—mostly handguns—are used in about 19,000 suicides each year. Among young people from 10 to 19, more than 1,400 suicides are committed with guns each year.

Caution Is Necessary

The belief of many gun advocates that teaching children how to use a gun properly will prevent accidents is belied by one West Coast surgeon's account. The surgeon left the operating room to tell a young couple that their little boy was dead, having accidentally shot himself while playing with his father's handgun. The boy's father, who said he was a member of the National Rifle Association, "became visibly angry, saying, 'I taught the dumb kid how to use it right.'"

The emergency nurses point out that 1.2 million children are likely to be left alone in homes with guns. They urge that children be taught, not how to use a gun, but never, ever, to play with one and that if they find a gun, to leave it alone and tell an adult about it. Parents should explain the difference between gun violence on television and in films and the real-life consequences of gun use.

People who have guns should always store them unloaded, separate from their ammunition, and secured with a gun lock, gun alarm or other

> *"Although many people say they own a gun for self-protection . . . the gun is more likely to be used against them."*

tamper-proof device that prevents unauthorized use or renders the gun inoperable. Trigger locks are not adequate protection. The weapon should be stored in a locked gun cabinet, safe or gun vault inaccessible to children. Forty percent of gun owners keep their guns in a bedroom or closet, where children and burglars can easily find them. Studies in several cities show that about 30 percent of families with children keep loaded guns in the home.

Even when parents are conscientious about gun safety, their neighbors, relatives and the parents of their friends may be less so. Parents would be wise to discuss gun safety with the adults in every household their children are likely to visit.

Gun Ownership Is Not Effective Self-Defense for Women

by Ann Jones

About the author: *Ann Jones is the author of* Women Who Kill *and* Next Time, She'll Be Dead: Battering and How to Stop It.

December 23, 1993. I open a copy of *USA Today* to the headline "Holiday Rush on Firearms." I read that "legions of Americans" are buying guns for Christmas, spurred by "a fear of crime and a dread of gun control." Afraid that passage of the Brady Bill is only the first step toward gun-control legislation that will leave them unarmed in a nation of gunslingers, the legions are giving gun dealers what one calls their best sales year in two decades. Santa Claus, on the other hand, is having a hard time. On the same day, the New York *Times* reports that Santa has been recalled from the malls of Denver because a mysterious letter writer threatens to blow "that Fatso" away. Christmas-spirited cops dress up in Santa suits, safely within the walls of police stations, and listen to the wish lists of kids who probably hope for Uzis of their own.

It's all there, in a single day's news, even during the season officially dedicated to peace on earth. Pick up any paper and read the daily dispatches from the domestic war zone. You'll find the record of violent acts that threaten everything we once thought precious or safe. And these days you'll find as well the stories of gun shoppers, male and female, who share the desperate conviction that only our own readiness to do violence can protect us from violence.

Random Violence Anxiety

Interviewed in *People,* President Bill Clinton says: "Nearly everybody who lives in any kind of an urban area today, and increasingly in medium-size and small towns, feels a significantly higher level of personal insecurity than they did a few years ago. They look over their shoulders more, they worry more about

Reprinted from Ann Jones, "Living with Guns, Playing with Fire," *Ms.*, May/June 1994, by permission of the author.

who they speak to on the street. There is a level of anxiety there that didn't exist, because nearly everybody knows somebody who has been victimized."

That anxiety about random violence currently inspires yet another crackdown on crime in the United States. Both Republicans and Democrats rant about law and order. They team up to throw good money after bad, opting to build "boot camps" and jails and still more prisons, though already, in the ones we have, we lock up more of our citizenry per capita than any other nation on earth. On television, in between violent entertainment programs, news programs examine our violent society, interviewing cops and convicts and drug pushers and teenage gang members and even children who are shooting and being shot at in unprecedented numbers. Health and Human Services Secretary Donna Shalala reports that if current trends continue, gunshots will replace car crashes as the leading cause of death by injury in the U.S. by the year 2003. "Among young adults ages 25 to 34," she says, "the crossover has [already] occurred on a nationwide basis." And "Americans," as the president says, "look over their shoulders."

> *"The crime that poses the greatest danger to women [is] rape and/or assault by a current or former boyfriend or husband."*

What About Domestic Violence?

Missing from this national debate on crime is any mention of the crime that poses the greatest danger to women: rape and/or assault by a current or former boyfriend or husband. Battering is now the single leading cause of injury to U.S. women between the ages of 15 and 44, sending more than a million women every year to doctors' offices or emergency rooms for treatment. It drives women into the streets, too: 50 percent of homeless women and kids across the U.S. are fleeing from male violence. It figures in one quarter of all suicide attempts by women and in one half of all suicide attempts by African American women. It also accounts for untold damage to fetuses in utero; 25 to 30 percent of pregnant women are battered, according to the National Coalition Against Domestic Violence. And every day in the U.S. four women are murdered by men who say they love them.

Generally, battering does not count as "crime." As recently as 1991, only 17 states recorded incidents of male violence against women in the home, and most confined reporting to "serious" bodily injury, rape, and murder. Officially, battering does not even count as "violence." In the "family violence" establishment, academics (mostly male) have applied innocuous labels such as "spouse abuse" or "partner abuse" to obscure both the severity of violent acts performed at home and the gender of the perpetrators. What we've learned to call "domestic violence" has come to seem but a pale imitation of the real thing. This is hardly what we expected when in 1970 feminists began one of the most dramatic social reform efforts in the nation's history: we brought the issue of battering out of the private home and into public consciousness. Yet in just two decades, male violence has been so thoroughly "domesticated" once again that even some feminists say they've had enough of cringing victims. They want to talk about *power.*

Gun Lobby Tactics

Enter the National Rifle Association (NRA). With deficits deepening, membership declining, and no pal in the White House, the NRA spent almost $29 million in 1992 but couldn't shoot down the Brady Bill. Undoubtedly depressed at the result, the NRA turns for comfort—where else?—to women. It finds feminist leaders preoccupied with an in-house argument—Are we *for* victims or *against* them?—and cleverly launches an appeal to both sides. Always adept at marketing, the NRA taps into the sentiments of those women who extol women's power and reject what they call "victim feminism." At the same time, it plays to the real terror of millions of U.S. women who are still victimized by men who are their partners or lovers. "Refuse To Be a Victim," the NRA says glibly, couching its ad campaign in the feminist language of choice, cynically co-opted from the campaign for reproductive rights. Appealing at once to women's empowerment and to women's fear, the NRA's ad campaign could not be more timely or better planned.

"As individual ownership of guns increasingly menaces public health and safety, more and more women take a stand against 'macho' myths and for the general welfare."

Don't think for a minute they have our best interests at heart. During campaigns in several states for legislation authorizing police to confiscate guns from men who assault women or violate restraining orders, the NRA said *nothing.* We're simply warm bodies in the great untapped female market for armaments. No one knows for sure how many women own guns; estimates range from 11 percent to the NRA's 17 percent, but everyone agrees that relatively few of the 211 million firearms in this country belong to women.

Susceptible Victims?

Like teenagers seduced by cigarette advertisers, or African Americans targeted with booze billboards, women too are a "special" market. We too have a pocket to be picked. Which is why women today face the question: to buy or not to buy a gun? It's a dilemma. And troublesome. It leaves women torn. Your mind says one thing, your gut another. Your beliefs and your instincts may not match up at all.

We're supposed to be society's peacemakers, or so tradition and conditioning tell us. And most U.S. women do consistently favor gun control. While many male lawmakers knuckle under year after year to the NRA lobby, prominent women, both in and out of Congress, stand up to them and help to redefine the issue. The final vote on the Brady Bill makes the gender gap plain: in the House, 51 percent of men voted for passage, while 81 percent of women were for the bill; in the Senate, it was 60 percent of men, 100 percent of women.

The "right to bear arms" (so dear to the NRA) is, after all, not an individual right but a collective right, for the purpose of maintaining a state militia. And as individual ownership of guns increasingly menaces public health and safety, more and more women take a stand against "macho" myths and for the general welfare, which is what the men who wrote the Second Amendment had in mind in the first place. Surgeon General Joycelyn Elders labels gun violence "one of the leading public health issues in America," implying that guns, like any other product that potentially threatens public health—cigarettes, for example, or food additives—should be subject to strict regulation and taxation. Hillary Rodham Clinton says she thinks a campaign to tax guns and ammunition as health hazards—the proceeds to go to health care reform—is a good idea. And Representative Nita Lowey (D.-N.Y.) attacks the NRA head-on.

Reactions to an Incident

But then there's Lorena Bobbitt. Although she armed herself with a plain kitchen knife rather than a gun, her dramatic refusal to be a victim anymore produced one of those metaphoric moments when the dark side of gender relations suddenly lies exposed. The same male commentators who matter-of-factly report rape, torture, and genocide in Bosnia launched the full ballistic vocabulary to describe Lorena Bobbitt's act: ghastly, unforgivable, unthinkable. Yet women could think it, and worse, laugh. Lorena Bobbitt's crime was that she made it look so easy—a stroke of a sharp knife.

I mention this because the widespread understanding among women of Lorena Bobbitt's act, even as one feminist spokesperson after another publicly condemned it, reveals a certain off-the-record vein of vengefulness, a mother lode of anger, a vast buildup of unrequited insults and injuries. Mostly we pretend it's not there. We're ladylike and polite. But there it is, welling up from time to time when you least expect it. Women exchange high fives in the street when Lorena Bobbitt is acquitted. Women cheer in the movie theater when Louise pulls the trigger

> *"The threat of violence, if it makes you play by its rules, is just as deadly to the spirit as violence itself."*

on that scumbag wanna-be rapist in the parking lot. It's like living on an emotional fault line; we go along calmly and then one day, boom, some little incident sets us quaking with laughter that smacks of sweet revenge.

This behavior disturbs men, who do their best to make women in general and feminists in particular disavow it. Some men say we hate them. Some men say—

get this!—that we condone violence against them. But some men try to sell us guns. "Refuse To Be a Victim," they say—though only on their terms and with their products. All the while male violence against women continues unabated.

> *"Having a gun in your home makes it three times as likely that someone will be killed there."*

A battering every 15 seconds, a rape every 46 seconds, a femicide every two hours. Women don't choose to be victims, but these days there's no end of opportunities in that line.

Women are fearful, yes. With good reason. But we're also beyond fear. We're fed up. That's what the cheering is about, and the high fives, and the laughter. Sweet revenge. Women's interest in guns—such as it is—isn't just about fear. It's about fighting back.

A Personal Example

I know something about fighting back myself—and about the consolations of a gun. In 1969 I took a job teaching at an African American college in the South, a job some local white citizens thought unsuitable for a white woman. They encouraged me to go back home. They drove down my street at all hours, shouting and waving a Confederate flag. They beat my dog nearly to death. They fired buckshot at my house. A black friend of mine, a former marine, gave me a handgun, a .38 special, and he and I made conspicuous trips to the public shooting range for target practice.

After that, the racists left me alone. But they left me diminished, too. I'd grown up with guns and knew how to handle them, but for complicated reasons—personal and political—I'd promised myself not to use them anymore. Then, in the face of the white citizens' welcome, my principles had simply vanished.

As a kid, I'd hunted with my dad from the time I was big enough to fire a shotgun without being flattened by the recoil. It was a great pleasure during those growing-up years, walking the damp brown autumn woods and cornfields of northern Wisconsin with a .20 gauge under my arm, watching for the sudden thunder of partridge or pheasant on the rise. But at 18 I shot my first deer, and as I watched it die in the snow, the deadly and irrevocable consequence of what I was doing came home to me. I couldn't stop weeping. (Yes, I know, "just like a girl.") I never went hunting again, but because the shotgun had been a gift from my father, I kept it.

Lessons Learned

Many years later, on April 4, 1968, Martin Luther King, Jr., was gunned down in Memphis. I borrowed a canoe, paddled to the middle of a lake near my home, and dropped my old shotgun over the side. It was a ridiculous gesture, I suppose, impelled by grief and fury at the slaughter of Dr. King and the collective dream he had inspired. But I wanted to rid the world of guns and all the violence and death they seemed to represent; at least I could get rid of mine. The nonviolent path of Dr. King would be my own. Only a year later, I went South and lost my resolution to a bunch of hopped-up racists waving a Confederate flag.

A long time after that, life gave me a second chance, and I failed again. While I was investigating a murder for one of my books, a man whispered death threats into my answering machine. Similar threats, cut and pasted together from newspapers, arrived unstamped in the mailbox, apparently delivered by hand. Someone broke into the house when I was away and, as a calling card, left all the doors and windows open wide. I searched through my things for that old .38 special, loaded it, and kept it on my desk while I wrote. At night I put it under my pillow. When I left the house, I took it along to have it handy when I came home again and searched every corner, every closet, every cubbyhole before sitting down once more at my desk. For six months, that gun made it possible for me to go through the motions of life and to go on working. But this time I understood the lesson I'd only half-learned in that southern town: the threat of violence, if it makes you play by its rules, is just as deadly to the spirit as violence itself. It wasn't a gun I needed. It was courage.

What Fear Can Do

Now when I read of women buying guns to gain a sense of power and control it makes me sad, for I imagine them afflicted with the same incapacitating fear and the same profound anger at being made to feel afraid. I think of all the survivors of battering and stalking and attempted murder I've talked to over the years. And some I never had a chance to meet, women like April LaSalata. In February 1988, her ex-husband, Anthony, broke into her home on Long Island, New York, armed with a sawed-off rifle and a knife, and stabbed her several times in the chest. She survived, and he was charged with attempted murder— then released on $25,000 bail. The county prosecutor begged the judge to increase the bail and hold LaSalata in jail. Request denied. April LaSalata applied for a permit to carry a gun to protect herself. Permit denied. In January 1989, Anthony waited for April to return from work, then shot her twice in the head on her own doorstep. She was 34.

If April LaSalata had been granted that gun permit, could she have saved herself? Maybe so. Maybe not.

Guns Require Responsibility

As a practical matter, leaving the human drama aside and looking at the studies and the numbers, it doesn't make much sense to own a gun. Having a gun in your home makes it three times as likely that someone will be killed there. And that someone may be you or your child. With children in the house, the only way to keep a gun safely is to break it down, hide it, and hide the bullets elsewhere—and in that condition it's of no use in an emergency. On the other hand, having a gun at the ready endangers children who may play with it or use it as a weapon. Between 1979 and 1991, nearly 50,000 children under the age of 20 were killed, by accident or design, with firearms, reports the Children's Defense Fund. Having a gun at the ready may also be fatal for you, if you're on the losing end of a struggle with an intruder. But a woman is much less likely to be attacked by an intruder or by a stranger in a public area than by the man she lives with. Bring a gun into the house, and he might use it on you. Any family member might use it to attempt suicide; unlike sleeping pills, a gun is a virtually faultless suicide weapon, offering no second chance. About 48 percent of deaths caused by firearms are suicides.

But suppose you actually manage to use your gun to wound or kill an attacker in self-defense. If you've shot an unknown intruder with a legally licensed gun, you may or may not have to stand trial. But if you've shot the man you live with, or used to live with, your troubles have only just begun. I've spent too much time in too

> *"When we took up the fight for women's rights, the right to bear arms was not what we had in mind."*

many prisons talking to too many women who say they killed batterers in self-defense, and who are now locked up for 15 or 20 years or life without parole, to think that "justifiable" homicide is easily justified when a woman pulls the trigger on a man. Consider the anguish these women go through, and their terrible loss of freedom. Still, it's better than being dead.

Empowering Without Guns

But if we want to talk about power, and having it, and using it for the safety and protection and greater empowerment of women, should we be talking about guns at all? I remember a conversation years ago with a group of women in an Indiana prison. Each had killed a husband or boyfriend and was serving a long sentence. One said, "When I get out of here, I'll never have a gun around the house again." Said another: "If I ever get out of here, I'll never have a man around the house," tracing her problem to its source.

How do we arm women with awareness and the courage to live free of violence? And more to the point, how do we stop violent men? That's not a job to be done piecemeal by lone women, armed with pearl-handled pistols, picking off batterers and rapists one by one. It's a job for the collective power of women and men.

It should never have to be up to the April LaSalatas of the world to arm themselves and shoot it out with men who are trying to kill them. The law could have saved April, and should have, and would have, if women mattered. Men continue to rape and batter and assault and kill—in a word, to victimize—women. But if those women don't matter in our society, then why should women matter to the courts or the cops or all those congressmen so diligently building prisons to lock up everybody but batterers?

Troubling Cultural Obstacles

I'm all for empowering victims, and after the relentless crime wave that men have waged undeterred against women all these years—even, and especially, in the so-called safety of home—I'd sure like to see us get our own back. Still, I think it's fair to say that when we took up the fight for women's rights, the right to bear arms was not what we had in mind. We imagined a just country in which cops and courts would defend, if need be, a woman's constitutional right to be free from bodily harm. We imagined an egalitarian world where people of all races and backgrounds and ages and both sexes could live together in harmony and cooperation, a world where classes and gender conflict would disappear, where there would be no cause for warfare and violence. Idealistic? Yes. But it seemed to me, and still does, the only kind of world worth struggling for.

Instead we live now in a country where every two minutes somebody gets shot. Where every 14 minutes somebody dies from a gunshot wound. Where every 2 hours a child is killed by someone with a gun. We live in a country where in 1991 guns killed 38,317 people. Where every day four men track down and kill the women they claim to love. A world where popular, state-of-the-art, so-called feminist Naomi Wolf cites pistol-packin mamas in NRA publications as splendid examples of "pioneer feminism."

Maybe I'd be safer if I bought another handgun and practiced up. Maybe I'd be safer still with an Uzi. But safer for what? That's not the world I want to live in. Remember that old peace slogan from the days of war in Vietnam: "Someday they'll give a war and nobody will come." I'm still working on that. And in the meantime, if you want to pack a piece in the gunslinger society, please don't mistake your hardware for power.

Chapter 5

What Measures Would Reduce Gun Violence?

Ways to Reduce Gun Violence: An Overview

by Michael D'Antonio

About the author: *Michael D'Antonio is a Pulitzer Prize–winning journalist who writes frequently about social issues.*

A gunman shoots up a post office in New Jersey. Another attacks a restaurant in Texas. A rash of car-jackings strikes Georgia. Any rational person would be alarmed by these horrible crimes against innocent people. And we are. National polls consistently show that violent crime is one of America's greatest concerns.

But we don't need polls to tell us this. We know it when we stop at a crowded intersection and suddenly get the urge to lock the doors. We feel it when bloody images from the nightly news fill our minds.

We are right to feel afraid. When a sniper shoots a diner sitting near a restaurant window, or when a woman is abducted outside a supermarket, we all know we could have been the victim. Schools, shopping malls, offices, and even our cars are no longer safe spaces.

But although we feel threatened, we are not paralyzed by fear. Restoring safety to public spaces has become a national cause. Smart, passionate people are standing up to the tide of violence. And in many cases women lead the crusade.

"The public is fed up with violence and is saying that enough is enough," says sociologist Amitai Etzioni, Ph.D., director of the Center for Communication Policy Studies in Washington, D.C. "There is no American who has not been touched—in some way—by violence. We are now seeing a number of concrete responses to this problem. Creative solutions are being tried all over. We have reason to be optimistic."

The experts on safety, violence, and community affairs that *Redbook* consulted suggested ten ways that America can stop violence and increase peace. Many have already met with success.

Community Policing

Already under way in many cities, community policing gets police officers out of patrol cars and onto street beats, where they can see and build relationships

Reprinted from Michael D'Antonio, "How You (Yes, You!) Can Stop Violence in Your Town," *Redbook*, February 1996, by permission of the author.

with the people they serve. Some community policing plans involve opening substations in neighborhoods and establishing citizen advisory committees for every precinct. Community policing has worked in many cities and towns. The Los Angeles Police Department says almost all crime figures are down, thanks in part to its citywide community policing program. Crime has also decreased in parts of Chicago, where officers hold open forums every month, where they work with citizens to set patrol priorities and find ways to prevent violence. Community policing is considered so effective that Congress has set aside $8.8 billion to fund programs nationwide. . . .

> *"There is no American who has not been touched—in some way—by violence."*

Bullet Control

Most Americans favor more restrictions on guns—but experts on all sides agree that strict gun control is politically unfeasible because of the lobbying power of the National Rifle Association and other anti-gun control groups. Even if we could control the sale of new guns, enough guns already exist to last us a century. Noting these roadblocks, Senator Daniel Patrick Moynihan of New York, a Democrat, suggests an ingenious alternative: heavy taxes and controls on the purchase of bullets.

Though Congress has yet to approve Moynihan's idea, some cities and towns already try to regulate ammunition. In California, specifically in Pasadena, Santa Monica, and Los Angeles, those purchasing ammunition must fill out registration cards and provide proof of their age. These programs have been in effect since 1995, and it's too early to tell if they are helping. However, bullet regulation has already proved an effective way to bypass the stalemated debate over guns. . . .

Rehabilitating Criminals

Get-tough policies for prisoners have gained political favor—as the return of chain gangs in the South shows—but society may actually be better off with a more positive approach. Wardens who have made prisons cleaner, expanded education programs, and reduced inmate stress have actually cut costs, reduced violence, and decreased recidivism. This approach has been successful at the federal Correctional Institution McKean County in Bradford, Pennsylvania, and has been adopted by the Corrections Corporation of America, which operates prisons under government contracts.

Perhaps the most unusual method for curbing inmates' violent tendencies is to teach them transcendental meditation and related stress-reduction techniques such as meditation and yoga. The argument for this approach is outlined in *Crime Vaccine* by J.B. Marcus, an Iowa attorney, who has written extensively on crime prevention. Meditation techniques had some success in California, Michigan, Massachusetts, Minnesota, and Vermont. . . .

Safe Corridors

In many urban neighborhoods adults take to the streets every morning and afternoon to guarantee safe passage for children walking to and from school. In North Philadelphia, for example, where churches organized one such effort, street crime has decreased substantially, and children, adults, and older persons now find the sidewalks much safer. . . .

Harlem educator Geoffrey Canada takes the concept one step further in his recent book, *Fist Stick Knife Gun.* He proposes a peace officer corps of neighborhood residents trained in conflict resolution to help avert violent confrontations.

The idea behind both this and the safe corridor plan is simple and can be applied anywhere: The watchful eyes and ears of residents are a neighborhood's best defense. A neighborhood that's alert, proactive, and works closely with local police is simply too much trouble for the bad guys.

Defensible Spaces

This kind of planned community features cul-de-sacs and short streets that may end in tiny parks and play areas, and houses with expansive front porches set on quiet streets. All these design elements can make a neighborhood safer because they increase contact among neighbors and make it difficult for dangerous outsiders to get in and out.

> *"Most experts . . . acknowledge the connection between the mayhem portrayed in the media and real-life violence."*

One of the most effective uses of defensible space can be seen in Five Oaks, a neighborhood in Dayton, that has turned more than 35 streets into dead ends and cul-de-sacs. According to a study of Five Oaks, the design scheme made the neighborhood quieter and less subject to heavy traffic, and helped cut violent crime in half. The defensible space concept, developed by architect and city planner Oscar Newman, is being implemented or considered in cities and towns around the country. . . .

Blocking Out TV Violence

Most experts and many in the media business acknowledge the connection between the mayhem portrayed in the media and real-life violence. Thousands of violent TV and film images can desensitize viewers, especially young ones, to the realities of violence. It's not a matter of direct cause and effect but, rather, influence. One University of Washington researcher says television violence plays a role in about half of all murders in America.

A device called the V-chip would allow parents to program a television set to lock out those programs that feature violence. Congress has already proposed ordering TV manufacturers to make the chip available in new sets, but some TV network executives have vowed to fight it as a form of censorship. For the chip to work, broadcasters would have to code their programs, a process that would lead to obvious conflicts over how programs might be rated.

Meanwhile, parents have two other choices (short of banning TV) that they can act on today. The Kid Control remote from TCI is shaped like a dinosaur or puppy and has buttons for only kid-friendly channels like PBS, the Disney Channel, and the Discovery Channel. . . . And Primestar, a digital minidish satellite system, lets parents lock out certain channels and movies with particular ratings. . . .

Conflict Resolution

Called peace education, conflict resolution, or peer mediation, antiviolence training is being tried in schools across the country. Experts in crime and violence, noting that young people commit the vast majority of violent crimes, hope the peacemaking skills learned in school will calm the impulses that lead to violence on the street. In Baltimore a public school program developed by researchers at Johns Hopkins University has cut the level of violence among students in half.

"Conflict-resolution programs in schools work best when they are followed up by adults in the community getting involved in the kids' lives," says Laura Ross Greiner, assistant director of the Center for the Study and Prevention of Violence at the University of Colorado. This kind of follow-up can be as simple as the example set by a woman in Los Angeles, Alice Harris. She noticed that teenage boys had no recreation programs and too much time on their hands. She installed a basketball hoop on her garage and invited them to play. Soon she was offering milk, cookies, and motherly advice. She has since helped several youngsters go on to college and has widened her effort to include other neighborhood parents.

Safer Guns

Gun manufacturers are the largest producers of hazardous consumer products exempt from government regulation. The American Bar Association has suggested empowering the Consumer Product Safety Commission to help gun makers redesign weapons to make them safer to operate.

Locks, safety switches, and other devices would make it much more difficult for young people to commit either accidental or intentional shootings. Readily available guns that are too easy to use represent a very real hazard. One study in Oklahoma found that 93 percent of accidental shoot-

> *"Experts in crime and violence . . . hope the peacemaking skills learned in school will calm the impulses that lead to violence on the street."*

ings by minors occurred when children were left unsupervised. The U.S. General Accounting Office has estimated that one-third of all accidental shootings could be prevented by installing simple safety devices on guns. . . .

Public Awareness Campaigns

In Boston and Los Angeles, as well as many other cities, billboards and TV spots aim to make violence socially unacceptable. Many national organizations, including the National Crime Prevention Council, the American Academy of Pediatrics, and the American Medical Association, are conducting antiviolence publicity campaigns. The aim is to show adults and kids what they can do to make their communities safer, and spur them to action. In the Boston area a series of billboards showing children's faces implores people to end violence. Television networks use top stars to remind viewers that smart people walk away from dangerous situations. Saatchi & Saatchi advertising agency has donated its services to produce a series of highly dramatic antiviolence commercials to air as a public service.

> *"Locks, safety switches, and other devices would make it much more difficult for young people to commit either accidental or intentional shootings."*

Although the effect of public relations efforts is difficult to measure, participants in a concerted antiviolence campaign in Los Angeles believe these efforts have contributed to the recent decrease in murders in that city. . . . The Center to Prevent Handgun Violence . . . also develops and implements antiviolence education programs.

Citizen Action Groups

In scores of communities, individuals and newly formed groups hold rallies, conduct vigils, march through neighborhoods, and pressure politicians, all to stop violence. These organizations, often led by concerned mothers and survivors of violence, offer support to families struck by crime and work with authorities to make neighborhoods safer. In Charleston, Massachusetts, an antiviolence campaign led by local mothers convinced government authorities to crack down on violent crime. In Los Angeles Lorna Hawkins, 43, a woman who has lost two sons to street violence, has taken her grief to the airwaves with an antiviolence program called *Drive-By Agony*.

Experts are not surprised to discover brave women leading the effort against violence. Women often take a stand where men fear to tread. "Mothers still have a symbolic power that is effective," says Deborah Prothrow-Stith, M.D., a professor of public health practice at Harvard University School of Public Health. "Mothers are often able to move police and officials to take action, and when they speak out, the media pays attention too."

Two national organizations [Save Our Sons and Daughters and Parents of Murdered Children] have been formed to help survivors of violence work in their own communities. . . .

No one proposal or program guarantees a safe society. But taken together, these ideas and initiatives reflect a groundswell of concern and action against violence, explains Laura Ross Greiner. "We have noticed a greater awareness of the violence issue in part because people feel they are directly threatened," she says. "And when people feel threatened, they become more active, creative, and innovative."

At a national conference on violence prevention—the first ever—hundreds of experts and community leaders shared ideas for a broad-scale peace campaign. Susan B. Sorenson, Ph.D, an associate professor in violence prevention at UCLA, attended the conference and was impressed by the depth of public concern about this problem.

"Random, unpredictable acts may be something we have to tolerate in society," says Dr. Sorenson. "But in general people are saying they want to prevent the kinds of violence that are more common." Dr. Sorenson expects that ordinary citizens will lead the way to a safer society by creating constructive outlets for their outrage, in the way the famed Mothers Against Drunk Driving helped citizens combat another deadly scourge. "The good news is, those kinds of organizations are coming, because we are really ready for it," adds Dr. Sorenson. "I think we can be optimistic about it."

Spiritual Involvement Would Reduce Gun Violence

by Caleb Rosado

About the author: *Caleb Rosado is a sociology professor at Humboldt State University in Arcata, California.*

"I'm the big man. I got the gun. Why does she have this attitude?"

This was the way a 16-year-old explained killing a mother of three. While Christine Schweiger's 10-year-old daughter watched in horror, two teenagers ordered her to her knees outside a Popeye's Famous Fried Chicken restaurant in Milwaukee and demanded her money. When she said she didn't have any, one of the youths blew away most of her head with a 12-gauge, sawed-off shotgun.

Many years ago, Mao Zedong said that "power grows out of the barrel of a gun." Mao's maxim is true today in America. For many people, especially young African-American and Latino males in this nation's urban communities, their only source of power and self-esteem comes from a gun. But while the power Mao referred to was political, the violent abuse of power that society is currently plagued with is "driven more by greed." So suggests Jesse Jackson: Today's youth, he reminds us, are "not shooting for food and clothes. They're shooting for territory, conquest, gold, diamonds, cars."

In other words, the violence we witness is *power with an attitude*, as reflected in the reasoning of the teen who killed Christine Schweiger. It is power that blames the victim for not cooperating with its evil intentions. It justifies itself with a cold, conscienceless attitude that believes its victims deserved what they got. It is like the adulteress of Proverbs 30:20, who "eats, and wipes her mouth, and says, 'I have done no wrong.'"

Why is human life regarded in certain sectors of society as having such little value that, on a whim—without provocation—one human being will blow away another, with no remorse whatsoever? Whether the incident is the Rodney King

Reprinted from Caleb Rosado, "America the Brutal," *Christianity Today*, August 15, 1994, by permission of the author.

and Reginald Denny beatings, or the Polly Klaas kidnapping-murder, or the Menendez brothers slaying their parents, the pattern is the same—violence without remorse, power with an attitude, an attitude that says, "You don't deserve to live."

How did we get to such a state of madness, and is there any way to achieve sanity?

We need to understand that violence does not occur in a social vacuum. Our values channel, shape, encourage, or discourage violent behavior.

Neither is the violence epidemic one-dimensional. The causal factors are historical, sociological, economical, political, psychological, theological, and spiritual. Let me suggest several reasons from these varied disciplines, each of which would not by itself be a sufficient explanation. Collectively, however, they provide a formidable argument for why we are in the present amoral morass of violence.

> *"We need to understand that violence does not occur in a social vacuum. Our values channel, shape, encourage, or discourage violent behavior."*

The Land of Cowboys

In American society, violence is, first, *a cultural-historical value*. The potential for violence was established from the foundations of our nation, with the Second Amendment to the Constitution in 1791: "A well-regulated militia, being necessary to the security of a free State, the right of the people to keep and bear arms, shall not be infringed." Today, even though the military use of privately owned arms has long disappeared, owning and displaying guns remains a fundamental right in American society.

Later, in the expansion of the nation at the expense of the native population, guns became the means by which the ill-devised Manifest Destiny of land appropriation was achieved. Two guns especially played a key role. The first was the Colt Revolver, patented in 1836 by Samuel Colt. Euphemistically labeled the "Peacemaker," it was better known as "the gun that won the West." The second was the Gatling Gun, a mechanically operated machine gun patented in 1862. Because the gun was capable of firing 350 rounds a minute through its rotating multiple barrels, it was believed to be the gun to end all wars. It did the opposite; it escalated violence.

Both weapons were part of a frontier mentality in American history. This mindset, combined with the ideology of rugged individualism, gave rise to the image of the American cowboy as the independent, "I-go-where-I-want-to-go, do-what-I-want-to-do" fellow, popularized in Hollywood Westerns, which, interestingly, have made a comeback in the nineties.

In our time, gun violence is an almost uniquely American problem, placing the U.S. in a league of its own. In 1990, handguns killed only 22 people in

Great Britain, 68 in Canada, and 87 in Japan; in the U.S., 10,567.

Today's heavily armed "urban cowboys," roaming the streets at night in their multi-*horse*-powered vehicles, are a re-emergence of the nineteenth-century outlaws who terrorized towns such as Tombstone, Deadwood, Dodge City, and Abilene. Nighttime has become our new frontier. Many of the characteristics of the old land frontier—sparse population, isolated settlements, individualism, boredom, acceptance of deviance, nearly everyone carrying a gun, lawlessness, and violence—are visible in the time frontier of night.

Entertainment Value

Second, in American society, *violence is an integral part of the social fabric of the entertainment industry.* James M. Henslin poignantly observes:

> It may seem bizarre to members of other cultures, but murder is a major form of entertainment in American society. Night after night we watch shootings, strangulations, stabbings, slashings, beatings, bombings, and various other forms of mutilation and mayhem flashing across our television screens—all in living color.

Rap music, music videos, video games, and movies, especially the slasher movies targeted at a teenage audience, are all part of the booming multibillion-dollar entertainment industry. Together they have become a modern Pied Piper, luring our children and robbing them of their childhood through fear and violence, from which many never return. Sadly, entertainment is the number-one prod-

> *"In our time, gun violence is an almost uniquely American problem, placing the U.S. in a league of its own."*

uct the U.S. exports to the rest of the world. That raises the question, will the violence that dominates American culture soon dominate other countries, as they drink from the "broken cisterns" of selected American values?

Deviant Individualism

Third, violence in American society is *a byproduct of disconnectedness.* Emile Durkheim, the pioneering sociologist, suggested that violence is a product of people's disconnections from others and from their moral community, in large measure due to the upheaval brought on by rapid social change. Those who lack social bonds are more likely to commit violent acts.

Because of adverse conditions, many people today find themselves alone— economically, emotionally, socially, and spiritually. Thus, what armed youth gangs, serial killers, disgruntled postal employees, racist skinheads, and child killers have in common is this: they all experience a sense of disconnectedness from society.

Sociologists Roger Finke and Rodney Stark clarify this theory:

> The real basis of the moral order is human relationships. Most of us conform

to laws and social norms most of the time because to do otherwise would risk our relationships with others. When we are alone, even the most respectable of us act in ways we would not were anyone present. People who have no relationships with family or close friends, or whose relationships are with persons far away, are essentially alone all the time. They do not risk their attachments if they are detected in deviant behavior, because they have none to lose.

Opposition Culture

When people find themselves disconnected from the societal rewards of wealth, power, and prestige, due to layoffs, lack of job opportunity, or being locked out of the system for political reasons, a sense of frustration develops, which may erupt in violence. Sometimes this frustration may gain access to social rewards by alternative means. For example, since no one is going to get rich working for McDonald's at $4.25 an hour, why not sell crack for $500 a day? The drug economy thus becomes an "employment agency" for many people locked out of the system.

When people find themselves locked out of the structures and rewards of the larger society, they tend to construct their own group, even if this group is regarded as deviant by society. Why? Because when one feels rejected, one can in turn reject the rejecters and everything they stand for by forming a subculture with its own value system and code of conduct—"the code of the streets."

In a recent *Newsweek*, University of Pennsylvania sociologist Elijah Anderson called this the "oppositional culture" of the streets. "It is a culture with its own code of behavior, based on gangsta bravado and gangsta respect, and it is a powerful force in the inner city. It subverts the values of hope, work, love and civility, and it condones and romanticizes violence." Many of today's urban youth, especially nighttimers, live in a different world from the rest of us, the daytimers. These two worlds neither interact nor relate.

The Ramifications of Disrespect

Because of the cultural value that males should be the primary family breadwinners, males locked out of the system through joblessness and racism tend to experience the most social and psychological strain. This strain is manifested in a sense of powerlessness and inferiority. But since these traits are perceived in gang life as weaknesses, one has to "front" (do impression management) in order to convey the opposite. The result is an overriding concern with *respect*. When coupled

> *"Violence is a product of people's disconnections from others and from their moral community."*

with the psycho-cultural need to express a macho image, the slightest demonstration of disrespect can result in an instant display of violence. Because their fragile self-images are hanging by a thin thread of self-worth, males are the most involved in crime.

Saturday night—our most disconnected time of the week—is also "the most dangerous time of the week," according to Henslin. "During weekends," he says, "when murders are more frequent, people feel less constrained by schedules and responsibilities, and they are likely to get out in public and, not insignificantly, do more drinking than usual. This increases the likelihood of quarrels, with the peak coming on the traditional 'Saturday night out.'" Indeed, it is not coincidental that cheap handguns are called "Saturday-night specials."

> *"Immediate strategies [are] available to churches and individual Christians who are willing to invest themselves in addressing our nation's epidemic of violence."*

Fourth, violence in America is in part *the legacy of self-hatred.* The United States has a unique history as a nation of nations. Unfortunately, its diverse peoples have not always accepted one another. We have a long and violent history of rejecting the "stranger," especially the one who is seen as different by virtue of color or culture.

Throughout our history, there have been two ways of becoming an American: one for the cultural minorities, the other for the racial minorities. The former—the Irish, the Germans, the Italians, the Jews—had to assimilate and be accepted by discarding their ethnic identification and their culture. Painful though that process was, the invisible gates to the majority's world were then opened to them because they were white. For the second group, identified by racial stigma, the issue was more complex. Their distinctiveness was biological and, as a result, the shedding of culture made little difference. They have rarely been seen as "genuine" Americans, but only as hyphenated Americans: African-Americans, Asian-Americans, Hispanic-Americans, or Native Americans.

The social rejection of persons of color can result in a legacy of self-hatred, a sense that life is meaningless, that a people is without value, worth, power, and hope. It should come as no surprise when this social trauma spills over into rage and violence in the streets. In his autobiography, *Makes Me Want to Holler,* Nathan McCall reminds us that the consequence of teaching people to hate themselves is violence to themselves. This violence is expressed in killing another person like oneself, because my brother is an extension of myself. The result is black-on-black violence. "If my life does not matter," McCall says, "your life does not matter either, since neither one of us has a future."

The Birth of Stereotypes

When Jesus said, "You shall love your neighbor as yourself," he gave us the inverse principle of how this happens. If I must use my self-regard as a yardstick to measure my response to my brother, then when I have no self-esteem, I have no standard to live by. And if all I feel for myself is hatred, then all I feel for you, as an extension of myself, is also hatred.

In view of all this, one can understand why young African-American, Asian-American, and Latino males are the most involved in violent crime—and why members of these groups turn on each other. Economically and politically blocked from societal rewards, and daily experiencing self-hatred and a lack of respect, they attack each other through a "horizontal violence."

This violence feeds the media, which, in turn, feed our stereotypes, which ultimately feed our fears and behaviors, even among us persons of color toward our own. Thus, Jesse Jackson himself admitted, in a 1993 speech decrying black-on-black violence: "There is nothing more painful to me at this stage in my life than to walk down the street and hear footsteps and start thinking about robbery—then look around and see somebody white and feel relieved." America is now collecting on a 400-year debt of violent dehumanization of persons of color.

An Absence of Godliness

Fifth, violence in American society reflects *a lack of the fear of God.* The carnage in our cities raises a crucial question: Where is God? Or, more precisely, where is the sense of the holiness and awesomeness of God to whom one must give account? The Bible calls this sense the "fear of God." It does not mean fear in our usual sense of being afraid. It means rather to quake or tremble in the presence of a Being so holy, so morally superior, so removed from evil, that in his presence, human boasting, human pride, human arrogance vanish as we bow in speechless humility, reverence, and adoration of the One beyond understanding.

For this reason, Proverbs declares, "The fear of the Lord is the beginning of wisdom." Any correct understanding of the human condition begins with a sense of the presence of God in human affairs. When the fear of God is missing, evil, corruption, and violence prevail. "Fools say in their hearts, 'There is no God.' They are corrupt, they do abominable deeds; there is no one who does good" (Ps. 14: 1).

If God is the source of life, then anything that unjustly takes life separates us from God. But the question is: Is the taking of life that which separates us from God, or is our separation from God that which makes it easy to take life?

Surely it is a reciprocal relationship, but the spark of that action lies in our separation from God. The psalmist says, "Transgression speaks to the wicked deep in their hearts" (36: 1). Why? "There is no fear of God before their eyes." Abraham

> *"Churches must . . . spend their energies educating their members about responsible gun ownership."*

went down to Egypt and feared for his life. He declared, "I thought, 'There is no fear of God at all in this place, and they will kill me'" (Gen. 20: 11).

Where God is not feared, life is cheap.

The church may very well be the most important institution to mediate change in our American cities. As *Sojourners* editor Jim Wallis observes, "The cruel and endemic economic injustice, soul-killing materialism, life-destroying drug traffic, pervasive racism, unprecedented breakdown of family life and structure, and almost total collapse of moral values that have created this culture of violence are, at heart, spiritual issues."

As the apostle Paul reminds us, "Our struggle is not against flesh and blood, but against . . . the spiritual forces of evil in the heavenly realm" (Eph. 6:12, NIV). Many Christians across the nation have recognized that our crisis is indeed a spiritual one and are responding with bold and innovative initiatives to deal with the problem head-on.

A coalition of seven Boston churches devised a ten-point plan for how churches can reach out to their inner-city neighborhoods. Their ambitious points of action are focused on building relationships and showing viable ways that the body of Christ can live out its call in urban communities. They include: commissioning missionaries to do pastoral work in the urban areas with the most violent and troubled young people; developing church teams to evangelize youth involved in gangs and drug trafficking; forming community-based economic-development programs; establishing ministry links between suburban and downtown churches. . . .

Sincere Strategies

In addition to the Boston coalition's plan, there are other, more immediate strategies available to churches and individual Christians who are willing to invest themselves in addressing our nation's epidemic of violence.

First, we can *support creative ways to deal with the proliferation of illegal firearms* in our communities—such as the "buy-back" programs that many major cities have recently implemented, offering gym shoes and sporting-event tickets in exchange for guns. Churches must also spend their energies educating their members about responsible gun ownership. "All who draw the sword will die by the sword," said Jesus (Matt. 26:52, NIV). His solemn warning was a call for nonviolence that speaks volumes to our present crisis.

Second, we can *fight for a more responsible entertainment industry* that will put human welfare above profit. We need to protest bad TV programming and film releases and support positive alternatives. The moneychangers in the temple of Mammon are just as amoral and callous as the young gunmen who kill on the streets. The only difference is that Hollywood investors do it through socially acceptable means. Both attitudes are just as murderous for their insensitivity.

Education Is Key

Third, *we can put our resources—both our money and energies—into jobs and education, not prisons.* For many young people today, crime is the only option available for gaining respectability. We can change that by giving them the option of obtaining a quality education. Comparing four-year costs for college to those for incarceration offers a jarring commentary. Four years at a public university costs on the average $23,892; at a private university, $59,644. But four years in a federal prison costs $80,288. If one can help prevent the other, simple math tells us which is the wise investment.

Swede Roskam, a Chicago Christian businessman, has made that investment. In 1983, Roskam founded Educational Assistance Limited (EAL), a nonprofit organization that provides financial assistance to aspiring college students in our nation's inner cities. EAL secures donations of excess inventory items like computers, furniture, and office supplies from major corporations, and then gives the items to colleges and universities in exchange for scholarship credits for needy youth. Since 1983, the program has helped 1,300 students receive their college degrees. Roskam's resourcefulness has given many kids an education beyond the "school of the streets."

Families Count

Fourth, *we can work to build positive attachments.* Families need to be strengthened. Support networks need to be developed in communities. We are all, in a sense, members of "gangs." Some groupings are positive, while others perpetrate destruction. We need to move people from deviant gangs to socially constructive ones. Churches and individual Christians can play a key role here, becoming "family" for the estranged and disconnected persons in our communities.

Consider Kathy Dudley, a wife and mother of two, who has courageously forged her dream for urban renewal with Voice of Hope Ministries (VOH) on Dallas's rough and impoverished West Side. Dudley's efforts provide West Dallas youth with weekly "Bible clubs," job training, and after-school activities. Since 1982, VOH has spawned more than a dozen college graduates. "Our presence has significantly curbed the amount of gang violence in this community," says Dudley. More visionary churches and individuals like Dudley are needed to give our urban young people a sense of belonging and purpose.

Valuing More than the Self

Fifth, *we must teach self-respect and an awareness of our value to God.* We need to encourage our children to reject rejection and not themselves. Audre Lorde, the African-American poet, tells us, "It is a waste of time hating a mirror or its reflection instead of stopping the hand that makes glass distortions." Black and Latino youth today are being deflated by social mirrors of self-hate and, as a result, are killing themselves. What they need is our help in "stopping the hand that makes glass with distortions." Ultimate self-respect comes when we recognize our value to God—that he created us in his own image and paid an awesome price for our redemption, thereby endowing the human soul with great value. Churches that embody and communicate this wisdom to the spiritually and economically disheartened people of our communities can save lives that otherwise would be erased by violence.

Finally, and most important, *we must restore to our communities a sense of awe toward God.* Martin Luther observed that the "natural" person cannot fear God, for the natural does not comprehend the spiritual. The fear of God is only experienced through the "spiritual" dimension. Unfortunately, this is often the least developed dimension in people's lives. This is why people are, in ever-increasing numbers, searching for some form of spirituality—an intangible reality that provides a sense of security and meaningful purpose. A renewed sense of God's awesomeness will supply the security and purpose our culture is seeking. Only by being assured of God's love for us do we learn to love ourselves. And only by being assured of God's love for all people do we learn to imitate his example (Matt. 5:44–48).

Respect the Past

Driving home from San Francisco one day, I pulled off Highway 101 to pay tribute at the informal memorial set up there in remembrance of Polly Klaas, the 12-year-old girl who was kidnapped from her home during a slumber party and later killed. It was a sobering experience, recalling her death at the hands of a heartless killer. Of all the kind words expressed there on cards, paper scraps, and wood, one moved me to the core. It simply read: "For a brief moment an angel rested here."

If Polly's life had been respected, if her abductor had seen the sacred in her, she would still be with us.

We, too, must learn to glimpse that unique image of God that dwells in every person. As we do, we can begin the process of rebuilding a society where differences can be valued and where children like Polly will be safe.

Controlling Gun Manufacturers Would Reduce Gun Violence

by William Greider

About the author: *William Greider, political editor for* Rolling Stone, *is the author of* One World, Ready or Not: The Manic Logic of Global Capitalism.

While talk shows and right-wing preachers obsess about the moral depravity of youth culture, the usual political adversaries line up for yet another long-running congressional struggle over various gun-control measures. The National Rifle Association knows that people are upset by the spectacle of gun-toting students and hopes to soften its image with Charlton Heston as its president.

Meanwhile, Handgun Control Inc., the leading advocacy group of reformers, unveils a grab bag of modest legislative ideas for reducing the bloodshed, such as mandatory trigger locks for handguns and criminal liability for careless parents who let their weapons turn small children into accidental killers.

HCI's various proposals sound reasonable enough (and might do some good on the margins), but the problem is, they are too reasonable. What's promised is another long and tedious slog through Washington's political labyrinth in search of very limited objectives. We did that already—with the "Brady Bill," which instituted a mandatory waiting period for the purchase of handguns, along with other incremental measures—while the random gun violence continues to proliferate new forms of pointless tragedy.

Different Actions

This time around, though Washington doesn't seem to get it yet, the outcome can be dramatically different. Public attitudes on the need for real action have shifted significantly, including among gun owners, and genuine progress is within reach. A new reform dynamic is under way on many different fronts, from public-health advocates to handgun manufacturers and the trial lawyers who are suing the companies on behalf of victims. For instance, Cease Fire Inc. (a national educational campaign launched by Jann S. Wenner, editor and publisher of *Rolling Stone*) broadcasts hard-hitting public-service announcements on television that warn parents that a handgun in their homes can be fatal to their children and their friends.

> *"What's required is serious safety regulation of this very dangerous product [guns]—the crucial first step toward drastically reducing its numbers."*

Together, these energies are going to refocus the debate on the nature of the guns themselves rather than on the behavior of people, whether kids or gun owners. What's required is serious safety regulation of this very dangerous product—the crucial first step toward drastically reducing its numbers.

What makes this breakthrough possible is a newly designed handgun that won't shoot if it's being held in the wrong hands—whether the shooter is a small child, or a depressed teenager attempting suicide, or even a felon who stole the weapon from someone's home. The technology exists. Working prototypes have already been developed. People should be able to buy them by the year 2000.

This innovation won't eliminate the gun problem by a long shot—an estimated 65 million pistols and revolvers are in the hands of American civilians. But it changes everything in the political debate and opens the way for real reform.

Smart in Various Ways

Colt's Manufacturing Co., the venerable firearms manufacturer in Connecticut, calls its version the Smart Gun. The company has been financially troubled but hopes to steal the lead on competitors while avoiding potential lawsuits and the rising public outrage aimed at firearms.

Gun-control advocates prefer to call the technology the "personalized" or "childproof" gun. They do not think this promising development should wait solely on the marketplace.

A reform organization called Ceasefire New Jersey is already pushing a bi-partisan bill in the legislature to require that all new handguns sold in the state be equipped with the owner-control technology. Bryan Miller, a former businessman who heads the group, predicts that once New Jersey acts, other states will swiftly follow. His brother Michael, an FBI agent, was killed in a crazed incident of random shooting back in 1994.

"Why am I so upbeat? That's just the way I am," Miller says. "But I also think our bill in New Jersey is going to happen, and we're going to save some lives and have measurable impact—a decline in accidental child deaths and a decline in teenage suicides. And that's going to make it easier to do the next thing.

"I believe this country is at the start of a major sea change in its attitudes about guns that will lead to gun-safety measures and will dramatically cut down gun deaths and injuries. It's going to take time, but it's going to happen. My opinion: Ten years from now, you won't be able to buy a handgun in this country that's not childproof. And we're going to lead the way in New Jersey."

After all the recent tragedies, does this sound too optimistic? I don't think so. The firearms industry is looking at the same confluence of political forces that Miller sees, and it is taking them very seriously. Gun makers also observe what happened to another industry that stonewalled public concern—tobacco. They are anxious to avoid a similar fate for guns.

The Childproof Gun

The outline for a childproof gun is actually 100 years old. Smith & Wesson used to manufacture a handgun with a safety lever on the grip that young children couldn't operate while simultaneously pulling the trigger. In this age of semiconductor chips and electronic locking codes, it ought to be easy enough to produce a more sophisticated version—a gun that fires only if the owner is personally pulling the trigger.

That's what Professor Stephen P. Teret, director of the Johns Hopkins Center for Gun Policy and Research, believes. Teret is a former trial lawyer who has spent nearly twenty years in public-health research—a scholar who studies public-safety questions with a supple sense of how reforms can be achieved on many fronts. The professor is motivated partly by the memory of friends whose twenty-two-month-old son, while in a caretaker's home, was shot in his crib by a four-year-old who happened to find a handgun in the night table.

> *"This country is at the start of a major sea change in its attitudes about guns that will lead to gun-safety measures."*

"That's just obscene," Teret says. "It's even more obscene because it didn't have to happen. There's no reason in the world why anyone should want to have a handgun that's operable by a four-year-old."

Success from Experiment and Accident

In 1992, Teret decided to stage a cheap experiment. The Injury Prevention Center at Johns Hopkins' School of Public Health, where he teaches, gave $2,000 and a revolver to three undergraduate engineering students. Their senior project, Teret told them, was to reconfigure this handgun, using existing technologies, so that only its authorized user could make it shoot.

"And they did it," the professor exclaims. "They used 'touch memory' technology—a chip in a ring the gun owner wears that connects with the gun and matches the authorized code. That's when I knew this was going to happen: If engineering students could do it, I had no doubt the industry can do it."

As the professor searched for ways to promote the concept, his cause was advanced by an accidental encounter. On a long flight home from Los Angeles,

Teret's seatmate happened to be Andrea Camp, spokeswoman for Rep. Pat Schroeder of Colorado, herself a social reformer on many fronts. For five hours, Teret elaborated to his captive audience the life-saving potential of new gun technologies.

Back in Washington, Camp briefed her boss. And Schroeder (who retired from Congress last year) began pushing various federal agencies, from the Pentagon to the Justice Department, to put down some real money toward exploring the idea.

An Idea Materializes

In 1994, the National Institute of Justice responded to her nudging and gave $650,000 to Sandia National Laboratories to research the technology. Then it awarded a $500,000 grant to Colt to refine its working prototype.

Colt's Smart Gun uses a transponder, a tiny transmitter that the authorized user would wear on a wristband, which sends a matching code to a receiver in the handgun's grip and enables the weapon to function. This concept is not so different, really, from the electronic keys that tenants use to operate an apartment elevator or that homeowners use to open an overhead garage door or unlock their cars.

The original objective of the Justice Department grants was to protect police. One of every six law-enforcement officers who gets fatally shot is killed by his own gun or his partner's, typically when an assailant seizes the weapon and turns it on the officer. If the officer's weapon could not be fired by a stranger, lives would be saved, for sure.

Technology is never foolproof, of course, and so the government says it will sponsor extensive field testing by police before the safety device is cleared for distribution. But this is a big leap forward. Reformers like Teret know that what works for police officers can work for others—a safety device far more certain than other options.

Trigger locks, which Handgun Control hopes to require in its legislation proposal, are already available to gun owners as add-ons, but they require a diligent owner, and the quality of the locks can be poor. Parental-liability laws, likewise, already exist in fifteen states, but whether they have had much impact is in dispute. In many instances when kids are killed accidentally by a parent's handgun, prosecutors are reluctant to add to the tragedy by prosecuting the owner as a felon.

> *"It ought to be easy enough to produce . . . a gun that fires only if the owner is personally pulling the trigger."*

"I'm very excited about personalized handguns," says Teret. "I think this is a solution to debates that have been gridlocked for the last several decades. People scream at each other about what's the meaning of the Second Amendment or whether we need guns to defend ourselves in dangerous situations. This provides a safe haven in the traditional storm over gun policy. It will save lives. It won't take anyone's gun away."

Indeed, once they are available, Colt's Smart Guns or other versions should open a vast new market for gun sales based on greater safety, just as air bags became a new feature for selling automobiles. Since gun sales have been flat in the late 1990s, the industry has an obvious stake in developing new market potential.

> *"One of every six law-enforcement officers who gets fatally shot is killed by his own gun or his partner's."*

But in other ways, this new brand of gun points threateningly at the firearms industry itself. It will have to dodge the bullet.

As a political strategy, the leading gun makers have decided they are no longer going to wear the "black hat" in the gun debate and stand shoulder to shoulder with the NRA against gun-control legislation. "We have allowed ourselves to sit back and ignore the problem, thus becoming part of it," Colt's CEO and president, Ron Stewart, wrote in the trade magazine *American Firearms Industry.* "Silence is acceptance. Our responses to the anti-gun lobby are ill-postured, defensive and pathetically inadequate."

The American Shooting Sports Council, a trade group for firearms makers, began the peacemaking offensive last year with an appearance in the White House's Rose Garden with President Clinton and a promise of a voluntary program to provide child-safety locks with all its handguns. The NRA was not amused to see its old ally making nice with the political leader it loathes.

"We made a decision a couple of years ago that the firearms industry was going to take a different tack from the tobacco industry," explains Bob Ricker, the council's director of government affairs. "We all saw those tobacco executives appear before congressional committees and make ridiculous assertions. We understand firearms are dangerous tools, and the general public understands that, too. We think the industry can bring a lot to this safety debate, whether it's accidental discharge or criminal misuse."

Colt's chief executive has proposed what is blasphemy to the NRA. Stewart calls for "a comprehensive federal firearms law, including the creation of federal gun permits" in order to pre-empt contradictory requirements from a proliferation of state laws. The gun lobby, as we have known it, is splitting up. An NRA spokesman says it has no objection to marketing the safer handguns—the NRA is always for safety—just so long as it doesn't become a legislative requirement.

Who Is Liable?

Meanwhile, however, the manufacturers are facing a very serious threat on another front: lawsuits by victims and their families. It took several decades of litigation before tobacco companies were cornered by clearly established legal liability, but guns are now more vulnerable because of the new technology. A potential breakthrough case is pending in Oakland, California, filed against Beretta U.S.A. Corp. by Lynn and Griffin Dix for the shooting of their fifteen-year-old son Kenzo four years ago.

The core argument in the Dix case is that the manufacturer is liable because Beretta failed to apply available safety technology in the gun that killed Kenzo. (Beretta argues that the technology wasn't available yet.) This definition of liability is long-established in product-safety litigation, and the introduction of "personalized" gun locks will raise the hurdle much higher. If some new guns are sold with this safeguard, then all other gun makers will be in the cross hairs, too.

"Whether it turns out to be Oakland or somewhere else," Professor Teret predicts, "eventually the gun manufacturers are going to lose a case for failing to provide the safest possible gun. Once that happens, they won't be able to afford not to have these new devices in their guns."

Teret is confident of the outcome because he played a part in launching the same dynamic that forced the adoption of air bags in cars. For nearly twenty years, the auto companies used their political clout to stymie this safety feature and even refused to offer air bags as an option, though the technology existed. As a former trial lawyer, Teret urged other plaintiffs' lawyers to challenge the industry's stonewalling with damage suits. In 1984, Ford saw that it was losing a lawsuit brought by an eighteen-year-old girl in Birmingham, Alabama, and so it settled for $1.8 million.

> *"We understand firearms are dangerous tools, and the general public understands that, too."*

"That one settlement caused a tidal wave of litigation against auto manufacturers for failure to provide air bags," Teret explains. The car industry surrendered. When politics are stalemated, litigation can be a more effective tool for advancing public health.

Forcing Safety

"It's easier to convince twelve jurors to do something than it is the U.S. Congress," the professor observes. "None of the jurors are seeking to get re-elected."

The gun industry faces the same threat. As these developments unfold, the companies themselves may jump on the bandwagon, competing with one another over who makes the safest gun, just as car companies now do with their products. Bryan Miller imagines manufacturers luring customers by offering fifty-dollar buyback bonuses for older, more dangerous guns.

One market force unleashed by this innovation may cut in the other direction and shrink the market of potential buyers: the rising price of handguns. At least initially, the "personalized" feature is expected to add $300 or more to the price tag and could double the cost of some of the cheaper handguns. In time the cost impact should fall, just as it did for computers and cell phones.

As the public recognizes the safety potential, the legal regulation and higher safety standards should become more obvious and acceptable, perhaps even in Washington. For instance, the federal law proposed by Handgun Control Inc. would unshackle the U.S. Consumer Products Safety Commission and authorize it to study the new technologies for handguns. At present, as reformers like to point out, the commission investigates and regulates the safety of toy guns but is prohibited by law from looking into real guns.

Technology, litigation, market forces, public opinion, regulation—those are the dynamics driving the gun debate in a new direction, interacting with each other and promising real progress. They all pivot on the same point: This is not about rap music or deranged teenagers or careless gun owners—it's about guns.

Curbing Easy Access

There's a downside. This new safety device, assuming it works, will not by itself solve the gun problem in its full dimensions (no one claims it will). The "childproof" gun does not confront a major source of gun deaths—homicide. Whether it's family, friends or strangers doing the shooting, homicides account for more than forty percent of the 36,000 or so firearms deaths every year (and seventy percent of handgun deaths for those age nineteen and younger).

Accidents should be reduced, but if a gun owner wants to shoot his wife (or vice versa), a Smart Gun isn't going to stop him. On the other hand, the new mechanism should have a significant impact on reducing suicides, especially among people nineteen years old and younger (roughly a fourth of their gun deaths are caused by suicide). Furthermore, a significant number of the guns that felons use in crimes are originally stolen from homes. This technology will at least shrink the easy access that criminals have to new firepower.

A more sophisticated objection from some reformers goes like this: The real problem is that America is awash in millions of handguns owned by private citizens, and the only real solution is to ban them, except perhaps for limited circumstances.

"Our concern," says Kristen Rand of the Violence Policy Center, "is that people will view this as a magic bullet—no pun intended." Conceivably, she adds, this feature will merely allow the firearms industry to turn over the market—selling safer guns to people who already own guns—while the older, less-safe weapons will continue to exist and do harm.

> *"Eventually the gun manufacturers are going to lose a case for failing to provide the safest possible gun."*

Prohibition may be the ultimate solution (I've written as much myself), but it's not in the cards, not now or for many years. Before anything like that can occur, the nation must undergo deep social change—not just anger but a new understanding that the gun problem can be solved. The Smart Gun turns the political debate in the right direction and begins this essential process of educating and altering popular attitudes. Once safer guns are in general use, people will see that the problem hasn't gone away. That could build the political predicate for a more aggressive campaign of eradication.

If this sounds too wishful, remember what happened to tobacco. The deep shift in public attitudes on smoking took many years of education and agitation by reformers, as well as new scientific evidence and litigation. Gun reform is not going to take anywhere near that long. The companies can see what lies ahead for them. And Americans can see the victims right now.

Holding Gun Manufacturers Accountable Would Reduce Gun-Related Deaths

by Sarah Brady

About the author: Sarah Brady heads Handgun Control, Inc., a gun control organization. Her husband, former White House press secretary James Brady, was severely wounded by John W. Hinckley Jr. in a 1981 attempt to assassinate President Ronald Reagan.

Imagine how your holiday plans might have changed if you had learned that thousands of children and teens suffer sickness and death every year after eating Thanksgiving turkey. Imagine if public health researchers consistently traced a link between turkey and higher death rates among children. Even more terrifying, imagine if the turkey industry denied it had any responsibility to prevent these deaths and government agencies could do nothing to require the turkey industry to grow healthier birds, even though they knew how.

Don't worry, your Thanksgiving turkey was safe. But another preventable epidemic has swept across our nation. It lives in our homes and it attacks our young disproportionately—it is an epidemic of gun death and injury.

Children Clearly Suffer

The Centers for Disease Control and Prevention estimate that nearly 1.2 million latchkey children have access to loaded and unlocked firearms in their homes. It is no surprise, therefore, that children and teenagers cause more than 10,000 unintentional shootings each year in which at least 800 people die. In addition, about 1,900 children and teenagers attempt suicide with a firearm every year. More than three-fourths of them are successful.

For years, the gun industry has known of technology that would prevent the majority of these deaths and injuries. "Personalized guns"—weapons that can only be fired by the owner—would stop the curious child, the suicidal teenager

Reprinted, by permission, from Sarah Brady, "A Way to Cut the Deadly Toll," *Los Angeles Times*, November 29, 1996.

and the thief from firing a gun found in a drawer or closet. The gun industry made a business decision not to develop and market this technology—a decision that contributes to thousands of unintentional shootings every year and costs hundreds of lives. Among these gun manufacturers is a cluster of Saturday Night Special makers located in Southern California—an area known as the "Ring of Fire."

Gun Manufacturers at Work

Only in September 1996 did Colt's Manufacturing Co. finally unveil a prototype of a personalized handgun. To fire the gun, the user must wear a radio-frequency tag (which can be placed in a ring or wrist band) to transmit a signal recognized by a chip placed in the gun. Though Colt was careful to state that this prototype was intended only for police use, the gun was heralded by others as a way to prevent unintentional shootings that occur when children find handguns that have been stored unlocked in the home.

While gun manufacturers have been reluctant to implement such safety features, they continue to create guns that are deadlier—more compact, more concealable and more powerful. The gun industry then markets these increasingly lethal guns by playing on our fear of crime in their advertising and implicitly encouraging the dangerous storage and handling of firearms.

"While gun manufacturers have been reluctant to implement safety features, they continue to create guns that are deadlier."

In one Beretta ad, for example, a pistol lies on a night stand with a bullet placed deliberately beside it. A woman and two young children peer innocently out of a photograph sitting next to the gun. The alarm clock shows 11:25 p.m. The headline reads, "Tip the odds in your favor." The ad illustrates precisely how the gun bought for protection is often the most dangerous, as it is usually stored unlocked and loaded for use at a moment's notice.

Urge Corporate Responsibility

The makers of most consumer products, including turkeys, teddy bears and even toy guns—none of which are inherently lethal—are subject to stricter safety standards than are gun manufacturers. Only one death was reported between 1988 and 1992 as a result of eating bad turkey meat, yet regulations require turkeys to go through a minimum of seven major inspections before hitting the supermarket shelves. Guns, designed to kill, claim the lives of 38,000 people every year and no regulation requires gun manufacturers to make safer guns.

The gun lobby has ensured that this madness will continue by pressuring Congress to exempt the gun industry from regulation by the Consumer Product Safety Commission. Gun manufacturers are the least regulated consumer product industry. But this is beginning to change. In Massachusetts, the attorney general is taking steps to impose safety standards on handguns. This is the direction we must go.

If any other consumer product took as many lives as guns do, we would see a public outcry so great that the manufacturer would be forced to make the product safer. We must demand the same level of responsibility from gun makers.

Treating Gun Violence as a Public Health Issue Could Reduce the Problem

by George M. Anderson

About the author: *George Anderson is an associate editor of* America, *a weekly news journal.*

Many Americans tend to regard gun violence as primarily a crime issue, and consequently look to stricter laws, longer prison sentences and more prisons as the answer. Increasingly, however, other approaches are being explored. One entails viewing it as a public health crisis. A series of interviews with health professionals around the country revealed both the growth of this approach and the gravity of the problem of firearms violence in the United States.

Among the foremost groups promoting the public health aspect is the Federal Centers for Disease Control in Atlanta, Ga. The director of its violence prevention division, James Mercy, M.D., commented on the need to widen the public's understanding of the questions involved. "Although firearm violence is typically seen as a crime issue, in fact there are more firearms-related deaths by suicide than there are deaths by homicide—48 percent as compared to 46 percent," he said. "So we're trying to broaden the picture to show that it's not just the criminals who are using guns."

Dr. Mercy and others who are alarmed at the increase in handgun injuries and deaths hope that out of this broadened perspective, a perspective based on scientific inquiry, Americans will begin to move more cautiously in regard to the purchase and ownership of firearms.

Getting Information to the Public

"The public often buys without taking into account the risks," Dr. Mercy said. "There is little evidence to show that handguns have a protective effect. On the contrary; in comparison with homes in the same neighborhood without guns,

Reprinted from George M. Anderson, "Gun Control: New Approaches," *America*, March 11, 1995, by permission of the author.

when there's a gun in the household, chances of its being used for suicide increase fivefold, and threefold for homicide in situations like family disputes. What's needed," he added, "is to get out accurate information so that potential buyers can make informed judgments—for example, about the heightened risk of injury or death when there are children in the home."

Efforts to highlight the risks of handgun ownership have been made more difficult, however, by the advertising campaigns of gun manufacturers that present what advocates of gun control regard as misinformation, particularly with regard to the protection claim. "Some companies are trying to expand their markets by targeting women," Dr. Mercy said, "suggesting that women have most to fear from strangers, whereas the greatest danger of violence is from co-habitants."

> *"Although firearm violence is typically seen as a crime issue . . . there are more firearms-related deaths by suicide than there are deaths by homicide."*

Persuading the Vulnerable

An 82-page study released late in 1994 by the Washington-based Violence Policy Center, called "Female Persuasion," explores this very issue. The author of the study, Susan Glick—the center's health policy analyst—observed that when the handgun market for white males became saturated in the 1980's and began to slump, the industry started focusing on women. "The firearms industry and pro-gun groups like the National Rifle Association have mounted a marketing campaign based on a professed concern for women's safety from crime and violence," Ms. Glick said. "As part of this approach, the industry presents female handgun ownership as a male bastion falling to women's equality. But the primary marketing tactic is not equality but fear. The pitch to women is simple: You're a woman, some stranger is going to rape you, so you'd better buy a handgun."

Her study reproduces magazine advertisements for guns that show, among others, a mother tucking her little girl into bed at night. The caption at the top reads: "Self-protection is more than your right—it's your responsibility." At the bottom of the advertisement two Colt pistols are displayed, with the comment: "Like a home fire extinguisher, it may be better to have it and not need it, than to need it and not have it."

Children Are Top Priority

The fact that Ms. Glick is the Violence Policy Center's health policy analyst shows that gun violence is increasingly coming to be perceived as a health matter. One result of this expanding perception is that seemingly diverse groups around the country have also begun to address the issue, especially from the child-safety point of view. The Children's Defense Fund, for example, has developed a series of public service announcements that focus on the toll guns take on children.

"There's a firearm in over 40 percent of American households, so every time a child goes to play in a friend's home, there's nearly a 50-50 chance that the home will have one," said Hattie Ruttenberg, the Children's Defense Fund's spokesperson on the issue. "We're trying to educate parents about the dangers."

The child-safety approach is one that has also been taken up by the Carter Center in Atlanta, which has been working on a project called "Not Even One"—meaning that the firearm death of even one child is unacceptable. Fred D. Smith, assistant director of the Carter Center's Interfaith Health Program, described the project in the course of another telephone conversation.

A National Coalition

"We've been looking at the idea of response teams. Every time a child is killed in a particular locality, the residents, the faith community and the local health department would all come together to investigate and see what could be done to prevent its happening again," he said. Mr. Smith noted that the protocol for a demonstration project along these lines is scheduled for implementation sometime in 1995. He added that the Centers for Disease Control has been involved in the planning in an advisory capacity and that the Interfaith Health Program networks with the Children's Defense Fund on the firearms question. Both, in turn, are in

> *"If handguns are killing people, steps can be taken both to demonstrate their hazards and to stem their proliferation."*

touch with the Violence Policy Center. Linkages like these point to the gradual formation of what might be considered a loosely knit nationwide coalition. Indeed, the Carter Center's report on "Not Even One" speaks of the need to establish a common voice, through which a movement could be built to alter public thinking.

One group moving specifically in this direction is the Chicago-based HELP Network. HELP is an acronym for Handgun Epidemic Lowering Plan. It was begun in 1993 by two physicians at Children's Memorial Medical Center in Chicago. It includes as member organizations the American Academy of Pediatrics, the American College of Physicians, the American Medical Association, along with more regionally based groups like the Connecticut Childhood Injury Prevention Center. HELP's mission is to foster public health approaches to ending the death, disability and suffering caused by handguns.

Making Connections

Another health-related group that has joined in the effort to reduce firearms deaths is Physicians for Social Responsibility. Although its primary commitments have traditionally been directed toward the elimination of weapons of mass destruction, the connection between large-scale armaments and handguns is now part of their focus. I spoke about the matter with Ann Smith, a fellow at Physicians for Social Responsibility's main office in Washington, D.C.; Ms. Smith is coordinator for its violence prevention program, with guns in the home as a primary area of concentration.

"We're just starting our program," she said, "and it's interesting to see that other groups that deal with anti-nuclear issues are also seeing the connection on the local scale. Global peace and inner city peace are very connected. People talk about guns out of their emotions," Ms. Smith continued, "but what's needed is to educate at the grass-roots level in such a way as to show that there are verifiable statistics that demonstrate, for instance, the dangers of guns in the home." From the epidemiological standpoint, Ms. Smith drew a parallel with malaria. When it became known that malaria was transmitted by mosquitoes and that mosquitoes were found especially in swampy areas, steps could be taken to reduce their presence there. Similarly, if handguns are killing people, steps can be taken both to demonstrate their hazards and to stem their proliferation.

A Hazardous Consumer Product

Dr. Smith noted that health-related groups have also been focusing on the lack of regulation within the firearms industry, which they see as further contributing to the high levels of handgun injuries and deaths. The regulatory aspect of the situation has led to another approach being pursued to reduce the violence. This is being studied by Stephen Teret at the newly created Center for Gun Policy and Research at the Johns Hopkins School of Public Health in Baltimore. An attorney with a master's degree in public health, Mr. Teret commented about regulation.

"We've been allowing ourselves to look only at the user of the gun, but we should also be looking at the manufacturer who makes it—in other words, not just at who pulls the trigger, but at who makes the trigger," he said. "What's needed is to see guns as a consumer product that should be regulated like any other potentially dangerous product."

> *"The first step toward regulation is to regard firearms as hazardous consumer products."*

"As it is now, though," Mr. Teret continued, "manufacturers in the United States can design and make as many guns as they like, in a completely unfettered way. As a result, given what guns can do in terms of injuries, manufacturers are implicitly making health policy decisions of a life and death nature without any public scrutiny."

The Mood of Congress

In a 1994 publication called "Cease Fire," the Violence Policy Center contends that the first step toward regulation is to regard firearms as hazardous consumer products. The second is to create what it terms "a workable regulatory framework," one that sets safety standards and restricts the availability of certain types of firearms. The Government agency charged with regulating the firearms industry is the Bureau of Alcohol, Tobacco and Firearms, a division of the Department of the Treasury. Its authority, however, is very limited. What the Violence Policy Center therefore recommends is that the B.A.T.F. be granted greater powers of regulation. But given the changing Congress, such a move is unlikely.

> *"The goal [of reducing gun violence] should be to shift the discussion from a criminal justice perspective to one centered on public health."*

Indeed, some observers fear that efforts will be made to repeal initiatives already in place, like the ban on certain types of assault weapons in the Crime Bill. Among these observers is Garen Wintemute, M.D., an emergency room physician in Sacramento, Calif., who is also affiliated with the University of California at Davis. As an indication of Congress's anti-regulatory mood, he pointed out that the Subcommittee on Crime of the House Judiciary Committee had originally planned two hearings, one for November 1994, the other for January 1995. "The first hearing was to have been on the misleading ads used by gun manufacturers to market guns to women," Dr. Wintemute said. "The second was going to examine the involvement of handguns in crime. Both were canceled after the November elections."

Doctors' Observations

Besides his work as an emergency room physician, Dr. Wintemute—who, like Mr. Teret, was cross trained in public health—is the author of *Ring of Fire*, published by the Violence Prevention Research Program at the University of California at Davis. "The title comes from the presence of the six large companies in the Los Angeles area that make 80 percent of the cheap handguns, the Saturday night specials, sold in the United States," Dr. Wintemute said. "The weapons manufactured by these six companies are disproportionately involved in gun violence around the country."

Like Mr. Teret, Dr. Wintemute sees a parallel between firearm violence and highway deaths. "Both types of trauma are major health problems, but we've treated them differently from the product safety standpoint," he said. "Until the 1960's, if there was a traffic accident, the person at fault was 'the nut behind the wheel,' so the blame was just on the user of the product. Then it came to be realized that cars could be regulated and made safer with devices like seat belts and air bags, which, along with improvements in highway design, have cut traffic fatalities in half over the past 30 years." But, he went on to observe, at the policy level we have deliberately chosen not to consider firearms as a product. We've kept the blinders on."

He added that among the surgeons he works with in emergency room situations the realization is growing that there is a better way of dealing with the firearms injuries they see than simply addressing the consequences—namely, through preventive measures that would keep the injuries from happening in the first place. Among these measures would be the kind of increased focus on the manufacturer advocated by Mr. Teret and the Violence Policy Center.

Prevention Through Restriction

As for prevention, especially with respect to children, Mr. Teret pointed out that from 1880 until the 1930's Smith & Wesson made handguns with a safety device, a metal lever that had to be depressed before the user could pull the trigger. "A small child's hand is too little to deal with both at once," Mr. Teret said, "but even though this model was effective, Smith & Wesson stopped making it. Now it is manufacturing the LadySmith, which targets women as buyers. But since it's marketed with young women in mind, it could easily find itself in the same environment as a child. Why isn't it childproof?" Mr. Teret asked. "Because no one forces the company to make it that way."

"With . . . emphasis on gun violence as a health, regulatory and safety products issue, a beginning has been made in the search for solutions to a problem that is old and worsening."

From his background as an attorney, Mr. Teret believes that in cases of children accidentally injured or killed by handguns in the home, lawsuits could be successfully brought against the manufacturers. Although suits brought in the 1980's on the basis of accidental injuries were unsuccessful, he feels that others based more specifically on the failure to childproof would be, in his words, "eminently winnable."

As yet another approach—through litigation—Mr. Teret mentioned that the Johns Hopkins Center for Gun Policy Research is also engaged in a project focusing on false advertising, similar to the work being done in this area by the Violence Policy Center. But for the election results, this project would have been the basis for the cancelled hearing on the subject by the House Subcommittee on Crime. "We're gathering ads that have a gun-in-the-house-protects message, and we're putting them together with epidemiological data that points to increased danger when there's a gun around," he said. "Then, if it seems likely that the Federal Trade Commission would act on the findings, we'll present it with the data."

Focusing on Child Safety

Mr. Teret's own concern with the child-safety aspect arises from the personal tragedy of close friends. "They had a 22-month-old baby, David, whom they left at the home of their regular sitter, the wife of a policeman. One day the sitter took David upstairs to her room for a nap, and while she was out, her own four-year-old took the father's gun and shot David. After that I started asking myself why should a four-year-old have been able to fire the gun in the first place." His belief in the value of child-proofing is corroborated by a 1991 study by the United States General Accounting Office called "Accidental Shootings." The study found that a childproof safety device could have prevented every unintentional shooting in which a child under six killed him- or herself or someone else.

Although not accidental for the most part, the toll that gun violence has taken on older children, especially in inner-city neighborhoods, has reached what are considered epidemic proportions. According to an article in the *Journal of the American Medical Association* in 1992, gun homicide is the leading cause of death among African-American males between the ages of 15 and 19. Dr. Mercy observed that from 1985 to 1991 alone the homicide rate for this group increased by 190 percent. "And the average age of the perpetrator has been getting younger," he said. "In 1985 the age range for those most likely to be arrested for homicide was 20 to 24, but by 1991 it had dropped to the 15- to 19-year age range." The fact that handguns are so easily available to these and even younger children again illustrates the lack of regulatory measures that would limit accessibility.

A Positive Supplement

The 1994 Crime Bill does include a provision that makes it a Federal crime for anyone under 18 to possess a handgun without proper adult supervision, and a second conviction could result in a year's incarceration in a juvenile facility. But it is doubtful whether a law of this kind, with its after-the-fact emphasis on punishment, will do much to deter inner-city youth from carrying firearms. As Dr. Mercy pointed out, those who carry them are largely motivated by fear. "And when they carry guns out of fear, that leads to more violence, which escalates the fear, like the nuclear build-up," he said.

The health and regulatory approach will not take the place of legislative initiatives like the Brady Bill, but in the view of Dr. Mercy and others the goal should be to shift the discussion from a criminal justice perspective to one centered on public health. That groups as seemingly disparate as Handgun Control, Inc., and the American Academy of Pediatrics are working together, through the former's Pediatricians' Project, is an indication that this shift is beginning to take place and that increased networking is occurring among a wide variety of organizations. Dr. Wintemute noted that whereas in 1990 there were only a handful of groups committed to reducing firearm violence, now there are many.

Adequate Funding

Another sign of this increased commitment is the fact that foundations are providing significant levels of funding for such organizations. Both HELP and the Johns Hopkins Center for Gun Policy and Research are funded by the Joyce

Foundation in Chicago, which has taken on gun violence as a special project among its other programs that deal with areas as wide-ranging as conservation and elections reform. The Joyce Foundation also provides funding for the Advocacy Institute in Washington, D.C., which, as part of its Gun Violence Project, plans to design a computer network that will link groups around the country interested in the issue. Similarly, the Pacific Center for Violence Prevention at San Francisco General Hospital received a grant of $7.5 million from The California Wellness Foundation. The Pacific Center's director, Andrew McGuire, said that grants to violence prevention groups are relatively new, and that some foundations are placing funds into a pool, thereby forming a consortium of foundations looking at the larger violence issue.

A Foundation for Positive Change

Part of the Pacific Center's three-pronged effort is the banning of so-called Saturday night specials of the kind described in Dr. Wintemute's book, *Ring of Fire*. Another is the elimination of California's preemption law in regard to firearms. Mr. McGuire said that this type of law, which exists in 33 states, precludes local governments from passing statutes that would be more restrictive than the firearms statutes of their state. "It ties the hands of city and county councils," he said. By way of contrast, he noted that in Illinois, which does not have a preemption law, the town of Morton Grove was able to pass an ordinance banning handguns. Public education is still another aspect of the Pacific Center's efforts, and through a separate $2 million grant from The Wellness Foundation to a political consultancy firm, it is conducting a statewide public education campaign aimed at reducing youth-related gun violence.

Public education will not be easy, however, and may take decades. As Susan Glick observed, it is hard, even with epidemiological studies and statistics at hand, to chip away at deeply entrenched misperceptions in matters like the desire to own a gun for reasons of protection. Nor will public education alone be enough to address some of the deeper social causes of gun violence, like poverty and the combined role of drug distribution and money. To deal with these, Dr. Mercy said, other new policy approaches will be called for. But at least with the emphasis on gun violence as a health, regulatory and safety products issue, a beginning has been made in the search for solutions to a problem that is old and worsening.

Responsible Gun Ownership Would Reduce Gun Violence

by Bart Kendrick

About the author: *Bart Kendrick writes for* Gun News Digest, *a journal for gun advocates.*

The love affair with mechanized tools has kept American men dreaming of levers and gears since long before the Industrial Revolution. It's been an unending fascination with tools that empowers their lives and accelerates their wheels toward progress. This steady progress and improved performance has mingled a subtle hum of giddy pleasure with the resonance of machines at work.

The Industrial Revolution was a wider stone for stepping than many dreamt. Simple life made easier by simple machines moved us ever more rapidly toward building complex systems to handle complex tasks. Regardless of advances, the mechanical advantage that controls most automated activity is still the inclined plane. Gears, levers, wheels and the work each perform depend on the angled slope of an inclined plane between two tangential points. Gears mesh to turn wheels because an inclined plane provides the mechanical advantage for one part to easily move another. The force required for one levered inclined plane to start a chain of events will vary, but it's safe to say a small force can usually deliver dramatic results.

The Mechanics of Guns

One example of dramatic results involving inclined planes on fulcrums are levers that cause the discharge of a loaded firearm. Firing starts and finishes in a fraction of a second . . . it's an event that takes less time than making a fist. Adding to the drama is how exerting just a few pounds of pressure at point "A" imposes hundreds of foot-pounds of energy on an object at a distant point "B."

Consider this simple sequence: An index finger exerting maybe 3 to 7 pounds

Reprinted, by permission, from Bart Kendrick, "The Inclined Plane, Gun Control, and the Second Amendment," *Gun News Digest*, Summer 1997.

pressure on a trigger (a levered inclined plane) moves a second levered inclined plane (the sear) releasing a third lever (the hammer) allowing it to move. The hammer drops its weight on the cartridge's primer, exploding it to ignite the powder charge. The powder's greater explosive energy sends a bullet, the projectile, into flight at a tremendous speed. The hurtled projectile hits a distant object with considerable foot-pounds of energy. The structure and composition of the object hit is changed by the impact of the projectile's mass.

Time Factors

Dramatic, lightning fast, irrevocable and irreparable. The value and performance of the inclined plane in this example is efficient beyond any doubt. A massive amount of force was delivered because a minimal amount of initial energy used a mechanical advantage.

Likewise, an automobile can impart a massive amount of force on a distant object after it gets to where the object is. Follow the process: opening, getting in and closing the car door, adjusting the mirrors, turning the ignition on, putting the car into gear, starting off, directing it along a selected pathway and gaining speed. Then, on finding the object to be hit, steering the car at and into it. Time elapsed . . . certainly more than a few minutes.

The crash and resulting damage might be dramatic, irrevocable and irreparable, but the act took more thought and time than making a fist. Multiple steps were needed before damage was done and quite possibly there was time, if not opportunity, for intercession and/or damage prevention.

Tools Are Not Responsible

Clearly, tools of any kind cannot perform without an outside factor taking control of them. Rolling pins don't roll by themselves and ball bats need someone to swing them. The same is true of mechanized tools—cars need a driver to move and firearms a finger to pull the trigger to shoot. Regardless of the tool, its use depends entirely on the user. Consequently, appropriate owner and user tool control is imperative. Left alone, tools remain in a static condition until someone imposes their control and puts them to use.

The possession and use of tools, but especially tools that can cause lethal damage, suggests they should only be allowed under the control of a responsible person. Toward that end, states issue licenses to regulate who can participate in certain activities; drivers licenses to operate an automobile, sporting licenses and various

> *"Clearly, tools of any kind cannot perform without an outside factor taking control of them."*

kinds of permits to own, possess and carry firearms, to name just a few. Unfortunately, not everyone who participates in license-required activity has a license and when caught in violation of law, is held accountable. Accountability, as we know all too well, follows violent, illegal or irresponsible acts committed; acts, perhaps equally as irrevocable and irreparable as the resulting damage caused by the projectile from a discharged firearm or vehicle ramming another object.

Intentional and deliberate acts aside, the overwhelming difference between massive destruction done by a car (or, for that matter, a rolling pin or ball bat) and a firearm is elapsed time. Hitting a distant object with a car, rolling pin or bat takes minutes or at least a few seconds, and multiple sequential acts. A distant object

> *"The need for laws and control does not stem from the devices, but specific owners and/or users."*

hit by the projectile from a loaded firearm takes a fraction of a second and involves one finger's pressure against a levered inclined plane. The last, an act taking less time than making a fist.

Some Laws Are Needed

Enforced regulation of laws, written or otherwise, lets people know that irresponsible behavior will not be tolerated. Automobiles haven't been banned to prevent auto accidents; instead, traffic laws are more aggressively enforced. To regulate hunting, a mandated condition for obtaining a license is to pass better education and safety courses. In these and most other activities requiring licenses, a responsible society willingly accepts logical and practical regulation when its value is recognized and it is unilaterally enforced.

Aggressively enforced firearms laws can diminish firearms incidents like traffic laws prevent auto accidents. The need for laws and control does not stem from the devices, but specific owners and/or users. That does not, however, remove the need for some additional forms of gun control to prevent the potential for damage. Most reasonable people agree that the need for such gun control exists.

Determining Rules

The purpose for gun control is preventing access to firearms and ammunitions by irresponsible parties. That poses a few problems: who is irresponsible; how much control is necessary to prevent access, and who makes the determination in each circumstance?

Who is an irresponsible person? Candidates include children, criminals, persons known or who display certain mental, emotional and/or physical incapacity. Others in this group are substance abusers or individuals who must depend on a medication for stability over extended periods of time. There are possibly more who could be added to this list, including anyone who has not received any firearms safety and education training or been instructed in the firearm's safe and proper use.

There are, interestingly enough, laws covering just about every irresponsible party on the list. In fact, there are also laws to ensure that a responsible party is not left unchecked indefinitely. And, deciding who is irresponsible and who makes that determination are elements of gun control already in place. Who the decision-makers are, how they were chosen and how well they do their respective jobs are factors over which most of us have little or no control.

Absolutely Responsible?

Unauthorized access is the problem and how to prevent it from being a factor is the question. Licensed activity, structured environments and circumstances of real and present danger are the only times that firearms and ammunition should *not* be locked away. Ideally, we would find firearms without locks only under the control of a person who has met all criteria for being considered "responsible." The only time that irresponsible access could then become the factor (under ideal conditions) is when the "responsible" party fails in the security obligation or has the loaded firearm wrested from his/her control. There are laws to handle security violators (an after-the-fact remedy) and the involved firearms are confiscated from the violator. Those firearms will more than likely be destroyed. Under the condition where the in-use-control factor is lost, with whom and where the firearm goes and how it will be used is unknown unless immediately recovered by authorities or another "responsible" person.

> *"Thinking that absolute enforcement, control and/or restriction singly or collectively prevents unauthorized access to firearms is not likely nor is it practical."*

Thinking in terms of anything "absolute" is an ideal we might strive to achieve. And, while firearm's enthusiasts may try, they most likely cannot improve upon the absolute efficiency of the inclined plane. It functions to discharge a firearm in exactly the manner of its design. Thinking that absolute enforcement, control and/or restriction singly or collectively prevents unauthorized access to firearms is not likely nor is it practical. There simply is not an absolute solution to any of the concerns expressed.

Laws are not enforced, statistics of incidents are misquoted and, yes, there are owners who do not take firearms ownership seriously enough to be fully responsible. All are factors which work against responsible people being free to enjoy firearms possession and use. The most positive steps to take to continue that use and enjoyment is for firearms owners to exercise strict control, preach prevention and enforcement, and work diligently to remove firearms from the possession of those less committed to preserving our Second Amendment Rights. Then, we will have moved closer to gun control.

Getting Involved Can Help Reduce Gun Violence

by The Michigan Partnership to Prevent Gun Violence

About the author: *The Michigan Partnership to Prevent Gun Violence is a coalition of law enforcement, medical, and public health professionals who promote the reduction and prevention of gun violence in Michigan.*

One of the most important things you as a citizen can do to help stop gun violence is to let your elected officials and/or the media know how you feel about the issues. All too often, citizen input is only received at election time, if then. As legislation is introduced and debated, your voiced opinion can have an important impact on the local, state, or national level.

Contacting Your Elected Officials

You may contact your elected officials by phone, person to person by appointment or at community events, by letter, or through e-mail. E-mail is fast replacing snail mail as the medium for contacting political policymakers because it is cheaper, easier, and faster. Regular mail (or "snail mail") is slower, but it gives the elected official a piece of paper from a "real person" to carry into committee meetings to reinforce his arguments. Regardless of the method of communication you choose—the most important thing is to do it—and do it now. If your elected official hears from only 10 people on a particular issue, she/he feels he has been hit by a landslide. Your voice counts.

Let's review some basic principles about communicating with your representatives—they have not changed, regardless of the medium used.

- It is important to contact your political policymakers early in the process, before a bill is passed. Once a bad measure is passed into law, it is much more difficult to change the law.
- It is important to contact your elected officials often on the same issue. They face several decision-making points—they are asked to be sponsors of the bill before it is introduced, they vote in committee, and they vote again

Reprinted from "What You Can Do to Stop Gun Violence: Contact Your Elected Officials," at www.mppgv.org/stopgv.htm, by permission of the Michigan Partnership to Prevent Gun Violence.

in the full session. They are under great pressure at each point and need your support.

- Get involved with a group of people of like interests and join in common action. There is strength in numbers—and more people to share the work!
- You can't catch flies with vinegar. A firm, friendly approach to communicating your opinion is far better than an angry letter. Be respectful.
- Get familiar with the legislative process. Ask a legislator or elected official for a "Citizens Guide" to state, local or national government processes.
- Before contacting any elected official, make sure you understand the major points at issue. Tell the elected official that these points are important to you. If you are communicating about a particular bill, use its name and/or bill number.
- If the contact method you are using is the telephone or a personal visit, prepare a short draft of what you want to say ahead of time.
- Tell the elected official that you are a citizen and/or volunteer acting out of personal interest and concern. Always identify yourself. Being anonymous detracts from your credibility.
- If you want a response, don't forget to give your address and/or telephone number and/or e-mail address.
- Contact your elected official whether they agree or disagree with your perspective. Those who agree will be glad for your encouragement, while those who disagree need help changing their minds!
- Be brief. A short, concise, to the point statement in your own words will beat out a dozen pages of statistics any day.

Contacting the Media

The media in our local communities have an important role to play in the gun violence debate. For example, television can contribute to the gun violence problem by fostering a frontier mentality through a barrage of programs that imply that use of a gun is an acceptable way to handle conflicts. Television may also be a source of family-oriented programming or public service announcements that can promote non-violent means of resolving conflict. Therefore, it is important to monitor the media and take an active role in providing feedback regarding

> *"One of the most important things you as a citizen can do to help stop gun violence is to let your elected officials and/or the media know how you feel about the issues."*

the appropriateness of programming. The important thing is to pick a level of involvement you are comfortable with and do something! Here is a list of things you can do to impact the media messages in your community.

- Monitor your children's TV watching. Spend time with them watching and discussing television shows. Let them know when programs promote values that are contrary to yours as well as when they reflect your values. Declare programs that consistently promote gun violence as "off limits" and tell your kids why.

- Write letters to the OP-ED section of your local paper responding to news items involving gun violence. Point out how those everyday tragedies could have been prevented through responsible gun ownership such as keeping the gun unloaded and unlocked, or making a decision against gun ownership if appropriate.

> *"The media in our local communities have an important role to play in the gun violence debate."*

- Form a group of people from your church, neighborhood, school, club or other places who are interested in promoting gun violence prevention. Together, write letters to the editor requesting more space be given to examining the issues surrounding gun violence.
- Have your group hold a press conference to announce your plans to stop gun violence in your community. Contact your local police and see if they can suggest an officer who could participate in your group's activities.
- Call in and participate on radio talk shows when gun violence prevention is the topic.
- Have your group write letters to the local TV stations deploring the excessive amount of violence that is being shown on particular shows. Vow not to watch them, and send a copy of your letters to program sponsors.
- Contact a gun violence prevention group for assistance on how to proceed in your local community. (Links to such groups in many states can be found on the Internet at www.mppgv.org under the "links" section.)
- Contact your local public access TV and see if they can provide help on producing a show on gun violence.
- Form a "phone tree" of people who will promise to write a letter in response to a particularly odious and violent program, advertisement, or article that condones irresponsible gun use.
- Ask media representatives to participate in your group and give you advice on accessing the media.

Bibliography

Books

Jack Anderson — *Inside the NRA: Armed and Dangerous, an Expose*. Beverly Hills, CA: Dove, 1996.

Lorelei Apel — *Dealing with Weapons at School and at Home*. New York: PowerKids, 1996.

Geoffrey Canada — *Fist, Stick, Knife, Gun: A Personal History of Violence in America*. Boston: Beacon, 1995.

Vic Cox — *Guns, Violence, and Teens*. Springfield, NJ: Enslow, 1997.

Edward F. Dolan and Margaret M. Scariano — *Guns in the United States*. New York: Franklin Watts, 1994.

Raymond B. Flannery — *Violence in America: Coping with Drugs, Distressed Families, Inadequate Schooling, and Acts of Hate*. New York: Continuum, 1997.

James Gilligan — *Violence: Our Deadly Epidemic and Its Causes*. New York: G.P. Putnam, 1996.

Deborah Hitzeroth — *Guns: Tools of Destructive Force*. San Diego: Lucent Books, 1994.

Gary Kleck — *Targeting Guns: Firearms and Their Control*. New York: Aldine de Gruyter, 1997.

David B. Kopel — *Guns: Who Should Have Them?* Amherst, NY: Prometheus, 1995.

Wayne R. LaPierre — *Guns, Crime, and Freedom*. Washington, DC: Regnery, 1995.

Erik Larson — *Lethal Passage: How the Travel of a Single Handgun Exposes the Rotts of America's Gun Crisis*. New York: Crown, 1994.

John R. Lott Jr. — *More Guns, Less Crime: Understanding Crime and Gun Control Laws*. Chicago: University of Chicago, 1998.

Maryann Miller — *Working Together Against Gun Violence*. Rev. ed. New York: Rosen, 1997.

James M. Murray — *Fifty Things You Can Do About Guns*. San Francisco: Robert D. Reed, 1994.

Guns and Violence

Rachel Ellenberg Shulson	*Guns: What You Should Know*. Morton Grove, IL: A. Whitman, 1997.
Robert J. Spitzer	*The Politics of Gun Control*. Chatham, NJ: Chatham House, 1995.
Josh Sugarman	*National Rifle Association: Money, Firepower, and Fear*. Washington, DC: National Press, 1992.
William Weir	*A Well Regulated Militia: The Battle over Gun Control*. New Haven, CT: Archon, 1997.
Stanley "Tookie" Williams and Barbara Cottman Becnel	*Guns and Weapons*. New York: Rosen, 1996.
Franklin E. Zimring and Gordon Hawkins	*Crime Is Not the Problem*. New York: Oxford University Press, 1997.

Periodicals

Eric Alterman	"Grace Under Fire," *Rolling Stone*, June 1, 1996.
David C. Anderson	"Assault Rifles: Dirt Cheap . . . and Legal!" *New York Times Magazine*, May 24, 1998.
Bruce B. Auster	"Guns and Money," *U.S. News & World Report*, August 10, 1998.
Luther M. Boggs Jr.	"Gun Town U.S.A., Revisited," *National Review*, August 15, 1994.
David Brauer and John McCormick	"The Boys Behind the Ambush," *Newsweek*, April 6, 1998.
Gail Lumet Buckley	"The Gun Cult," *America*, October 19, 1996.
Dana Charry and Ellen Charry	"The Crisis of Violence," *Christian Century*, July 15, 1998.
Robert Dreyfus	"The NRA's Last Hurrah?" *Rolling Stone*, October 31, 1996.
Economist	"Hey, Anybody Want a Gun?" May 16, 1998.
Howard Fineman	"Friendly Fire," *Newsweek*, May 8, 1995.
Ted Gest	"Firearms Folk," *U.S. News & World Report*, January 13, 1997.
Edward L. Glaeser and Spencer Glendon	"Who Owns Guns? Criminals, Victims, and the Culture of Violence," *American Economic Review*, May 1998.
Stephen Goode	"NRA: Exposed or Demonized?" *Insight*, February 3, 1997. Available from PO Box 581367, Minneapolis, MN 55458-1367.
Barbara Grizzuti Harrison	"Cease Fire," *Mother Jones*, March/April 1997.
David Heim	"American Mayhem: School Shootings," *Christian Century*, June 3, 1998.

Bibliography

Philip J. Hilts	"The New Battle over Handguns," *Good Housekeeping*, June 1997.
Albert R. Hunt	"Teen Violence Spawned by Guns and Cultural Rot," *Wall Street Journal*, June 11, 1998.
Tina Johnstone	"I'm Fighting the War Against Guns," *Ladies' Home Journal*, March 1998.
Jeffrey Klein	"A War of All Against All," *Mother Jones*, July/August 1996.
Richard Lacayo and Zed Nelson	"Still Under the Gun," *Time*, July 6, 1998.
Benilde Little	"How Can We Stop Youth Violence?" *Essence*, August 1996.
John R. Lott Jr. and David B. Mustard	"Crime, Deterrence, and Right-to-Carry Concealed Handguns," *Journal of Legal Studies*, January 1997.
Tanya K. Metaksa	"Banning Guns and Taxing Your Rights," *American Rifleman*, June 1998. Available from 11250 Waples Mill Rd., Fairfax, VA 22030.
Lawrence Minard	"Don't Outlaw It—Red Tape It," *Forbes*, April 7, 1997.
David D. Polsby	"From the Hip," *National Review*, April 24, 1997.
Jeremy Rabkin	"Guns in Your Political Future," *American Spectator*, November 1996.
Larry Reibstein and John Engern	"One Strike and You're Out," *Newsweek*, December 23, 1996.
Daniel Seligman	"Gun Control, New York–Style," *Fortune*, October 28, 1996.
Bruce Shapiro	"Running Against the Gun: McCarthy on Long Island," *Nation*, November 11, 1996.
Josh Sugarman and Kristen Rand	"Cease Fire," *Rolling Stone*, March 10, 1994.
William R. Tonso	"Shooting Blind," *Reason*, November 1995.
Patricia J. Williams	"The NRA's ABCs," *Nation*, August 10, 1998.
Chris Oliver Wilson	"Disarming News: Why Bobbies Have No Guns," *U.S. News & World Report*, February 9, 1998.
Gordon Witkin and Katia Hettner	"The Fight to Bear Arms," *U.S. News & World Report*, May 22, 1995.
Franklin Zimring and Gordon Hawkins	"Concealed Handguns: The Counterfeit Deterrent," *Responsive Community*, Spring 1997. Available from 2130 H Street, NW, Suite 714, Washington, DC 20052.

Organizations to Contact

The editors have compiled the following list of organizations concerned with the issues debated in this book. The descriptions are derived from materials provided by the organizations. All have publications or information available for interested readers. The list was compiled on the date of publication of the present volume; the information provided here may change. Be aware that many organizations take several weeks or longer to respond to inquiries, so allow as much time as possible.

American Civil Liberties Union (ACLU)
132 W. 43rd St., New York, NY 10036
(212) 944-9800 • fax: (212) 869-9065

The ACLU champions the rights set forth in the Declaration of Independence and the U.S. Constitution. The ACLU interprets the Second Amendment as a guarantee for states to form militias, not as a guarantee of the individual right to own and bear firearms. Consequently, the organization believes that gun control is constitutional and, since guns are dangerous, it is necessary. The ACLU publishes the semiannual *Civil Liberties* in addition to policy statements and reports.

Campaign for an Effective Crime Policy (CECP)
918 F St. NW, Suite 501, Washington, DC 20004
(202) 628-1903 • fax: (202) 628-1091
e-mail: carter@crimepolicy.com • website: http://www.sproject.com/home.htm

CECP's purpose is to promote information, ideas, discussion, and debate about criminal justice policy and to advocate alternative sentencing policies. The campaign's core document, available to the public, is the book *A Call for Rational Debate on Crime and Punishment*.

Canadians Concerned About Violence in Entertainment (C-CAVE)
167 Glen Rd., Toronto, ON M4W 2W8 CANADA
(416) 961-0853 • fax: (416) 929-2720

C-CAVE conducts research on the harmful effects violence in the media has on society and provides its findings to both the Canadian government and the public. The organization's committees research issues of violence against women and children, sports violence, and pornography. C-CAVE disseminates educational materials, including periodic news updates.

Cato Institute
1000 Massachusetts Ave. NW, Washington, DC 20001
(202) 842-0200 • fax: (202) 842-3490

The Cato Institute is a libertarian public-policy research foundation. It evaluates government policies and offers reform proposals in its publication *Policy Analysis*. Topics include "Crime, Police, and Root Causes" and "Prison Blues: How America's Foolish Sentencing Policies Endanger Public Safety." In addition, the institute publishes the bimonthly newsletter *Cato Policy Report* and the triannual *Cato Journal*.

Citizens Committee for the Right to Keep and Bear Arms
12500 NE Tenth Pl., Bellevue, WA 98005
(206) 454-4911 • fax: (206) 451-3959

The committee believes that the U.S. Constitution's Second Amendment guarantees and protects the right of individual Americans to own guns. It works to educate the public concerning this right and to lobby legislators to prevent the passage of gun-control laws. The committee is affiliated with the Second Amendment Foundation and has more than six hundred thousand members. It publishes the books *Gun Laws of America, Gun Rights Fact Book, Origin of the Second Amendment,* and *Point Blank: Guns and Violence in America.*

Coalition to Stop Gun Violence (CSGV)
1000 16th St. NW, Suite 603, Washington, DC 20002
(202) 530-0340 • fax: (202) 530-0331
e-mail: noguns@aol.com • website: http://www.gunfree.org

Formerly the National Coalition to Ban Handguns, CSGV lobbies at the local, state, and federal levels to ban the sale of handguns and assault weapons to individuals. It also litigates cases against firearms makers. Its publications include various informational sheets on gun violence and the papers "Overrated: The NRA's Role in the 1994 Elections" and "The Unspoken Tragedy: Firearm Suicide in the United States."

Doctors for Integrity in Policy Research (DIPR)
5201 Norris Canyon Rd., Suite 140, San Ramon, CA 94583
(925) 277-0333 • fax: (925) 820-5118
e-mail: EdgarSuter@aol.com

DIPR is a national think tank of approximately five hundred medical-school professors, researchers, and practicing physicians who are committed to exposing biased and incompetent research, editorial censorship, and unsound public policy. It believes that substandard science is extremely prevalent in medical literature on guns and violence. DIPR publishes the papers "Guns in Medical Literature: A Failure of Peer Reviews," "'Assault Weapons' Revisited: An Analysis of the AMA Report," and "Gun Control Revisited: Religion or Science?"

Educational Fund to End Handgun Violence
1000 16th St. NW, Suite 603, Washington, DC 20036-5705
(202) 530-5888 • fax: (202) 530-0331
e-mail: edfund@aol.com • website: http://www.gunfree.inter.net

The fund is a nonprofit educational charity dedicated to ending gun violence, especially violence against children. It provides information concerning handgun violence and firearms marketing, production, and design. The fund sponsors educational programs and publishes the quarterly newsletter *Firearm Litigation Reporter,* the manual *Grass Roots Organizing,* and the booklet *Kids and Guns: A National Disgrace.*

Handgun Control, Inc.
1225 Eye St. NW, Suite 1100, Washington, DC 20005
(202) 898-0792 • fax: (202) 371-9615

A citizens' lobby working for the federal regulation of the manufacture, sale, and civilian possession of handguns and automatic weapons, the organization successfully promoted the passage of the Brady Bill, which mandates a five-day waiting period for the purchase of handguns. The lobby publishes the quarterly newsletter *Progress Report* and the book *Guns Don't Die—People Do* as well as legislative reports and pamphlets.

Independence Institute
14142 Denver West Pkwy., Suite 101, Golden, CO 80401
(303) 279-6536 • fax: (303) 279-4176

The Independence Institute is a pro–free market think tank that supports gun ownership as both a civil liberty and a constitutional right. Its publications include books and booklets opposing gun control, such as *Children and Guns: Sensible Solutions, The Assault Weapon Panic: "Political Correctness" Takes Aim at the Constitution,* and *The Samurai, the Mountie, and the Cowboy.*

Jews for the Preservation of Firearms Ownership (JPFO)
2872 S. Wentworth Ave., Milwaukee, WI 53207
(414) 769-0760 • fax: (414) 483-8435

JPFO is an educational organization that believes Jewish law mandates self-defense. Its primary goal is the elimination of the idea that gun control is a socially useful public policy in any country. JPFO publishes the quarterly *Firearms Sentinel* and the comic book *"Gun Control" Kills Kids!* as well as the books *Gun Control: Gateway to Tyranny* and *Lethal Laws.*

The Lawyer's Second Amendment Society
18034 Ventura Blvd., No. 329, Encino, CA 91316
(818) 734-3066
e-mail: rkbaesq@ix.netcom.com

The society is a nationwide network of attorneys and others who are interested in preserving the right to keep and bear arms. It attempts to educate citizens about what it believes is their inalienable right, provided by the Constitution's framers, to defend themselves with firearms if necessary. The society publishes the *Liberty Poll* newsletter six times a year.

National Council on Crime and Delinquency (NCCD)
685 Market St., Suite 620, San Francisco, CA 94105
(415) 896-6223 • fax: (415) 896-5109

NCCD is a nonprofit organization that works to reduce crime and delinquency. It conducts research on crime control issues and provides reform guidelines for the criminal justice system. NCCD publications include the quarterly *FOCUS Research Briefs*, the journal *Crime and Delinquency*, and semiannual policy-paper booklets.

National Crime Prevention Council (NCPC)
1700 K. St. NW, 2nd Fl., Washington, DC 20006-3817
(202) 466-6272 • fax: (202) 296-1356
e-mail: tcc@ncpc.org • website: http://www.ncpc.org/

NCPC is a branch of the U.S. Department of Justice. Through its programs and educational materials, the council works to teach Americans how to reduce crime and to address its causes. It provides readers with information on gun control and gun violence. NCPC's publications include the newsletter *Catalyst*, which is published ten times a year, the book *Reducing Gun Violence: What Communities Can Do*, and the booklet *Making Children, Families, and Communities Safer from Violence.*

National Organization for Victim Assistance (NOVA)
1757 Park Rd. NW, Washington, DC 20010
(202) 232-6682 • (800) TRY-NOVA • fax: (202) 462-2255
e-mail: NOVA@try-nova.org

NOVA serves as a national forum for victim advocacy by assisting victims of crime, providing education and technical assistance to those who assist victims, and serving as a membership organization for supporters of the victims movement. NOVA publishes the monthly *NOVA Newsletter.*

National Rifle Association of America (NRA)
11250 Waples Mill Rd., Fairfax, VA 22030
(703) 267-1000 • fax: (703) 267-3989
website: http://www.nra.org

With nearly three million members, the NRA is America's largest organization of gun owners. It is also the primary lobbying group for those who oppose gun control laws. The NRA believes that such laws violate the U.S. Constitution and do nothing to reduce crime. In addition to its monthly magazines *American Rifleman, American Hunter,* and *Incites,* the NRA publishes numerous books, bibliographies, reports, and pamphlets on gun ownership, gun safety, and gun control.

Second Amendment Foundation
12500 NE Tenth Pl., Bellevue, WA 98005
(206) 454-7012 • fax: (206) 451-3959

The foundation is dedicated to informing Americans about their Second Amendment right to keep and bear firearms. It believes that gun-control laws violate this right. The foundation publishes the quarterly newsletter *Second Amendment Reporter,* the *Gottlieb/Tartaro Report,* and the magazines *Gun Week* and *Women and Guns.*

U.S. Department of Justice
Office of Justice Programs
Box 6000, Rockville, MD 20850
(800) 732-3277

The Department of Justice protects citizens by maintaining effective law enforcement, crime prevention, crime detection, and prosecution and rehabilitation of offenders. Through its Office of Justice Programs, the department operates the National Institute of Justice, the Office of Juvenile Justice and Delinquency Prevention, and the Bureau of Justice Statistics. Its publications include fact sheets, research packets, bibliographies, the semiannual journal *Juvenile Justice,* and the books *Questions and Answers in Lethal and Non-Lethal Violence: Proceedings of the Second Annual Workshop of the Homicide Research Working Group* and *Partnerships to Prevent Youth Violence.*

Violence Policy Center
2000 P St. NW, Suite 200, Washington, DC 20036
(202) 822-8200 • fax: (202) 822-8202

The center is an educational foundation that conducts research on firearms violence. It works to educate the public concerning the dangers of guns and supports gun-control measures. The center's publications include the report "Cease Fire: A Comprehensive Strategy to Reduce Firearms Violence" and the books *NRA: Money, Firepower, and Fear* and *Assault Weapons and Accessories in America.*

Index

Index

Index

Voice of Hope Ministries, 177

Waco, Texas incident, 94, 96
Walker, Sam, 126
Wallis, Jim, 176
War on Drugs, 134
Washington, D.C., 69, 73, 140, 152, 164
  Advocacy Institute, 197
  ban on handguns in, 107
  killing of Capitol police officers in, 104
Washington, George, 115
Washington, Tom, 71
Weaver, Beth, 84
Weaver, Randy, 94
Weiner, Jennifer, 32
Wenner, Jann S., 180
Williams, David C., 93
Wilson, Lamarr, 25
Wintemute, Garen, 194, 196, 197
Wisconsin, 32, 33, 72

Wolf, Naomi, 162
women, 72, 139, 158
  anti-violence efforts of, 168, 169
  and desire to fight back, 159
  endangered by gun control, 85
  need to protect/empower, 75, 161–62
  as special market for advertising, 157,
    191
  as victims of male violence, 156–57
  see also rape
Wright, James D., 89, 90
Wright, Richard T., 78, 80
Wright, Shannon, 21
Wyoming, 55

Yale Law Journal, 93

Zedong, Mao, 170
Zimring, Franklin, 127, 131, 132